STAIRWAY TO TYRANNY

STAIRWAY TO TYRANNY

CORPORATE CREEP, GLOBALISM AND THE LOSS OF LIBERTY

H. L. DOWLESS

Algora Publishing
New York

Library of Congress Cataloging-in-Publication Data —

Names: Dowless, H. L., author.
Title: Stairway to tyranny: corporate creep, globalism and the loss of
    liberty / H.L. Dowless.
Description: New York: Algora Publishing, [2017] | Includes bibliographical
    references.
Identifiers: LCCN 2017015052 (print) | LCCN 2017020900 (ebook) | ISBN
    9781628942606 (pdf) | ISBN 9781628942583 (soft cover: alk. paper) | ISBN
    9781628942590 (hard cover: alk. paper)
Subjects: LCSH: Banks and banking—Political aspects—United States—History.
    | Corporations—Political aspects—United States—History. | Free
    enterprise—Political aspects—United States—History. |
    Globalization—Political aspects—History.
Classification: LCC HG2461 (ebook) | LCC HG2461 .D68 2017 (print) | DDC
    322/.30973—dc23
LC record available at https://lccn.loc.gov/2017015052

Printed in the United States

TABLE OF CONTENTS

INTRODUCTION

This book reviews the historical precedents that show how we in America are being set up for an authoritarian take-over, and it calls for all citizens to work together to stop it in its tracks. US history as we know it has been twisted and distorted to throw us off the trail, so that we misread the signs that indicate the danger we are in. Every major issue has been condensed into an emotional distraction for the purpose of concealing the facts.

Is America the exceptional nation, is it different? Is it the land of unassailable Liberty?

Can we believe that there is no danger of "fascism" or "totalitarianism" here? That there's no corporate stranglehold on the economy; no collusion between Washington and the bankers/businesses; no creeping laws that take private property away from hard-working families and individuals for the benefit of those at the top...?

Are we not, rather, smug and blind, walking right into the trap? Authority is being concentrated, our liberties are chipped away, and what little wealth we manage to scrape together is confiscated on more and more flimsy pretexts. The privately-held resource base that was supposed to be the bedrock of this country is being taken away, and the average citizen is turned into a feudal serf, a debt-slave, subservient to a central bank and the corporations it finances.

According to this author's investigations, the roots of the problem were planted in Colonial America, when the words on our fine founding documents said one thing but the structures that were the building blocks of the real new nation prepared for a different future. Now the end game is here. Within the next few years, we may wake up to see an America in the total grip of authoritarian rule. As Jefferson and the other founding fathers warned, this possibility is ever present and we must actively guard against it.

It's time to see our history in a new light and draw new conclusions. I hope the reader can find food for thought in the pages ahead.

The United States was founded amidst great debates and poetic rhetoric evoking ideals of individual rights, including private property rights, declaimed by men who desired to separate themselves from the forces of Corporation married with the Government/Banking cartel that controlled Great Britain.

In my previous book, *Reflections On the Loss of the Freeborn American Nation,* [1] I discussed how the Founders and their followers sought to escape the grasp of government-insider collusion that completely ignored citizen concerns. The great barrier of separation was the anointed Constitution — a document of divorce, if you will, intended to dissolve a poisonous union.

But the power always fights back. Evidence of this is tactfully tucked away inside the Constitution itself. The US is a *representative republic*, not a *democracy*. Yet we are consistently lulled to sleep with hallowed words assuring us that "every vote counts"! What is happening, in practice?

Overriding the interests of the actual citizen-voters, our system positively encourages bribes to candidates and elected representatives via "campaign contributions," not only by individual voters but by anonymous groups, by PACs and parties, corporations and whole industries. This came about despite the efforts of the intellectual Thomas Jefferson, the first American hero of the common man, who strongly advocated limiting the possibility of corruption via bribes to Representatives.

During the Washington administration, the first step was made to facilitate the consolidation of power in the hands of the corporate/bankers cartel, and that step was the presidential signing of the charter that established the First Bank of the United States, with no call for curbs to be placed upon currency values, gold and silver or otherwise. This gave the cartel the ability to inflate the value of the national currency, then deflate it, however suited their own interests — not the national interest. Among other things, they could use deflation to drive mortgage holders into default, allowing banks to foreclose on individual property owners.

Then insiders could snap up potentially valuable foreclosed properties and huge tracts of government land for pennies on the dollar. The value of the banknote could then be gradually moved higher, by reinserting gold into the bank to back the already issued banknotes; the local centralized banks would offer loans to the working public as property values were gradually

---

[1] https://www.amazon.com/Reflections-Loss-Freeborn-American-Nation/dp/162894207X

inflated, but the loans came at deceptively high interest rates, meaning that anyone who wished to exercise the right to own property ran the risk of quickly becoming highly indebted and having to pay three times over the asking price in the course of the loan, just to actually "own" the property.

Within about a year of that bank charter being signed, the collusion did exactly as Jefferson had warned they might, confirming the need to have safeguards on currency values and inside the system at large.

One shocking fraud was played out against veterans of the Revolutionary War. Individual states were made to pay off the national debt, without regard to which states had incurred debt and which had paid as they went along. Individual farmers saw their hard-won personal property confiscated, in view of individual states defaulting on their allotted share of the national debt.

The official record shows that insiders, speculators with connections, then bought up the apparently worthless banknotes from desperate veterans and local citizens who could no longer wait. Those with connections, and influence, in the nation's capital apparently knew beforehand that the value of the banknotes was going to be manipulated from almost zero to full face value in due course. The lowly individual only received 10 to 20 cents on the dollar, in gold, when selling to these speculators; but those who bought up the notes received the full face value following Hamilton's appeal to Congress for "*assumption,*" for the nation to "assume" the debt that had been incurred by various states...

Congressmen were witnesses to this great fraud, and they eventually fell into two opposing groups, depending on whether they considered it to their own benefit or not. Those two opposing groups evolved into official political parties, the Federalists and the Jeffersonian Democrats. The Federalists evolved into the modern day Republican Party, and the Jeffersonian Democrats, later on transformed into the Jacksonian Democrats, which in passage of time became known simply as the Democratic Party.

The Democrats espoused the Constitutional right of individuals to ascend the ladder of affluence, if they were able, through their own work and good decisions, and to elevate themselves to the top of society through their own merit. Their influence in government was totally eliminated with conclusion of the Civil War, as their side, the side that demanded restraints on the corrupt cartel, lost more than the war on the battlefield.

A greatly modified version of the Democrats would emerge in 1875 but its economic base had been wiped out, leaving it largely impotent at the national level. The DP served primarily as a state-based governmental body. From a practical point of view, this elitist, corrupt banking/corporate conglomerate (let's just refer to it as the CBCC) had taken over; and now they did not even have to deal with an organized opposition. Eventually the DP would devolve into its present day position as one of two legs supporting the US government.

And what is today's US system? We see a fascist corporate/government partnership, (that is "socialism" for the corporate owners) where the wealth and the power are concentrated in the hands of the .001% at the top, for the benefit of the .001% at the top, with a superficial gloss of pseudo-socialism, a minimal social safety net (welfare payments) that is used to divide and conquer the remaining 99.999%.

The Republican Party still maintains its original stance, strongly advocating the rule of corporations, the centralized banks and the Federal Reserve, with the collusion of government insiders (the complete US representative body minus a few lone voices). Strong words. But here is an example.

Before President Trump made her Ambassador to the UN, Governor of South Carolina Nikki Haley supported lower corporate taxes and opposed regulation of corporations. In inviting business (corporate entities) to move to South Carolina she said:

> "[I]f you come to South Carolina, the cost of doing business is going to be low here. We are going to make sure that you have a loyal, willing workforce [regulate to discourage worker mobility; regulate competition from individuals until citizens have no other choice to labor for the interests of the corporate aristocracy] and we are going to be one of the lowest union-participation [no check on the corporate interests to secure plebeian concerns] states in the country." [1]

Corporations currently furnish just 11% of our Federal tax collections. In 1945, corporations seem to have managed just fine while providing some 35% of the US Federal Tax revenue. Why is the working man left to cover the gap? Apparently, we have just as much voice in Washington as our Revolutionary forefathers had in London. [2]

Meanwhile the Democrats serve the power by convincing every individual that he or she is entitled to more, due to belonging to one or another "minority" or "disadvantaged" identity group — regardless of the effort individuals make (or fail to make) to earn their position in society.

---

[1] https://infogalactic.com/info/Nikki_Haley
[2] In fact, the General Accounting Office (GAO) studied the tax returns of all large U.S. companies in depth for 2008 through 2012 and found that 20% of large profitable companies paid no US corporate income tax at all. Moreover, profitable large U.S. companies as a whole paid only *14% of their pretax* income in U.S. corporate income taxes. That's not even close to the 35% statutory rate or even the 22% effective rate often cited by tax experts. But that latter rate includes foreign, state and local taxes, which wouldn't change even if the U.S. statutory rate were dropped to zero. *money.cnn.com/2016/04/13/pf/taxes/gao-corporate-taxes/*

To get our share of the crumbs of benefits magnanimously dangled before us, we are encouraged to identify ourselves with the poor, the retired, the children, the unemployed, the indigenous people, the refugees, the women-owned businesses, and minorities of every kind. Talk about pushing emotion over rational thinking! Even if you don't fit into one of their categories, you have to recognize their claim, sympathize with their pain, concede your guilt in having had an easier start, and quietly pay your taxes to cover more hand-outs. Even to the point where so many minorities have been carved out that there is no non-minority majority anymore.

Any concerns for the prosperity and rights of the common person as an individual has been sacrificed in the name of "progress."

During the years between the founding of the First Bank of the US and commencement of the Civil War, the two opposing factions waged a war of words inside Congress and even inside the White House. This impassioned conflict even erupted into fist fights inside the halls of US congress. At least one duel (between Alexander Hamilton and Aaron Burr, with Hamilton dying as a result) and two possible Presidential assassinations ensued, Zachary Taylor being one.

The CBCC created a distraction, even as far back as the Jackson administration, in the form of a divisive appeal to emotion for the masses, to garner support for a planned future invasion. Inflammatory subversive literature was distributed (much as the Internet and mass media are brimming with news and fake news today) advocating an outright attack on the economic base supporting Democrats. How dared they demand solid checks and safeguards on the banking system and functions of favoritism between corporate interests and their paid-off representative bodies, all of which who stood to gain financially from their collusion.

President Buchanan, in office just before the Civil War supported the Constitutionally endorsed right of the South [or any individual state] to secede. He declared in a Congressional address that tariff "extortion" had facilitated the move to secede; and with the exit of Confederated state representatives, he had no choice but to placate the opposing side, at least outwardly.

When the Representatives first exited from the Democratic convention in Charleston SC, resigning to assume their new positions inside the newly forming Confederate Congress, the Morrill Tariff of 1861 was ratified. This Act favored the corporate aristocracy and further intensified the animosity. And if such provocation resulted in armed conflict, well, the US Federal government assumed it would be short lived and would end in favor of the CBCC.

The corporate-dominated congress also endorsed a number of other acts. None of these acts were to the benefit of the citizens of the non-industrial Southern and Western states. However, the West was not at risk of an attack on a broad scale due to having very limited and unrepresented population base which could not mount any real opposition. The only possible exception here that might have favored, in some cases, the "lower orders" was the *Homestead Act*, but even here, one must proceed very cautiously before leaping into any rash assumptions.

The Morrill Act

The Morrill Act facilitated the foundation of the land grant colleges and was, in theory, intended to boost higher education. Federally-owned land was given to the *states* — *via corporations* — to sell, endeavoring to raise funds for the purpose of establishing schools. These institutions were established to instruct in "sustainable" agriculture, military science and engineering. Most of these colleges became the large state universities of today, like Texas A & M, but some few did become famous "corporate-influenced" private schools, such as Cornell University, the University of Delaware, and the Massachusetts Institute of Technology.

These colleges were financed on the backs of the most debt-free states at that time. The land grant system of financing colleges had no solid Constitutional backing, since it was endorsed by the Federal government *directly* into the hands of a corporate elite. In the end, individual states possessed the right to determine the grant and college establishment, since only the citizens inside an individual state could determine what was in their own best interests; the Federal government did not have the right to impose its own order, subject to rampant corruption. Buchanan himself said, in his Veto message:

> "The Federal Government, which makes the donation, has confessedly no Constitutional power to follow it into the states and enforce the application of the fund to the intended objects. As donors we shall possess no control over our own gift after it shall have passed from our hands. It is true that the state legislatures are required to stipulate that they will faithfully execute the trust in the manner prescribed by the bill."[1]

Buchanan feared that the college system would only stand as a clandestine method of misappropriating funds to serve the interests of a collective elitist few. The broad community was expected to embrace the concept, since

---

[1] "James Buchanan," The American Presidency Project. http://www.presidency.ucsb.edu/ws/?pid=68368.

the schools would sound like they were there to serve their interests. This sounded especially good to the least educated, including native Americans and the recently freed slaves. If the appropriation of funds was not even done properly, who would see to it that they were indeed used to serve the interests of the working people and not some privileged constituency?

As Buchanan himself warned:

> "It is extremely doubtful, to say the least, whether this bill would contribute to the advancement of agriculture and the mechanic arts—objects the dignity and value of which can not be too highly appreciated."

The Homestead Act

The Homestead Act was designed to distribute land to individual farmers, primarily in the West. The idea was to encourage people to populate the area as the railroad corporations expanded, and serve as a thriving customer base to the corporate ventures of the future. The question was, should this be done by the Federal government or by individual states, and at whose expense?

Obviously, at the expense of Southern citizens[1] and the native populations who already resident in the Western lands and who, by any common law understanding, owned them. Although it is omitted from the history we're taught in school, Buchanan rightly vetoed the bill, initially. But when the South was no longer represented, Buchanan had no alternative but to concede to the overwhelming and ominous majority.

The Pacific Railroad Acts 1862

This act authorized the Federal government to issue land and bonds directly to private railroad companies. No doubt the interests of the people were largely ignored in favor of corporations and banks. As a face-saver, before this act was passed, the Federal government issued grants to the individual states, and only *then* did the states deliver it to the corporations.

The National Banking Act

This act established a national currency. It facilitated the centralization of currency, but held no demand for the Jacksonian Democrats had only wanted the ability to gauge where that currency went and to whose benefit,

---

[1] "Congress instructed the Bureau to rent *forty acres of confiscated* or abandoned land to each freedman family." https://www.jstor.org/stable/4231584?seq=1#page_scan_tab_contents

and asked that the face value of such currency should be equal to the same amount in gold or silver. But no independent body was set up to safeguard these basic concerns; nor is there, to this day, any representative body to demand equal value in gold or silver for the stated face value on our banknotes.

The Revenue Act of 1861

This act facilitated the Federal extortion of funds to fight a war against the people of the United States when they stood up in opposition of the CBCC. The citizens were forced to finance the conflict via the nation's first hard income tax. A majority of Northerners with a colonial heritage *opposed* the war; this resulted in a mass Federal appeal to thousands of uneducated immigrants, who had no such heritage of organizing to oppose an extortionist absolute authority, and who had not been raised to cherish the idea of individual liberty.

Ironically, if the Federal government had not given so much money away to serve corporate interests via the land grants and other more indirect means, then it would have had enough revenue to fight a war against its own population anyway!

Buchanan spoke publicly in regard to the Constitutional backing of the institution of slavery, as did Frederick Douglass himself. Franklin Pierce did so as well, both presidents respecting the Constitutional rights of individual citizens who made the choice to own slaves.

Now, if presidents and our early families in the North understood the Constitution as allowing slavery, and who bore a blood connection to the time when the British colonies seceded from London, how were the masses compelled to change their views?

During the first two and a half years of the Civil War, the Federal government had a difficult time getting men to sign up for the fight. The first national military draft was called and literally thousands chose to leave rather than accede to the draft.[1] The Southern army excelled to a splendor in the field of battle, winning virtually every primary engagement.

Why did the citizens suddenly decide that the war was right; were their opinions changed, or was the population somehow changed?

There was, of course, a major shift going on in the population, but we rarely think of it in these terms. That element of the population in the Northern states who possessed a colonial heritage and strong sense of the Constitution was intentionally displaced by huge waves of Federally invited

---

[1] Thousands went to Canada; there were 200,000 Union deserters, and New York City experienced draft riots I 1863 that were put down by federal troops.

immigrants![1] This new workforce could be manipulated by divisive appeals to emotion, and persuaded to volunteer for a romanticized fight on the field of battle. Any Constitutional quibbles or regard for individual rights were not core concepts for them![2] It has been estimated that 43% to 50% of the Union army was made up of recent immigrants, but it is not mentioned in schoolbooks, strangely enough, as far as this researcher could determine.

Most recruited immigrants could not even read or write and were struggling in their own homelands due to personal incompatibility with the system, illogical personal choices, or a government or society bent on persecuting them. Promises of citizenship and work were highly attractive — as they are today. And the fight was expected to be a short one, anyway.

---

[1] http://time.com/3940428/civil-war-immigrant-soldiers/
[2] http://www.zocalopublicsquare.org/2015/06/30/the-civil-war-was-won-by-immigrant-soldiers/chronicles/who-we-were/

ABRAHAM LINCOLN: WHAT ARE WE TO MAKE OF HIM?

Abraham Lincoln certainly had his beginnings among the most humble of homes. We are all familiar with the image of a log cabin and a tall, skinny boy studying in the wee hours of the morning by the dreary light of swine tallow candles. As thinking, analytical individuals, however, we wonder at the very fact of this image being so strongly pushed.

Why did Lincoln labor so diligently, when he became president, in the name of the CBCC, if he truly hailed from humble origins? Maybe h had no choice, as they were now in absolute control. After all, by the time that Lincoln assumed the presidency, representatives from the Southern states had already largely vacated the halls of Congress and the *Star of the West* had already been fired upon.

The representative body remaining were the Republicans, since the Jacksonian democrats had largely removed themselves to serve inside the Confederate Congress. Lincoln had no one to back him if he opposed the business/banking cartel and its collusion now with virtually the entire US representative body. Anything else?

Is it possible that further back, Lincoln's blood line stemmed from the "gilded" British gentry, just as Washington's did? In fact, he was even said to have bragged frequently about his distant royal bloodline.

What if Lincoln silently aspired to reclaim his past blood origin in privilege and wealth?

What if his poor family and all the obstacles before him fired his ambition to reclaim "his place" in the upper classes, no matter what he was forced to sacrifice?

Perhaps his low standing is part of why he suffered from depression.[1] Let's try on some other possible clues.

Lincoln's sixth great grandfather, Richard Lincoln, was a churchwarden with his own coat of arms. Richard Lincoln's grave underneath the center aisle of Saint Andrews church in Hingham, Norfolk (England) confirms his genteel status. But he wrote his son out of his will due to a dispute, and those descendants struggled ever after.

Here, we must presume, lay a point where resentment must have festered with the passage of time.

The Lincoln family settled in America, moving frequently, and suffering adversity as was not all that uncommon at the time. Lincoln's grandfather Captain Abraham Lincoln moved the family from Virginia to Hardin County Kentucky. Captain Abraham Lincoln was slain by Indians in 1786.

The future president's father Thomas was forced to move in with other members of the family who had already settled there. Lincoln's mother appears to have been born out of wedlock, which also could have weighed on Lincoln's self-esteem.

Lincoln's father eventually acquired 816.5 acres of land in the state of Kentucky; with the passage of time, he lost all but 200 acres in court disputes over property titles. Thomas sold the remaining land and relocated the family to Indiana, where land titles were more secure. Thomas labored there as a farmer, cabinet maker and carpenter.

Lincoln's youth was difficult. On October 5, 1818, his mother Nancy died. On December 2, 1819, Lincoln's father remarried, taking a woman with three children of her own. Lincoln became very close to her, even calling her "mother" according to the official history.

Lincoln appeared to have not cared much for hard physical labor, preferring instead to read, write, do basic arithmetic and write poetry; all very suggestive of his general dissatisfaction for the standard plebeian way-of-life and position that both he and his family had been thrust into.

In early March, 1830, the Lincoln family moved to Macon county, Illinois. According to the official history, Abraham became distant from his father following their move from Indiana because of his father's lack of education, but he occasionally lent him money anyway. We may presume this anecdote to simply be another suggestion describing Abraham's genteel vision of himself. The family eventually determined to move to Coles County, but Abraham took a flat boat into Sangamon county instead, evidently hoping to associate with those on a higher social, economic, educational and intellectual realm.

---

[1] Shenk, Joshua Wolf (October 2005)." Lincoln's Great Depression". *The Atlantic.* Archived from the original on October 20, 2011.

Lincoln's first romantic interest was Ann Rutledge, but she died of typhoid at age 22. Lincoln eventually met a lady named Mary Todd, who interestingly enough *came from a slave-owning family*, suggesting that Lincoln himself held no real hard-line aversion to the institution of slavery.

What were his motivations for signing the Emancipation Proclamation? Whose interests did he really serve?

Lincoln and his wife had four children, of whom most died. Robert was the only child to live into adulthood and have children. All of this adversity appearing to strengthen Lincoln's resolve to reclaim his long lost family aristocracy. All of the Todds were slave owners or slave traders; Lincoln, however, was very close to them, even visiting them in their slave operated plantation estates. [1]

He ran for the Illinois General Assembly, but failed; perhaps he did not have powerful friends, money or education. This failure may have deepened his situational resentment and even further re-enforced his inner resolve to find success at all costs.

Things seemed to be looking up for Lincoln when he landed a job as postmaster in New Salem, Illinois. While working as post master, Lincoln began reading large numbers of law books. Lincoln's second try for the Illinois General Assembly was a success, and he was also admitted to the bar in 1836. Lincoln partnered with William Herndon in his law firm, a Republican.

Lincoln served for four terms in the Illinois house of representatives. The railroad companies were the biggest money there.

Samuel D. Lockwood was an Illinois state politician who served as the state's attorney general, secretary of state and supreme court justice. In 1824, as attorney general, he was given the authorization to hire the contractors who surveyed the route for the canal to follow. This could have only come about with Lincoln and others assisting him in gaining authority over the project, a potentially lucrative position and sure to lead to further benefits. Now Lincoln was finally getting close to a position that would allow him to begin to reclaim his family's long lost honor, wealth and status.

Lincoln supported Zachary Taylor's run for President. He had hoped to be appointed Commissioner of the General Land Office, a lucrative position with the advantage of back room deals from the corporations seeking the land grants as well. Upon resuming his prior law practice in Springfield, Illinois, he defended every corporate venture that came his way with the ongoing migration to the West, for the next 16 years. [2]

---

[1] *Free Soil, Free Labor, Free Men.* Eric Foner (1995), pp. 440–447.
[2] *Lincoln.* David Herbert Donald, (1996), p. 140

He also successfully defended Alton & Sangamon Railroad against an individual shareholder who had refused to pay up for an investment, since the railroad route that had previously been planned was abruptly "changed." The railroad company won out over the individual citizen, with Lincoln's help. From 1853 to 1860, one of Lincoln's largest clients was the Illinois Central Railroad.

The Great American Propaganda Effort

From 1850 onward, the issue of slavery came to be discussed more and more on emotional terms. We are taught that this was primarily due to the moral question involved. But that question was not new; what was new is that the legal basis and the rational considerations no longer carried weight. In fact, progress toward the end of slavery was already being made. The US Congress issued an act in 1807 that abolished the international slave trade, and most of the world was moving gradually away from it, and less than 10% of the Southern population even owned slaves; but at the same time, to operate any profitable large landed estate anywhere in the nation, it was necessary to employ them, since mechanized farm equipment did not exist. The greater issue was that the state Representatives from the South were the ones who demanded checks and balances on the national currency and on the government process in general that accommodated corruption.

By 1850 there had already been an attempt by the banking cartel, seeking absolute authority, to destroy the economic base of the South. The CBCC levied a series of tariffs that would damage the business of the South while enriching the banking cartel. Backed into a corner, the representatives of the South voiced their objections, and threatened to exercise yet another Constitutionally endorsed option, that is, to secede. Secession was also supported by the Tenth Amendment which limits the powers of the federal government, in conjunction with the preamble of the Declaration of Independence.

By the time of the Jackson administration, the new tactic of emotional suasion was also being employed.

Kansas was the scene of early battles between anti-slavery and pro-slavery populations. As Digital History explains,

> Because the Kansas-Nebraska Act [1854] stated that the future status of slavery in the territories was to be decided by popular vote, both antislavery Northerners and proslavery Southerners competed to win the region for their section.... For six years, proslavery and antislavery factions fought in Kansas as popular sovereignty degenerated into violence... the New England Emigrant Aid Company to promote the emigration of antislavery New Englanders to Kansas

to "vote to make it free"... Slaveholders from Missouri feared that the New England Emigrant Aid Company wanted to convert Kansas into a haven for runaway slaves.[1]

In addition, antislavery propaganda was being churned out in Lawrence and was distributed on both sides of the line. By 1856 proslavery activists attacked the town.

The New England Emigrant Aid Company was organized and funded from Massachusetts. They were joined in their work of funding and directing subversion by the American Anti-Slavery Society, based in New York City — the centers of US banking, then and now.

Rep. James C. Burney (Rep.-Ky)

Burney of Kentucky was affiliated, through Henry Clay, with a number of presidents and other high end government officials. Clay was an appointee of the Republican Party, essentially a descendent of the old Federalist party and was linked to the banking cartel seeking to dominate the direction of US government.

Lucy Stone

Lucy Stone was a gifted speaker and a minor writer; her husband, Henry Blackwell, however, had far-reaching political connections. Blackwell formed the Literary Club of Cincinnati (euphemism), which covertly produced and distributed propaganda aimed to incite. His political affiliations included Ainsworth Spotford, future president Rutherford B. Hayes, and Salmon P. Chase. Chase was secretary of the US Treasury under Lincoln, as well as serving on the halls of US senate prior to the election of Lincoln.

Augustine Clark

Augustine Clark was a Vermont attorney, prominent banker and politician. He served as Vermont State Treasurer. He was also a member of the National Republican Party, as we recall who it was that they descended from. In 1826 he was president of the Caledonia National Bank. He also served many terms in the Vermont House of Representatives 1824–1832. He supported William Wirt (a US attorney general) in his 1832 presidential candidacy.

By 1850 the forces of the CBCC had instituted a propaganda base in the form of a diversion, soaked heavily in an appeal to emotion, that was growing. By now it had spread over huge sections of the nation, even into

---

[1] http://www.digitalhistory.uh.edu/disp_textbook.cfm?smtID=2&psid=3280

areas that were predominantly against it. Not only that, virtual colonies had even been established from which the propaganda could be developed and sow seeds of conflict.

The links running from the agencies responsible for developing and distributing the propaganda, reaching into the highest level of banking and government, can simply no longer be ignored. The flames of war were being fanned by emotional appeals that easily won out over logic.

If the aggressive tariffs and propaganda succeeded in demolishing the Southern power base, the landscape would be leveled so that the development corporations could move in, take over large tracts of land, and also take over as the sole provider of services to the communities surrounding the plantation estates. Corporations in collusion could enter into the picture from other angles as well, in the gutted cities and towns, to profit from construction contracts financed via the centralized bank. And the people of the land would be taxed to pay back the bank.

Back To Lincoln

Lincoln had grown up surrounded by this propaganda. Lincoln also bore witness to the violence that resulted among the average men. By the 1850s the issue of slavery was paramount, not principally because of moral considerations, but because it was needed to extract the resources on large landed estates. These estates mainly produced raw products that were exchanged locally as well as internationally, while services and processed goods developed from the raw products were offered back to the surrounding public. The estates also offered financing options via family-owned banks. This local financing operation was what funded and supported the large Representative base that was calling for controls on currency value and safeguards against corruption in the inner workings of government.

Lincoln, working on behalf of the large corporations, sought to drastically limit any expansion of that Representative body. And when the time came, he facilitated the wholesale destruction of the economic base, and the physical landscape, the infrastructure, and the very people of the land.

Lincoln opposed the Kansas-Nebraska Act. The Act specified that average citizens on the ground could determine for themselves whether they desired slavery within their borders, by simple vote, rather than have that decision dictated by US Congress. Lincoln fought for that decision to be dictated in Washington, rather than left up to the plebeian people for their consensus.

Lincoln speeches were famous. His Peoria Speech demonstrates his moving terminology as he seeks to strike the legs out from under the landed estates and their Representatives in Washington. Making an overt appeal to emotion, he labels the supporting institution "a monstrous injustice," appealing to both the voter and to congressional senses of injustice. He went on to declare that "it deprives our republican example of its just influence in the world"; as if to say that Congressional facilitation of corruption and links to corporations and the centralized bank did not do so and much worse.

Lincoln was an ideal candidate for the Republican party, supported large corporations, centralized currency and banking, all working with their inside government collusion in absence of any checks and balances. In order to overcome the average man's resentment, Lincoln's humble background and modest status were emphasized, causing people to identify with him personally despite his protection of the very interests who oppressed them.

Thus men who would ordinarily vote Jacksonian Democrat, or Northern Democrat, would submit to the appeal for camaraderie and vote Republican instead; being misled into reasoning that *somehow* as they served corporate interests, the National Republicans would manage to serve those concerns of the enterprising individual as well. the strength of the appeal was evidenced by Lincoln's status at second place in the Republican National Convention of 1856 in the candidacy for Vice President.

Lincoln picked up the pace for the attack against all supports on the economy which allowed individuals to ascend into a level of wealth on par with the corporate aristocracy. His blatant attack heralded the events to come.

Lincoln opposed the *Dred Scott vs Sanford* decision rendered by the US supreme court, which ruled that "a negro, whose ancestors were imported ... and sold as slaves", even if he was freed, could not be an American citizen and therefore had no standing in federal court, and said that the federal government did not have the power to regulate slavery in federal territories.

He also supported Stephen Douglas, who opposed admitting Kansas as a slave-owning state, which would increase the number of Representatives demanding checks on currency and banking.

Because of his continuing attacks on individual property rights and the ability to get ahead through success in the agrarian model, Lincoln was nominated for US senate in 1858. By that time the issue of state secession was strong, since the Constitution supported it; and state leaders were on the verge of acting on that endorsed right. Lincoln gave his famous "House Divided" speech, where he strongly insinuated that he would virtually deny those states the right to divorce themselves from the Union if he came to power.

If the South seceded and set itself up as a separate nation, it would have stood in stark competition economically, politically, historically, culturally and socially to those states dominated by the CBCC. Perhaps, eventually the citizens in that area would even rise against the imposed lordship and extortion. To fend off such a nightmare, by 1858 we can observe a continued effort on the part of Lincoln to color the debate over slavery in heated moralistic hues.

Property ownership, and production wrought from that property, is still the clearest way for a family to move up the economic and social ladder. What the cartel sought was to wrest that Constitutionally endowed right from the citizenry.

The economy had already been intentionally crashed by the conspiring cartel, first by removing the gold backing all banknotes from the central bank. When the British reinserted the gold on their side, the resilient Southern plantations continued to profit while the Northern corporations supported by the de facto centralized bank suffered. This suggests that safeguarding the currency values was most vital for real people, if not for corporate "persons," and should be demanded.

To facilitate a complete crash of the US financial system, a ship carrying a huge gold haul equal to 6% of the entire national debt, the SS *Central America*, was sunk, preventing it from making it into the central bank. The result was more economic pain for the American citizen, to include the Southern states.

Within three years the largely debt free, independent Southern half of the nation once again was proving itself resilient, requiring another economic attack from the banking cartel. The 1858 Lincoln–Douglas debates "reframed America's argument about slavery and transformed Lincoln into a presidential contender." Smithsonian Magazine notes that the image-conscious Lincoln staged his appeal to the common man, while he was "actually a prosperous lawyer who enjoyed an upper-middle-class existence in an exclusive section of Springfield."[1] His speeches, during a severe nationwide economic drop, coincided with a rise in the economic stability of the largely debt-free Southern states.

Lincoln was making a hard line appeal to the masses for support, as we may observe inside the content of his addresses from the day. Lincoln's modest, school of hard knocks image, on the one side, and his absolute devotion to the conspiring cartel on the other, made him the supreme candidate.

Lincoln's 1860 speech at Cooper Union is further evidence. Among the strongest supporters was William H Seward, governor of New York state, the center of the centralized bank and an ex-lawyer of strong Federalist conviction. Another supporter was Samuel P Chase who would go on to become Secretary of Treasury. Chase was a strong supporter of a strong

---

[1] http://www.smithsonianmag.com/history/how-lincoln-bested-douglas-in-their-famous-debates-7558180/

centralized government, and the issue of currency with no backing in gold or silver to serve as a value check. He later on presided over the direct attack on President Andrew Johnson for possible impeachment in 1868.

When Johnson refused the demands of the CBCC, to treat harshly those who had made the ultimate sacrifice in the name of individual liberty, he was arraigned by the political inquisition and condemned, eventually being dismissed from office.

While Chase and Seward were presented to the public as Lincoln's rivals, their support recognized in Lincoln's Cooper-Union address strongly suggests this was a device intending to distract the plebeians from seeing who it was that sponsored Lincoln.

In 1860 at the Illinois Republican state convention held in Decatur, Lincoln received his first endorsement to run for US President. Lincoln's followers organized a campaign team that actively sought to embellish his modest beginning in an overt appeal to the masses for camaraderie. Who it was that in reality pushed Lincoln's Presidential nomination, might be revealed in our examination of just *who* the organizational leaders of the campaign were.

David Davis

A US senator from Illinois and an associate justice from the Supreme court, Davis was one of Lincoln's former law partners and one of Lincoln's primary body guards. He was educated at Yale University. He was born to a wealthy family in Maryland. From 1848–1862 Davis presided over the court of the Illinois eighth circuit, where Lincoln was practicing law. On October 17th 1862, Davis received a recess appointment from then President Lincoln to a seat on the US supreme court vacated by John Archibald Campbell, who had resigned in protest over Lincoln's intent to go to war with the seceding Southern states. This resignation verifies the illegality of the cartel now in absolute authority in America.

Norman Judd

Born in Rome, upstate New York, Judd received a liberal schooling. He studied law and was admitted to the bar in 1836, and commenced to practice law in his hometown. He moved to Chicago in 1836 and served as a member of the Illinois senate from 1844 to 1860. He served a delegate to the 1860 Republican national convention. He was appointed as minister plenipotentiary to the Kingdom of Prussia, a powerful unifying force in Germany, by Abraham Lincoln from March 6th, 1861 and served until 1865.

It appears that Lincoln was attempting to secure greater financial advantage for the corporations. Letters sent by Judd confirm that tolls on American goods being shipped down the river Elbe in 1861 had been effectively abolished.

Leonard Swett

Swett was a civil and criminal lawyer who advised and assisted Lincoln throughout his political career. Swett was dispatched to California to seize the New Almaden Mine (a mine that produced mercury needed the goldfields of California) in an order signed by then President Lincoln. In addition to his Federal duties, he anticipated payment of $10,000 (approximately $200,000 in present day money value) from a group of American investors.

Big money was circulating, with advantage to all within range. How this benefited Lincoln we may only suspect. Many of these investors were either associated with the Lincoln administration, and were directly involved in wresting away control of the mine from Baron Forbes Company, a British-Mexican firm that had been operating for the past 15 years and had been pursued in Federal court on at least six past occasions.

These investors organized a false front organization called the Quicksilver Mining Company. The Federal agent and the marshal sent in to neutralize the opposition were met at the gate by armed miners, who ardently resisted the attempt to seize the premises. Enforcement of the seizure was blocked by General George Wright, commander of the Department of the Pacific, a decision reinforced by a subsequent order of Henry Halleck, general in chief of the Union Armies, who believed that the order was unauthorized and clandestinely obtained.

Eventually the owners of the mine were forced to sell out. California also had a deep sentiment in favor of checks and balances that that ran heavily within the general population. No doubt, examples of corruption like this served to reinforce their conviction.

Another interesting question is, what do modern presidents mean when they hail Lincoln as a hero? What did President Obama, a constitutional scholar, we are told, really have in mind? And why was he such a supporter of the corporations?[1]

On May 18 at the Republican National Convention in Chicago, Lincoln's friends promised a win and manipulated a nomination on the third ballot. They manipulated the win by placing Hannibal Hamlin, a former Democrat/slave moderate from Maine, on the ballot for Vice President. Lincoln's

---

[1] http://www.cbsnews.com/news/critics-slam-obama-for-protecting-monsanto/

potential for success depended upon his ability to feign a moderate support for the individual's constitutional right to own slaves.

Hamlin also was a heavy supporter of what have been euphemistically labeled "internal improvements," which in reality amount to insider "development" contracts, money for which was designed to be extorted from those areas of the nation with economies supporting individual interests, that stood outside those areas controlled and dominated by the interests of the CBCC.

Certain large corporations had already placed a bid for such jobs by the time of the NRC; such as the Pennsylvania iron interests, now made confident that they would receive due consideration for their unconditional support of candidates, via tariffs tailor-made for them, at the expense of the common man.

The intent initiated, at least by the time of Jackson, was to provoke a conflict designed to destroy the economy supporting the Congress Representatives calling for checks on the government, banking and corporations.

Presidents Pierce and Buchanan both criticized the extortionist tariffs, and commoners had their doubts about it all — the Federal government had a difficult time getting new recruits to sign up for combat duty. Propagandist demagogues traveled the nation calling people to support Lincoln, using the same "common-man" appeal that the written media had used. Meanwhile the intention was to purloin the rights of any individual citizen to pursue wealth through the use of his property within the laws of the times.

Future Reflections

Those now in control of Washington and the CBCC know their own history far better than the overwhelming majority of Americans. And they well recall the Peasants Revolt and the French Revolution, the lead-up to which looked a bit similar to present-day America.

In order to resist these forces, people need to get beyond the divisions and fractionalizing "identity politics" so popular these days. Many of the social movements, protest movements, and non-profit groups we see are actually funded and guided behind the scenes by the very financiers and corporations we need to fight. "They have no conception of reasoned debate, toleration of disagreement, or respect for law. Rather than promote assimilation to the American norm, or what was the American norm — the only hope to keep the country from devolving into warring tribes — they promote identity politics. [1] They divide us, because they know that as long as Americans relate

---

[1] "The sprawling class from which the protesters come, not just in Washington or just recently, opposes the bedrock of our approximation of democracy. It

to events only from competing, narrow perspectives, there will be no coming together to create a coherent voice of protest. We need to stand together, despite our differences, if we are to stand up to our common enemy of control by the corporate/banking elite.

"The appeal to ethnic/religious identity as the sole definition of political selfhood is the perfect tool for manipulating the masses — and this is why the only possible output of identity politics is totalitarianism."[1]

Lincoln won the presidency on November 6, 1860, beating Democrat Stephen Douglas, John C Breckinridge of the Southern Democrats, and John Bell of the Constitutional Union Party. Lincoln has been hailed by our distorted history as a popular hero, the first President of the Republican Party — an interesting observation in view of whose interests that party really served (and still serves).

Was there a cartel payoff? Lincoln's victory was entirely due to support inside the Northern states and those of the West. Lincoln won only a plurality of the popular vote, but his victory in the electoral college was decisive: Lincoln had 180 and his opponents added together had only 123. There were fusion tickets in which all of Lincoln's opponents combined to support the same slate of Electors in New York, New Jersey, and Rhode Island, but even if the anti-Lincoln vote had been combined in every state, Lincoln still would have won a majority in the Electoral College.

The fusion tickets as well as the conclusive Electoral College vote may indicate that money was flowing to those who could control the final decision. The CBCC possessed that kind of money and in great abundance. The railroad companies moving Westward, for instance, were financed by Junius Morgan and George Peabody primarily, either directly or indirectly. The state of Illinois had been a center for the railroad business all of Lincoln's life.

Now they had their puppet inside the supreme office of the United States, the land of the free. The opposition had effectively removed itself, as the CBCC had presumed they would, by moving to secede.

Lincoln went on to heighten tensions by vilifying any who stood strong in opposition, saying, "I will suffer death before I consent ... to any concession or compromise which looks like buying the privilege to take possession

---

is not an economic divide.... They have no conception of reasoned debate, toleration of disagreement, or respect for law. Rather than promote assimilation to the American norm, or what was the American norm, the only hope to keep the country from devolving into warring tribes, they promote identity politics." Internal Secession and the Road to Ruin: A Tale of Two Countries, from *The Burning Platform*, Guest post by Fred Reed, at https://www.theburningplatform.com/

[1] "Identity Politics = Totalitarianism." Guest post on *Zero Hedge* by Charles Hugh-Smith via OfTwoMinds blog, http://www.zerohedge.com/news/2016-09-07/identity-politics-totalitarianism

of this government to which we have a constitutional right." By falsely portraying the opposition as anti-Constitution, and subtly suggesting that the pro-corporate conspiracy was in line with the Constitution and ideals of liberty. This statement was made in regard to the subject of Lincoln making compromise, [1] that was noted at the time as possessing the potential for defusing the tension and the negative situation at large. And he rejected a compromise that could have brought a bit of much needed calm.

The Corwin Amendment to the Constitution would have secured the constitutional right to own slaves in the states where this was practiced, and it prohibited government from interfering, since slavery was permitted under the constitution.

The Crittenden Compromise would have extended the Missouri Compromise line of 1820, and it would have also produced more Representatives of the Southern states who were calling for safeguards against the CBCC.

Lincoln adamantly rejected any form of compromise, saying, "I will suffer death before I consent to any concession or compromise which looks like buying the privilege to take possession of this government to which we [we who?] have a Constitutional right." [2]

Never mind that the CBCC had been doing just that from day one.

Lincoln made his way across the nation, giving speeches twisting the truth to make villains out of those who opposed the extortionist intent of the cartel. His message was largely rejected, and soon he feared the possibility of assassination. On February 23, Lincoln traveled to Washington D.C. in disguise, in order to give his inaugural address, and was placed under heavy military guard.

A final masquerade intending to feign a genuine solution to the mounting national tensions came about in an incident euphemistically labeled the Peace Conference of 1861. During the course of this conference, both issues of compromise were again discussed and debated with delegates from six "slave" states and six "free" states. of course, no such peace agreement was reached.

President James Buchanan had already negotiated an agreement with Governor Pickens of South Carolina, in which he agreed not to resupply South Carolina federal military installations with provisions or any sort of reinforcements. The ship *Star of the West*, a former mail carrier that had traveled the exact route of the SS *Central America*, and for the purpose of transporting gold from California back to the central banks of New York, made the shipment in spite of a Presidential order not to do so. Just as the

---

[1] Donald (1996), p. 268
[2] Donald (1996), p. 268

governor of South Carolina had warned to Buchanan, the ship was fired upon and was forced to turn back. All former Federal property inside South Carolina boundaries was seized, contrary to the agreement made by Buchanan.[1]

Now we find that Major Anderson was being ordered sternly by Lincoln himself to resupply Fort Sumter, the last remaining military installation inside the Confederated states not under Federal control. First there had been a promise that no aggressive actions would occur, and the ship *Star of the West* was fired upon, as the governor of South Carolina had said would be the case should such a violation occur! Now the US Federal government committed another act of aggression by seizing military installations on what amounted to foreign soil.

This was followed by the attempt to resupply Fort Sumter, a third overt act of US government aggression intending to provoke conflict. Lincoln, working under command of the cartel that was now in absolute control of US government functions, notified South Carolina Governor Francis W. Pickens that he was sending in additional supply ships to Fort Sumter (in another direct violation of Buchanan's agreement).

Pickens promptly issued the stern demand to both Lincoln and Major Anderson that Fort Sumter be evacuated immediately. Lincoln ordered Anderson to remain, leaving the Confederacy no choice but to force him out. Both Lincoln and the US Federal government were forcing the situation toward war.

At 0430, April 12, 1861, Confederate batteries opened fire with a tremendous thirty-four hour bombardment of the fort. Anderson and his command then complied with the order to evacuate, having fulfilled Lincoln's order to violate any agreed upon conditions of the peace arrangement between Buchanan and Governor Pickens. Propagandists who later reported the events could vilify the opposition by saying it was "those evil hotheads" who had fired the first shots.

Lincoln ordered all states to send in detachments totaling 75,000 men. Baltimore, Maryland, was the center for rail links running North. Mobs there attacked Federal troops who were changing trains. Local leaders burned critical bridge links to the capital to prevent Federal troop movement and put a halt to the war that the US Federal government was hell-bent on initiating. The Federal army leaders responded by arresting Maryland officials.

Lincoln followed by illegally suspending the right of Habeas Corpus without first going through Congress to do so, removing the civilian's right of protection from indefinite imprisonment by what amounted to a political

---

[1] http://americancivilwar.com/authors/Joseph_Ryan/Articles/Lincoln-Instigated-War/The-Buried-Fact-Record.html

inquisition. The US Constitution declares that citizens are innocent until proven guilty by a legitimate court of law. Lincoln's illegal suspension of HC resulted in the mass arrest of thousands labeled as sympathizers, with no benefit of trial by law, sending many innocents to their deaths inside what amounted to concentration camps. Congress avidly supported such action since there were no opposition members present to demand otherwise.

As Lincoln's crass abuse of authority continued unabated, citizens inside the border states and even beyond began to take notice. Lincoln's response was to send propagandist demagogues out to justify his disregard for Constitutional law. Foreign powers were also beginning to question Lincoln's disregard for legitimate Constitution-based authority inside the boundaries of his own nation. How trustworthy was he? He was waging war on that part of the nation that had been supplying 85% of the Federal budget; but they no longer had a voice in Washington.[1]

On August 6, 1861, Lincoln signed the Confiscation Act, allowing the confiscation of any property nationwide assumed to support economic base that allowed upward mobility. The US economy was supposed to be dominated by the central bank and their corporate interests.

General John C. Fremont proclaimed martial law within Missouri borders, in complete disregard for his own superiors or the concerns of the citizens of the state. He declared that any citizen found bearing arms could be court martialed and executed, disregarding the fact that one's right to bear arms was guaranteed by Constitution. Fremont was already under investigation for fraud and corruption.

The Trent affair nearly initiated war with Great Britain. The US navy illegally intercepted a British merchant ship, the *Trent*, on the high seas and seized two Confederate diplomats who were aiming to establish a relationship with Great Britain and France in a bid to secure foreign recognition of their national independence. Great Britain was appalled by this overt violation of neutrality rights and the crass insult to their national honor. There is a strong suggestion that the chief investors in the Bank of England had already sensed the American side's unreliability, as we can observe in the Panic of 1857. In the wake of increasing tension, Lincoln had no choice but to release the diplomats, yet still offered no formal apology for the violation of international rights.

Lincoln's second-in-command was Edwin Stanton, was a firm supporter of absolute rule by the corporation. The military would move to take control of all strategic points, dividing the opposing forces along the Mississippi River, for example, and defeating its military, rather than simply capturing

---

[1] https://snapoutofitamerica.wordpress.com/2014/01/20/the-terrible-truth-about-abraham-lincoln-and-the-confederate-war/

territory. But in spite of his enthusiasm, his blockade and his military ruthlessness, Lincoln's army was suffering major defeat in nearly every primary engagement, contrary to all professional estimations previously. His military lost the first battle of Bull Run, a major battle, leading to a sudden decision to retire by the Union general-in-chief, Winfield Scott.

Lincoln found a replacement in General George McClellan. McClellan promptly sent Lincoln a letter urging caution in his aggressive war campaign to subjugate the masses. McClellan lost the Peninsular Campaign, another major battle, and Lincoln replaced him with Henry Wagner Halleck in March 1862.

McClellan's letter prompted Lincoln to appoint John Pope as head of the new army of Virginia. Pope assured Lincoln that he could move forward with the proposed battle plan and capture the Confederate capital in Richmond. Pope, however, was soundly defeated during the second battle of Bull Run in the summer of 1862, to the exasperation and astonishment of all professional assessments regarding the situation. The SS *Virginia* also destroyed three Federal vessels, so the forces of corporation and their government collusion were losing both on land and at sea.

Though Lincoln had deposed Pope following the SBOBR, he restored him into authority over the forces in and around Washington DC, out of desperation. Lee's forces soon crossed the Potomac, leading to the battle of Antietam, one of the bloodiest Federal victories in history. Some have even gone as far as to label it a Pyrrhic victory (the 12 Massachusetts Infantry lost 67% of their forces), a loss despite technical victory. The results were inconclusive and virtually irrelevant, since McClellan's superior numbers (75,000 men versus Lee's 55,000-man army) still failed to achieve any real objective. Even Lincoln himself came to believe that the battle was merely a draw, rather than a decisive defeat that he had ardently hoped for.

Some 25% of the Federal forces were lost, with at least that same number more as later casualties due to failed amputation, mental disturbance and shock, and other ills. The massive loss of manpower, in spite of the huge numbers of foreign troops utilized so heavily by the Federal government, prompted a new call for man-power, in an unusual form.

The Emancipation Proclamation went into effect on January 1, 1863. This document declared that all slaves who escaped Confederate control into areas outside of that control were made free. The document was an appeal to emotion back down into slave ranks, as well as resting with their moralist sympathizers as being one of liberation; bearing the suggestion that by simply signing on, one was securing the liberty of all others in his identical situation. Let the real truth be self-evident in the very words of Lincoln:

"As a fit and necessary military measure, on January 1, 1863, all persons held as slaves in the Confederate states will thenceforward, and forever, be free."[1]

There were also false promises of forty acres (confiscated from the whites) and a mule, a promise grounded in the idea that for slaves to receive land via outright theft from the original owners could only be appropriate. That promise was never realized, whether it was just or not.

Efforts to placate always reveal veiled efforts of manipulation. No gift ever comes without a price. Because of the need for raw recruits, following activation of the EP on January 1863, Lincoln's battle strategy now held two primary objectives conjunction with a number of critical secondary goals; to strike in multiple areas and on multiple fronts, to initiate a program of total war against the families of those who stood strong in resistance, and to recruit new forces from among the slave population.

This struck at the very economy upon which the region stood, effectively knocking the supports out, since the investment made into the labor force was permanently lost when the slaves were released. Secondly, it allowed virtual legions of soldiers to extort their needs for sustenance from the local people of the land, who were already in short supply due to the blockade and a general draining situation of the war. Obviously, the aim was to leech the economic system dry, bringing chaos to the people.

Official history notes that Lincoln longed for a single decisive victory so that the Emancipation Proclamation could be proclaimed without being viewed as having being born of desperation.

With the plantation system demolished, and that route to prosperity crushed, the Southern model was finally being turned into dust. Very soon any hopes that the House of Representative could find enough voices to demand protections against corporate corruption, centralized banking and government officials, would be permanently eradicated.

Two of Lincoln's most trusted commanders, McClellan and Don Carlos Buell, refused to pursue the Confederate forces deeper into Virginia and Eastern Tennessee, sensing some suggestion of mistrust regarding Lincoln's motivations for his incessant determination. Lincoln refused to deal with questions regarding his motivation, so both generals were promptly replaced when the time was deemed appropriate for Lincoln to do so.

McClellan was replaced by Ambrose Burnside, and Buell was replaced by William Rosecrans. Burnside, determined to secure a victory, made an irrational advance across the Rappahannock River. He played directly into the hands of General Lee. Burnside was soundly defeated in the Battle of Fredericksburg, Virginia.

---

[1] Donald (1996), pp. 364–365

Federal desertions in 1863 were in the thousands, especially following the Battle of Fredericksburg. Foreign immigration again was needed since the local population was not highly motivated to fight for the North.

Following Burnside's dramatic defeat, Lincoln brought in Joseph Hooker, an advocate for an outright military dictatorship.

The mid-term elections in 1862 demonstrate that by that time, the folks in the industrial and banking states were beginning to tire of the Lincoln administration. Lincoln was blamed for badly underestimating Southern resiliency; for rising inflation resulting from endless printing of banknotes (not backed by gold); higher taxes; the continuing arrest of citizens charged with conspiracy on the basis of assumption without any benefit of trial; the military draft law(most citizens who bore a colonial heritage refused to enlist to fight innocent civilians on behalf of corporate interests; and fears that the Emancipation Proclamation would lead to massive hordes of ex-slaves saturating the employment market.

By spring of 1863, civilians were tired of seeing a rapid depletion of national resources, daily battle casualties in the form of amputees and mental patients, and gruesome battlefield death statistics. Hooker hastily made an attack just north of Richmond, directly confronting Lee. Rosecrans moved on Chattanooga, Tennessee, at about the same time; and Grant moved on Vicksburg, Mississippi, soon capturing a high strategic point from which to eventually control the Mississippi river. All of this was followed up with a naval attack on Charleston, South Carolina, sealing off a major port for moving supplies in and out, as well as striking at a symbolic center of the Secessionist effort.

At this stage, it would appear that Lincoln and his Federal government were in sheer desperation, struggling to create an opening in what had basically been an invincible Southern defense. One force may have possessed superiority in numbers, equipment and possibly technology; but the other possessed superiority in strategy, which is the surest element.

The Tide Begins To Turn

On July, 1863, the first major Federal victory occurred in Gettysburg, Pennsylvania. The entire world knows this monumental engagement as the Battle of Gettysburg. The battlefield logistics preceding the first shot turned out to be decisive. Why did Lee move to attack in the very face of such well-fortified positions? Why did Lee order a move across that great open field to attack an army fortified on distant granite hilltops, a natural fortress, when Washington D.C. was wide open, and from a practical point of view, virtually defenseless?

This move was in direct violation of Sun Tzu's "Thirteen Chapters" and the first supreme inviolable rule in master strategist Sun Tzu's command, "Always avoid an enemy at his strongest positions for the purpose of conserving resources to attack at his weakest points." In view of Lee's past line of successes, most certainly he knew of "The Thirteen Chapters" and had studied them at West Point Military Academy.

Longstreet seems to have advised Lee accordingly, but Lee's recorded response was, "But this is where the enemy is, and we will attack him here."[1]

The Threat That Changed History

Lee's own forces were at their weakest point — foot weary, low on supplies and in an open field. Was it really simply a costly "blunder"? Lee's hallowed memory is such that no one has ever dared to suggest that he may have had some conflicting impulses. Could his family have been threatened?

The official story is that "Confederate Gen. Robert E. Lee's detailed battle plans discovered by Union troops under a locust tree in a field," that "Acting on Lee's plans, Gen. George B. McClelland planned offensive attack which would become Battle of Antietam," and that the resulting Union "victory alter[ed the] fate of the entire Civil War."[2] In other words, Lee's plans were left in a most cordial fashion, as if to say, have a cigar on me.

Just four months prior, Lee's invalid, wheel-chair bound wife, had been captured by McClellan, according to the official history, only later to be released and promptly escorted across Union lines. We are not clear as to how long she was held or specifically when she was released.

This author highly suspects that much more was at work here than history is allowed to reveal.

Robert E Lee had three sons, but only one of them stands out. His name was William Henry Fitzhugh Lee, also known as "Rooney." This son was a brigadier general in the Confederate army. Rooney was seriously wounded at the Battle of Brandy Station in 1863, on June 9. He removed himself to Hickory Hill Plantation in Ashland, Virginia, so that he could be with his family on June 26, 1863. He was captured on the same day. The Battle of Gettysburg occurred on July 1–3, 1863. This would be distracting enough, for Lee, even if there were no explicit threats made.

On top of this, Orton Williams proposed to General Lee's daughter Agnes, in the parlor of the plantation home, but Agnes rejected his proposal. Apparently the travesty of war had turned Orton (Mary Custis Lee's cousin,

[1] https://snapoutofitamerica.wordpress.com/2014/01/20/the-terrible-truth-about-abraham-lincoln-and-the-confederate-war/

[2] Daily Mail.com: http://www.dailymail.co.uk/news/article-2203885/Civil-War-Robert-E-Lees-secret-Special-Orders-No-191-Union-soldiers-changed-fate-Antietam-Americas-bloodiest-day.html#ixzz4XqiT2Zug

a childhood sweetheart of Agnes, and a general family companion) into a hard, bitter man, unlike the easy going, loving nature that he had shown before. Orton was captured by the Federal army and hanged as a spy the following morning. He wrote a letter to Agnes proclaiming his innocence immediately before his execution, and the letter was obviously allowed and delivered by Federal authorities.

General Lee later wrote that the cruel deed was done simply to harm him and his family.

William Henry Fitzhugh Lee had been brought to the plantation home for recuperation. The Federal army learned of his whereabouts, more than likely through the efforts of Allan Pinkerton's detectives who also supplied Lincoln with personal security, and sent a raiding party to capture him. The official claim was that they were going to hold him as hostage for the purpose of making an exchange.

About two weeks after arriving, the family heard shots coming from the hickory grove down by the gate, suspecting only poachers hunting squirrels. Charlotte Wickham Lee sent William Henry Lee's youngest brother, Robert Jr., down to investigate. He spied the raiders approaching before they actually made it to the mansion.

Quickly turning his horse around, he made his way back to the Plantation office where his brother was. William Henry Fitzhugh Lee felt that the Federal army would make the honorable move and parole casualty soldiers, since he had always done so on their behalf. He did not realize that they were after him just as much as his brother.

Upon realizing the brutish truth, Robert Jr. escaped into the hedges and burrowed in, where he could observe the entire ensuing affair. Their faithful, aged servant Scott proceeded to take all of their horses to safety. The Federals captured William Henry Lee but later on released him, though we are not told how much time passed before doing so.

Not being content with their trophies, they proceeded to demand from Scott the locations of more horses and other goods. Scott refused to cooperate, so the Federal soldiers beat the old man to death with the barrels of their pistols. Rooney Lee was captured in the Plantation office and carted away on a stolen plantation wagon, while his shivering family watched. We know from the official historical record that Lincoln himself threatened Lee that both Rooney and his brother would hang, using the threat to manipulate judicial proceedings involving Federal officers captured by Confederate forces, and other events on the ground.

While Rooney was away in military prison at Fortress Monroe, his infant children are reported as having succumbed to scarlet fever and his wife is simply recorded as having "wasted away," dying on December 26, 1863, just over four months from the time of the battle of Gettysburg.

The Federals had also burned the manor at White House Landing (once the home of Rooney Lee) to the ground in late 1862, prior to the event described.

Before we conclude in this passage concerning Lee specifically and the strong suggestions of criminal conduct by Lincoln with his circle of corporate associates, we must recall an incident that occurred on Lee's primary place of residence in Arlington, Virginia at a time when the war was waning in the later part of 1863, into 1864.

Lee and his wife had vacated their primary property at Arlington early on. A ruthless, unconstitutional tax was levied on the property of Lee. As a direct result of tax default, Lee lost his wife's entire family estate, even though Mary Lee had sent an agent to the estate with money, positive intentions and instructions to pay the tax. The Federal government turned the agent away in disregard for the property owner's personal situation,[1] refusing to take the money from anyone other than the principals.

As an ultimate insult and to ensure that the Lee family could never again occupy the estate or its grounds, the bodies of dead Federal troops were buried in the midst of the estate front yard beginning on May 13, 1864. Most of the trees in the wooded grounds of the estate were cut down and used for construction projects, so that most of the oldest trees on the estate, and most of the valuable timber, were confiscated by the Federal government, a precursor of events to come at large for the most valuable of landed plebeian estates. These grounds were later made into the Arlington National Cemetery.

Take a glance at the condolence letter sent to Rooney by the great general, Lee himself, a father writing to his grieving son in the midst of raging war times.

Camp Orange Co: 24 Apl '64

I recd last night My dear Son your letter of the 22nd. It has given me great Comfort. God knows how I loved your dear dear Wife, how Sweet her memory is to me, & how I mourn her loss. My grief Could not be greater if you had been taken from me. You were both equally dear to me. My heart is too full to Speak on this Subject, nor Can I write. But my grief is not for her, but for ourselves. She is brighter & happier than ever, Safe from all evil & awaiting us in her Heavenly abode. May God in his Mercy enable us to join her in eternal praise to

---

[1] Mary Lee also suffered from severe rheumatoid arthritis and was wheelchair bound as a result.

our Lord & Saviour. Let us humbly bow ourselves before Him & offer perpetual prayer for pardon & forgiveness!

But we Cannot indulge in grief however mournful yet pleasing. Our Country demands all our thoughts, all our energies. To resist the powerful Combination now forming against us, will require every man at his place. If victorious we have everything to hope for in the future. If defeated nothing will be left us to live for. I have not heard what action has been taken by the Dept in reference to my recommendations Concerning the organization of the Cavy. But we have no time to wait & you had better join your brigade. This week will in all probability bring us active work & we must strike fast & strong. My whole trust is in God, & I am ready for whatever he may ordain. May he guide guard & Strengthen us is my Constant prayer!

Your devoted father

R E. Lee

The War Against Plebeian Liberty Rages On

With the Federal victory at Gettysburg, and Lee's blunder —— intentional or due to fatigue, frayed nerves, etc. — Lincoln threw everything into the fight.

By the end of 1863, twenty regiments of ex-slaves had been recruited by Lorenzo Thomas from the Mississippi Valley alone, and no doubt filled with propagandist notations to not only compel a raging battle vigor but to provide a constituency that could be manipulated to oppose the majority in any Constitutional stand against the demands of the banking cartel for generations to come. Such is the manner in which divisions among the masses are formed, first by appealing to the self-serving sentimentality of one demographic segment, justified by an imposed sense of having been wronged — especially be goading the younger generation to action.

Following Gettysburg, there was a change in command from General Meade down to Ulysses S Grant. With his opponent's forces now spread out, like water from a powerful creek scattered into a gentle broad run, he had experienced two decisive victories being first at Shiloh, Tennessee, then in the Vicksburg campaign, with Vicksburg carrying into June 1863.

Treatment of Victims

Grant's victory with the Vicksburg campaign impressed Lincoln, and not only for the victory itself but for Grant's ruthless and "dogged persistence," his outspoken advocacy for total warfare, unhindered by any moral scruples. Here was a military leader who did not hesitate to fire on mothers and children, getting the job done no matter what the cost in his own supplies or manpower or in civilian abuse. [1]

Other tactics included attacking on all fronts simultaneously, in conjunction with the idea of dividing to conquer, already gradually demonstrating their effectiveness in view of an enemy slowly bleeding to death from a dwindling of general resources and manpower, initially on the field of battle and now on the home-front as well.

Now, if under the rules of war this Party would take prisoner women and children, starve whole regions, and slaughter with abandon, what might they do in the near future when re-awakened Americans call for a restoration of their liberties? the greatest difference is that with today's technology, they will be in a position to execute their crimes with far more devastating efficiency.

The good news is that there are very basic techniques to defeat high technology systems. Such diverse groups as the Viet Cong and the South America Jivaro have used such tactics; and the famous strategist Sun Tzu has something to offer as well.

A solid, well organized nonviolent approach, even in the face of violence, may in fact prove to be the most effective in the end, as has been verified with the struggles of Gandhi and his revolt against the British Empire. The only exception in this analysis might be if we are struggling against what in reality is the development of a one world government, especially if the authoritarian one-world movement has already ruthlessly dominated huge tracts of national/ continental land across the planet.

The War Goes On

While Lincoln admired Grant, he also feared him as a political rival. Such a revered general might leverage his way into the White House. And now, Congress requested that Grant be given the rank of Lieutenant General, a position not held in the US military since the days of George Washington. Lincoln feared Grant was gaining a new glitter much too close for his own comfort.

Grant next demonstrated his boldness in an event known to history as the overland campaign. Losses were so great that an outcry all across the Federal states demanded an explanation for the death figures: a third of Grant's entire army!

However, the losses affected the Confederates even more, in combination with the scattered army and the general attrition rate. The Confederate army began to weaken. Grant crossed the James River, Virginia, imposing a siege and trench warfare outside Petersburg. Lincoln met with Grant and William Tecumseh Sherman to discuss the best way to meet the military objective of taking down the Confederate Army, and the real objective, how to destroy the economic base and break the morale of the population of the region that still dared to call for some controls over the banks/corporations/colluding politicians.

Sherman moved to Petersburg and destroyed three railroads leading out toward Richmond and beyond into other regions Southward. Sherman and Philip Sheridan carried the war directly to the civilians living in the Shenandoah Valley, attacking plantation estates and destroying what had taken generations to build up.

Federal officers intentionally encouraged soldiers, veterans and those on furlough to plunder, steal, rape, brutalize and murder. They even burned the livestock and crops, so that starvation would kill the citizens or drive them off their land, freeing the land up for later confiscation. This campaign was carried on from Virginia right on through the heart of Georgia, going directly toward the seashore beyond.

As the war raged on, Lincoln was open to no negotiations, only unconditional surrender. According to the book *Nathaniel Bedford Forrest*, a biography by Jack Hurst, Forrest met with Lee during the days of total warfare launched by the Federal troops in 1864. Forrest requested Lee to hand over the supreme command to him, laying a written plan of strategy before him to give assurance that he could come out victorious, regardless of the odds now cast before them. This plan was later affirmed by strategic experts at West Point as having potential for success, had it been adopted.

Forrest was an ingenious master in the art of guerrilla warfare, never losing any major engagement, even though he was outnumbered ten to one in many cases. But Lee refused his offer, saying the nation had suffered enough from the war and that it was time to see an end to the conflict.

On April 1, 1865, Grant's forces finally outflanked Lee's in the Battle of Five Forks, nearly encircling Petersburg, and the Confederate government immediately evacuated Richmond, capital city of the Confederacy. On April 9, 1865, Lee surrendered to Grant at Appomattox.

During the all-out Federal assault from late 1863 into 1865, the Federal government employed every effort to assault the civilian opposition.

Truth Reveals the Source

All through the history of warfare, invading forces have taken advantage of any divisions and rival groups they could find among the resisting society. Double agents (voluntary or bought or coerced), and those having mixed allegiances, have been used by the Roman Empire, the Spanish colonists, the

British, and now the Federal government against citizens of the Confederate territory.[2] The events were especially terrifying for those who were caught out in the hinterlands (ten to fifteen miles outside of town). The ploy began with the invader bribing anyone they could: criminal gangs, rival families, or others, with supplies or funds.

In this case, with the Emancipation Proclamation there was a ready-made field of individuals suddenly offered a new life — but empty handed and with no place to start. They were ripe for recruitment; no extra motivation was needed as there was only one way to survive. Even those who felt no particular animosity for the plantation families found they had no option but to take what they needed; there was no other source.

The real scope of the damage caused by this Federal policy of total warfare would not be realized until one or two generations had passed. The bitter feelings engendered by the abuses, the senseless slaughter and devastation waged by the Federal forces, left boiling rage and unmitigated hatred within the general population, that were destined to last for generations, for the merciless, wanton crimes committed against family, dear friends and associates in the past.

Later on, during the Reconstruction period, Federal authorities were extremely low on funds due to the massive expense of war. They could not finance an effective security platform or in 1864 proficient management program for the conquered Southern states; so they relied on the same methods to terrorize and intimidate local communities into submission.

Deep divisions had already been formed during the last two years of the war. These Federally encouraged crimes and feuds left wounds that would fester for generations, continuing to divide society and prevent any unified defense from springing up again. Divide and conquer, by any means possible.

Lincoln's Bid For Reelection

Lincoln was up for reelection in 1864 and knew that he would win with little in the way of opposition. On November 8, Lincoln was reelected in a landslide, carrying all but three states.

On March 4, 1865, Lincoln made his second inaugural address, in which he attempted to justify this needless human slaughter and destruction as being "God's will." Lincoln also attempted to justify the catastrophe of war by appealing to the now ex-slaves' sense of justice and the sense of duty of those the soldiers who had backed the CBCC, which now held more power and authority over American land and American citizenry than ever. Lincoln now was transposed into a higher authority, a potentate, not simply another American President.

As Lincoln himself declared,

> Fondly do we hope—fervently do we pray—that this mighty scourge of war may speedily pass away. Yet, if God wills that it continue, until all the wealth piled by the bondsman's 250 years of unrequited toil shall be sunk, and until every drop of blood drawn with the lash, shall be paid by another drawn with the sword, as was said 3,000 years ago, so still it must be said, "the judgments of the Lord, are true and righteous altogether". With malice toward none; with charity for all; with firmness in the right, as God gives us to see the right, let us strive on to finish the work we are in; to bind up the nation's wounds; to care for him who shall have borne the battle, and for his widow, and his orphan—to do all which may achieve and cherish a just and lasting peace, among ourselves, and with all nations.

Malice toward none?[1] Charity for all? the vanquished should swallow not only their defeat but the criminal, senseless brutality suffered; and despite the utter lack of charity from their conquerors, should pray in faith to God?

Lincoln appointed Andrew Johnson as Vice President on March 4, 1865. Johnson appeared tipsy (or ill?) during the ceremony, but Lincoln later assured everyone that no person needed to fear his intentions. Johnson was an ardent pro-Unionist who hailed from Tennessee. Many had advised Johnson to convince Lincoln that he should never be lenient with "traitors to the Union."

The Assassination of President Lincoln

Lincoln was shot on Good Friday, April 14, 1865, while attending the play "Our American Cousin," at Ford's Theater, merely five days after Lee's surrender at Appomattox, Virginia. An earlier attempt at assassinating Lincoln had been made in August 1864. Who was behind the plot and what was the larger game are the subject of many a book and outside our scope for now. Let's just see what happened next.

Lincoln lay dead, but the damage was already done: the defeated and disenfranchised portion of the nation that dreamed of somehow regaining their standing in the nation had nothing to fight with: no man power, no economic base, and nothing to build from. The only option was to bow before the callous master of the CBCC and the entire Representative body already inside the halls of Congress who backed them.

In an attempt to appeal to emotion and give the reign of absolute authority some justification, the story was told and retold, in everything from public speeches to schoolbooks, that slavery was brought to an end, with a Constitutional amendment, and that this great moral achievement

---

[1] https://confederateshop.com/my-two-cents/essays/publius/war-crimes-committed-by-federal-forces-during-the-civil-war/

was worth any cost. By repeating this notion, it came to be understood that this had been the goal of the war from the outset, which it was not. Never mind, this permanent destruction of the slave institution was done without any respect for the value of black lives, but only to destroy the economic base of those who opposed the CBCC.

The truth is that a sly twist had been placed inside the amendment. The legal right to own slaves had simply been taken from the individual and handed over to the corporation and government; with a false check pretending to safeguard people from any future attempt by corporations to enslave them, in stating that any legal label of slave was only to be assigned by legitimate court of law.

Bankers as Kingmakers

The states' right to print their own currency, backed by equal value in gold or silver, had been stolen in 1863. So too was the individual family's right to invest its earnings in its own bank for the purpose of providing lending services back to the public; the surest and one of the swiftest methods throughout history of massing a collective fortune.

Lincoln's death represented the end of Constitutional America, rather than the death of slavery.

And with the death of Lincoln, the coffers were empty: it has been estimated that only six months of national funds remained in the national Bank of New York and Treasury.

Think of that, then think about the position of Lincoln's Memorial in Washington, which glares over the Mall across from the Eccles (Federal Reserve Board) Building. Here sits the king whom the CBCC chose, he was the cartel's anointed leader who had supervised their complete conquest of the United States, while posing as a liberator.

Further, upon entering the Lincoln Memorial, one is struck by the sight of the visiting masses being forced to gaze upward at the enthroned figure of Lincoln lording over them. He sits just slightly to his own left. To the casual observer, he appears to be gazing cross at the Washington Monument. When one stands directly in front of Lincoln's figure, however, it can be seen that Lincoln is staring directly at the US Capitol. If he could turn his head 45° the left, his eyes would align perfectly with the Federal Reserve building.

The veiled message appears to be that Lincoln was working with the supreme powers of banking, and conquered not only the US citizen masses but the halls of Congress, with whom the bank rules the masses as a collective absolute authority, rather than in conjunction with a representative body that stands strong on behalf of America's citizen base, as the entire world has been led to believe.

A memorial for Lincoln had been proposed since the time of his death, but it was not until 1913 that Congress approved the commission's choice of design and location. That date of 1913 bears outstanding significance.

The monument was officially completed on May 30, 1922, being dedicated personally by William H Taft.

Taft presided over passage of the Sixteenth Amendment, which allowed Congress to levy an income tax irrespective of any state concerns or the people who reside therein. This amendment was made with no form of check or supervision to protect the tax payers.

When the South lost the Civil War, that sort of protection had been totally removed.

For that reason, this author chose years ago to stop voting. I will do so again only under one single condition, to be discussed later on. Rare are the situations where once may feel confident that a factual intent to serve the people of the land exists and no subterfuge to further limit our freedom.

For the last sixty years, it has been clear that there is no 'lesser of the two evils,' for the two parties are just legs on the same authoritative body, scheming continuously in their own service against the people and the nation in which they rule.

What would really serve the people would be the adoption of a joint resolution by two thirds of both Houses, proposing to the states an amendment to the Constitution granting to the Federal Government the right to levy and collect an income tax without apportionment among the states according to population, and, second, the enactment, as part of the pending revenue measure, either as a substitute for, or in addition to, the inheritance tax, of an excise tax upon all corporations measured by 2 % of their net income.

The First Dark Step Downward

The real truth in the entire affair concerning the Presidency of Lincoln was that the war Lincoln started was on behalf of the de facto central bank of New York, and the corporations that had grown up around it. The true purpose in any fake liberation was to increase manpower in the Federal armed forces and to destroy the economic base that supported the legislators representing those who defied the financial industry and the corporations supported by the bank.

State-issued currency was outlawed in 1863. State-issued currency would have provided an alternative to Federal currency not backed by specie, and if the State currency was appropriately backed by gold and silver, it would have been a strong rival. We may now comprehend the reasoning behind the state of Texas calling for all of its gold and the right to issue its own state currency in our present day and time.

The Constitution

At the National Archives in Washington D.C., the original Constitution is enshrined beneath protective glass in a controlled environment. No one is allowed to take photographs of any sort in the rotunda area. It is not clear why, but it makes one wonder why the photographic record has to be so controlled. What if one has a genuine interest in seeing precisely what is written there, for himself?

Since the documents are aged and the writing faded, as well as the style of handwriting from the day of signature being difficult to read, one is forced to exit the National Archive building and walk up the street a block to the Museum of American History. If one makes his way past Washington's tent and his false teeth, to the place where the artifacts from the Revolutionary war lie, at the end of the corridor is a chamber with an enlarged photograph of the original Constitutional document hanging up to cover the wall on the left hand side, and an enlarged copy printed in clearly legible modern day print on the right hand wall from it.

Here we may take special notice of the Tenth Amendment. The Constitution delegates authority to the Federal Government, and no authority specifically delegated to the Federal Government goes directly to the states and/or the people. Where is the order denying people the right to divorce from the Union of states, should the Federal government make demands that violate the Constitution and the collective will of the people in majority?

In short, for any authority at any time to declare that states do not have the right to secede from the Federal union by majority vote, is to say in the same breath that the Federal government has the right to abuse individual rights and state rights conjunctive with a flagrant violation of Constitutional law; and that the people within individual states have a right to do nothing more than simply tolerate this crass abuse in silence. The right of states to secede was a safeguard, ensuring that the Federal authority could not over step its bounds.

Blind submission to unchecked authority is inherently not a part of the American tradition, or the US would have never divorced itself from Great Britain. When leaders attempt to convince the United States citizen base otherwise, then what type of rule are they really attempting to force down upon the people of the nation? These are very serious questions that citizens will most certainly need to ponder in the coming years.

TEN AMENDMENTS -

What is this here for?

The Tenth Amendment

Now, let's make one last journey to the Civil War corridor located inside the National Museum of American History. We will pass artifacts from the battle of Gettysburg and the Emancipation Proclamation document. Just adjacent to the document is a gift shop. We keep on going past this, into the final chamber of the corridor. Here we may observe on the wall "The Amended Constitution To Preserve the Union."

The most striking, astonishing details of what really took place during this conflict show what the citizens of America in reality lost, rather than gained. Take notice again of the Tenth Amendment and how it was conceptualized throughout the legislative branch almost immediately following conclusion of the US Civil War. In the amended version, the actions taken by the Federal Government strongly appear to read as such:

The Constitution delegates authority to the Federal Government and the Federal Government down to the states and the people.

Recall the National Banking Act of 1863 literally forcing centralized currency on to the states, effectively eliminating any form of control on the de facto central bank of the day, which would manifest itself later as the Federal Reserve.

The Thirteenth Amendment Refines the Rules on Slavery

We all think slavery has been permanently banned. But look: the 13th Amendment provides that "Neither slavery nor involuntary servitude, except as a punishment for crime whereof the party shall have been duly convicted, shall exist within the United States, or any place subject to their jurisdiction." (https://www.ourdocuments.gov/) Note that slavery was *not* outlawed but is allowed to exist henceforth only if a legitimate court of law determined that as a penalty for a crime committed.

Having given us all a false sense of security, this leaves a path of manipulation open to the corporations working with the legal system, should they ever decide to do so, as this amendment was conceived to facilitate the transfer of legalized slavery from the individual person into the hands of government and corporation.

The Fourteenth Amendment Disenfranchises the South

At the same time, the Fourteenth Amendment was enacted in July of 1868, barely three years following the US Civil War. Any person searching for more validation of the Federal government making heavy use of recruited foreign soldiers for the purpose of displacing the citizen base and over-riding their views in respect to the Constitution, simply take notice of this amendment.

It was well known by Federal officials that citizens in the Southern states would seek vengeance on these former agents of the enemy who had made war against them, wantonly destroying their hard won property; these same villains who engaged in outright depraved criminal activity against its non-military civilians during the time of total warfare.

The idea in initiating the vendetta that the Federal government well knew was forthcoming would be to expel or outright eliminate these agents, since the war against forces of the de facto centralized bank was not over with, in the minds of the Anglo-Southern masses at large, who simply refused to give up on the American-made ideology of individual economic liberty just because Lee had surrendered at Appomattox.

This amendment also catered to corporate use of foreign labor by disdaining those who would design to work against it, regardless of where it was in the nation that these contesting groups might hail from.

The same rule of logic applied to former slaves, which is why the Fourteenth Amendment made a direct appeal to their interests. As we shall recall, the Federal Government also compelled the service of ex-slaves via the Emancipation Proclamation, heavily encouraging military service. These individuals were also virtual Federally sanctioned criminal agents of the total warfare effort on the Southern home front, as far as local citizens were concerned. When the war ended, rather than settle in the Northern states, the traitorous ex-slaves and Federal combat veterans remained on Southern soil, living among their very neighbors whom they had so savagely made war upon, with Federal encouragement, while hoping among themselves to benefit from purloined resources falsely promised by the US Federal Government. [3]

Hence, the USFG and its agents knew well that a vendetta was coming, and by 1868 it had already commenced, in view of the US Federal government's near bankrupt situation and its inability to provide security on its newly conquered soil. The Western states, including the west of Tennessee, for example, were being run by pro-Confederate guerrilla forces, assembling a form of police protection and criminal prosecution. This prevailing lawless situation of contesting citizenry left the Anglo-South with no choice but to provide for its own security via a series of paramilitary organizations, [4] pursuing the guilty in the most efficient manner available.

Examine the text of the Fourteenth Amendment here:

> Section 1. All persons born or naturalized in the United States, and subject to the jurisdiction thereof, are citizens of the United States and of the state wherein they reside. No state shall make or enforce any law which shall abridge the privileges or immunities of citizens of the United States; nor shall any state deprive any person of life, liberty, or property, without due process of law; nor deny to any person within its jurisdiction the equal protection of the laws.

> Section 2. Representatives shall be apportioned among the several states according to their respective numbers, counting the whole number of persons in each state, excluding Indians not taxed. But when the right to vote at any election for the choice of electors for President and Vice President of the United States, Representatives in Congress, the Executive and Judicial officers of a state, or the members of the Legislature thereof, is denied to any of the male inhabitants of

such state, being twenty-one years of age, and citizens of the United States, or in any way abridged, except for participation in rebellion, or other crime, the basis of representation therein shall be reduced in the proportion which the number of such male citizens shall bear to the whole number of male citizens twenty-one years of age in such state.

Section 3. No person shall be a Senator or Representative in Congress, or elector of President and Vice President, or hold any office, civil or military, under the United States, or under any state, who, having previously taken an oath, as a member of Congress, or as an officer of the United States, or as a member of any state legislature, or as an executive or judicial officer of any state, to support the Constitution of the United States, shall have engaged in insurrection or rebellion against the same, or given aid or comfort to the enemies thereof. But Congress may, by a vote of two-thirds of each House, remove such disability.

Section 4. The validity of the public debt of the United States, authorized by law, including debts incurred for payment of pensions and bounties for services in suppressing insurrection or rebellion, shall not be questioned. But neither the United States nor any state shall assume or pay any debt or obligation incurred in aid of insurrection or rebellion against the United States, or any claim for the loss or emancipation of any slave; but all such debts, obligations and claims shall be held illegal and void.

Section 5. The Congress shall have power to enforce, by appropriate legislation, the provisions of this article.

The Fifteenth Amendment appears to concur.

Section 1. The right of citizens of the United States to vote shall not be denied or abridged by the United States or by any state on account of race, color, or previous condition of servitude.

Section 2. The Congress shall have power to enforce this article by appropriate legislation.

Foreigners who had been invited to come and fight for the Union, in a bid to earn citizenship, together with blacks freed from slavery, were encouraged to settle in the now de-populated South, where so many men had been killed and land was laid waste. But their voting pattern would, of course, be opposite to that of the agrarian families whose estates they were usurping. Largely uneducated ex-slaves and illiterate foreigners held no understanding whatsoever of economic liberty broadly speaking, let alone the notion of a central bank and the ways it could extend its reach over enterprising individuals. Meanwhile, the white men were stripped of the right to vote. Now voters in the South would be voting directly against the interests of the main constituency.

Furthermore, the Southern economic base was completely broken. Money lending at interest is the surest method of attaining true wealth. Private lending banks were an important part of the plantation establishment, along with took works, a forge, and other services. But to the banking elites and their corporate pals, it only looked like uncontrollable competition. Better they should hold a monopoly on that activity!

As was intimated earlier in this work, legalized slavery was simply transferred from the hands of the individual to the hands of the government and corporation. In that light, consider the trend toward privatizing prisons in the US today, whereby profit-driven corporations own and manage the prison system, evolving into a thriving industrialized component. Demand for compulsory labor with no significant wage cost could very possibly soon outstrip the supply. And the 13th amendment is no safeguard against that.

It may sound like an overblown concern, to those who have not heard much about it. But major corporations are routinely taking advantage of the slave labor of prisoners, as is the US military industrial complex. Motorola, Compaq, Honeywell, Microsoft, Boeing, Revlon, Chevron, TWA, Victoria's Secret and Eddie Bauer, as well as IBM, Texas Instruments, Dell, Kmart, JCPenney and McDonald's are profiting. So are their shareholders, especially the major shareholders.[1]

The Rise of American Business

Industrial production in the Northern sector of the nation grew in step with the Industrial Revolution, the usual war-time boost, and soon thereafter with the rise of huge monopolies, such as the one owned by Andrew Carnegie and the steel industry. The trans-continental railroad and the development of the assembly line gave a tremendous impetus. And as businesses grew, the lending banks got their share. (Maybe more.)

People were happy to pursue the work when it could be found, since the nation had been engulfed in an economic collapse that lasted from 1873 until

---

[1] "The Pentagon and Slave Labor in U.S. Prisons," at Global Research. http://www.globalresearch.ca/the-pentagon-and-slave-labor-in-u-s-prisons/25376

1879, basically covering the US and Europe, where it lasted even longer. In Britain the economy appears to have stagnated for two decades.

While the depression was related in part to the natural flow of economies in general, the reality of an exceedingly low rate of funds available inside the Bank of New York and the Treasury suggests that the depression was also caused or exacerbated by the fact that every available resource that the Federal Government, and the South, possessed had been thrown into the war effort.

Now, there was no requirement that banknotes be backed in gold or silver, nothing to stop the printing press from rolling. The market was flooded with non-specie-backed notes. The idea or rather the hope was that the gradually rising corporate businesses would invest, produce and give their own form of value into these notes.

A major trend in this period was the explosive growth of the railroads, accompanied by over-speculation. Federal land in the West was being purchased in bulk by RR companies, and building projects were financed with loans specifically structured for simple corporate access.

Around these RR depots businesses sprang up and towns grew that were primarily owned and operated by the railroad corporations. Other causes are listed as being due to economic dislocation from the Franco–Prussian war, and massive property losses from the Chicago and Boston fires of 1871 and 1872.

The Panic of 1874

While some mega-businesses did make gains, the overall financial situation appeared to teeter even among the economic elites. With the coming of 1880, things began to feel as if they were calming, and it felt as if a period of gradually increasing prosperity might return for the next four years. Something went wrong somewhere along the way, however. Huge profits, huge corruption, huge gaps in accountability brought the predictable results.

Two huge Wall Street firms collapsed: Grant and Ward, and Marine National Bank of New York. The failure of these two firms caused a domino effect, where a multiplicity of firms fell.

Other causes of the collapse were acts of embezzlement, such as the situation of James C Eno who stole over three million dollars and fled to Canada. Even though the bank eventually replenished the missing amount, the fact that it could happen did not do much to build confidence in the financial system or in Wall Street.

The Depression of 1893

Certain sources tell us that the Panic of 1893 actually began in Argentina, which reminds us that industry and banking were, by this time, linked to the international world of finance. As we shall recall, by 1857 American business and banking had already assumed an international aspect, leading to negative cooperation seeking to manipulate the system at large, in favor of an elitist few. At this scale of lending and borrowing, few, after all, can participate.

The situation began to unravel with the banking firm Baring Brothers, in Argentina. An English merchant bank based in London, it was founded in 1762 and was owned by the German-based banking family Baring, who were merchants and moneylenders. A failure of the Argentine wheat crop and a coup in Buenos Aires ended further investments. Europeans from other areas began a run on gold in the US treasury, since all that they had to do was to cash in their dollar investments for exportable gold.

In spite of the tough economy, during the 1870s and 1880s the US had experienced some growth, but that was primarily due to high international commodity prices. The growth factor would have primarily come in the form of bank-purchased stock options in commodities or corporate executive stock option investments in commodities.

There again, the primary economic beneficiaries of the time period following the Civil War were the international banking and corporate leaders. The people on the ground were dealing with a continuing collapse.

Just thirteen days prior to the inauguration of President Grover Cleveland in 1885, the Philadelphia and Reading Railroad went into receivership, having greatly overextended itself through investments of non-gold backed banknotes into property development contracts. This company was most certainly not the only one.

As concern for the general state of the economy worsened, a mass run on the banks came about as people on rushed in to withdraw their hard-earned funds. This was followed by a credit crunch, causing foreign investors to sell American stocks to obtain American funds backed by purchases in gold from the US Treasury. Some 500 banks closed, 15,000 businesses failed and numerous farms ceased operation.

The unemployment rate was 35% in New York State and 43% in the state of Michigan, making this collapse even worse than the one in 1929. Soup kitchens opened up to feed the starving hordes. Large numbers of women resorted to prostitution, as reported by the records of the day. People lost their life savings when the banks went under. People who could not meet their mortgage obligations simply walked away; a scenario that sounds too familiar to us in the present day, and for many of the same reasons. The situation led to the Pullman Strike and more than 1,300 strikes nationwide, many of them violent, from Illinois, to the coal fields of Appalachia, to Idaho.

Just as Jefferson had predicted so long ago, without checks on the issuance of currency and throughout the system at large, corruption would prevail at the expense of the people on the ground.

The decline of gold reserves stored in the Treasury forced President Cleveland to borrow $65 million in gold from Wall Street banker J.P. Morgan and the Rothschild Banking Family of England, who charged the US government a hefty $7 million fee (approximately $140 million in today's currency) for bailing out the US system. This added 9.3% debt on top of that which the nation already had.

This is not part of any "conspiracy theory," but a short recitation of hard facts from the official historical record. Read this statement from a laborer during the Pullman Strike. The need for some sort of controls on the interests of corporations may be revealed.

Addressed to the American Railway Convention, 15 June 1894:

> Rents all over the city in every quarter have fallen, in some cases to one-half. Residences, compared with which ours are hovels, can be had a few miles away at the prices we have been contributing to make a millionaire a billionaire. What we pay $15 for in Pullman is leased for $8 in Roseland; and remember that just as no man or woman of our 4,000 toilers has ever felt the friendly pressure of George M. Pullman's hand, so no man or woman of us all has ever owned or can ever hope to own one inch of George M. Pullman's land. Why, even the very streets are his.
>
> Water which Pullman buys from the city at 8 cents a thousand gallons he retails to us at 500 percent advance and claims he is losing $400 a month on it. Gas which sells at 75 cents per thousand feet in Hyde Park, just north of us, he sells for $2.25. When we went to tell him our grievances, he said we were all his 'children'. Pullman, both the man and the town, is an ulcer on the body politic. He owns the houses, the schoolhouses, and churches of God in the town he gave his once humble name. [1]

In the 1894 elections, the Republican Party excelled. The Democratic Party was of course crushed by then, impotent on a national level, since its economic base had been destroyed. Lincoln had seen to that.[5]

---

[1]   Statement from the Pullman Strikers (June 15, 1894). In U.S. Strike Commission, *Report on the Chicago Strike of Jnne-July, 1894, by the United Stout Strike Commission* (Washington, DC: Government Printing Office, 1895). pp. 87-88. From History is a Weapon, at http://www.historyisaweapon.com/defcon1/pullmanstrikersstatement.html .

The depletion of funds caused by the war, the physical destruction of a large swath of the nation, the loss of men, were exacerbated by the ensuing economic catastrophes wrought by inflation. The uncontrolled printing of banknotes did bring about an explosion in corporate investment, in combination with unchecked corruption in the CBCC, but it created havoc.

In the South and parts of the West and Midwest, the dramatically weakened Democratic Party still dominated at the local level, and life struggled on with an unspoken intention of resurrecting the antebellum economic system in the South, with its focus on economic success built by individuals and families, not financier/corporate/government insider schemes. It is interesting to note that only two Democratic presidents were elected during the 75 year period between the Civil War and the Great Depression: Cleveland and Wilson.

During the period of Reconstruction, after the War, the Democratic Party had been exterminated at the national level. The Panic of 1893 continued until 1900.

In the new century, Woodrow Wilson came to the fore as a person of interest. Though he was a member of the Democratic Party on paper, his motivations were perfectly aligned with banking interests, not the concerns of the rank and file people. In brief, he had worked diligently to establish the Federal Reserve system. He, along with Taft, supported adoption of the Sixteenth Amendment which gave Congress the right to impose a national income tax (passed in 1909, ratified in 1913), forcing the citizenry to pay any debts incurred by Washington — such as war expenses. (Tariffs had been the preferred means heretofore; but the corporate powers of the Northeast didn't like that.)

That was just in time for the first World War. On the international stage, this war made the bankers rich just as the Civil War had done; and at its conclusion, the international bankers operating behind the Allied powers who set the terms of the "peace" again forced the debt down onto the side that lost, in this case the German/Austrian people.

Twelve years later, to divest themselves of the crushing extortionist demands of this treaty, the new German government took control of its currency away from these multi-national central banks, and removed the gold/silver backing. Their vast increase in production some four years later became known as "the first German economic miracle." A deeper discussion of this delicate matter would be very interesting but lies outside the scope of this writing.

The Panic of 1907 and the Federal Reserve

Starting in 1897, a gradual uptick in the economy generated a sense of optimism. By 1900 economic circumstances appeared to have at least stabilized, though people were dealing with a currency of unstable and often highly questionable value. This insecure feeling continued for the next seven years.

Technology had changed, in the meantime. Improved tractors and fertilizers now allowed huge landed estates to flourish, but without the necessity of slaves. Rice farms using the new harvesting machinery, combines and planters did well on the Mississippi delta, for example. And electricity was now becoming more commonplace in developed areas of the nation.

The problem with this development was, and is, that what is presented, sold or even imposed as progress, can soon make people dependent, no longer willing to live without it. We find outstanding examples in modern day "financing" of homes and automobiles, whereby people feel they have to "buy" something even if they cannot afford to own it; insurance of all sorts is required by law, and inescapable income and property tax leave individuals in financial bondage. There is no liberty when there is no way to opt out.

The panic of 1907 was caused by Augustus Heinze, a copper magnate, and his brother who tried to manipulate the value of the United Copper Company. The scheme failed, resulting in the collapse of New York City's third largest banking trust, the Knickerbocker Trust Company, and regional banks then withdrew funds from New York City banks. The New York Stock exchange fell by a whopping 50%!

Wall Street Banker J.P. Morgan pledged large sums of his own personal money, obviously hedging a bet on the economy moving back up and being able to earn some high-end interest rates in the process. He also convinced other New York bankers to do the same thing. The following year, senator Nelson W Aldrich, father-in-law of John D Rockefeller Jr., established and chaired a commission to investigate the crisis and propose future solutions, eventually leading to the creation of the Federal Reserve.

The circumstances suggest, to this author, that such crises were engineered or allowed at least in part for the purpose of legitimizing such a proposal in the first place.

The Central Bankers Gain Control of the US

The United States did not have an officially recognized centralized bank as such, at this time, and had not had one since the days of Jackson vetoing the charter on the Second Bank of the United States. By proxy, however, the Bank of New York once held all of the specie, and all other banks petitioned for that gold and silver as well as Federal banknotes/dollars, even locally operated state banks. And there were no bounds, no constraints, on what it could do in setting the face value on the bank notes issued (dollars); no requirement that the notes be backed by gold or silver matching the face value of the note. This was an open invitation to manipulation and corruption.

Independent state-owned banks were liquidated, along with banks owned by individual families, in 1863, as we recall, by the National Banking Act, which also served to centralize US currency into a single note, rather than state-issued notes, consequently exterminating any controls on manipulation of currency values.

Decades later, the temptation to keep the printing press running, churning out more dollars as needed, even enabled the debt-based funding of government social programs that were billed as "safety net" provisions but which fed the financial beast while dividing Americans and setting one group against another, while undermining the family itself that is the bedrock of any society. Social wrongs of the past are not righted by giving gifts in the present and future, and taking money from today's hard-pressed workers to make up for something an earlier generation may have done simply does not work. Now America's workforce is bound to service a system with a strong socialized platform that in reality is a way of enslaving the entire US working population.

The creation of the Federal Reserve was part of this mechanism. Following the panics around the end of the last century, efforts to stabilize the economic situation centered on the creation of an official centralized bank. And given the way the Morgans and Rockefellers, et al., had steed in back then, why not facilitate the future of national lending at large by these same families, in a manner that would take care of government by allowing it access to funds without question? the bankers would take care of themselves, no need to worry about that. Now comes the idea of guaranteeing an allotted interest payment by their own self-appointed collection agency, the IRS. Who is to take care of the actual people? Oh, well. Are we sure that slavery has ended?

The New Clandestine Centralized Bank

The Federal Reserve Bank sounds like a Federal institution; most people would assume it is part of, or belongs to, the Federal government — that is, the people of the United States. But that is an intentional deception. The Federal Reserve is a private corporate entity, and the shares are owned by commercial banks.

It does not operate according to instructions from the Government. It is independent. When government officials desire any type of financing, that is, when they want a loan, there is nothing in place either in the halls of

Congress, or in the home of the lender, to debate the wisdom of taking on more debt in the taxpayers' name. Voters have no method of determining what or when specific loans are being made, for what purpose.

The only statistics presented for public consumption are in the realm of a national debt so massive that few ordinary minds, including the writer of this text, can comprehend them. The figures are so huge that they can only be considered as abstractions, and the impact of this ever-increasing debt burden is masked with many subterfuges. In many ways, we cannot perceive any drastic rift in the course of daily life. As a college professor I know once (ironically) said, "The birds still sing and the cash registers ring. People still go out to eat, and jump in the pool to beat the heat, so why should I care about something I read in some book or hear on the television? What can I do about anything?" This complacency is pushed by the media, where subliminal messages are so powerful that the lies perpetuated are accepted en masse, even in the face of hard facts to the contrary.

The Next Phase of Conquest

It all began underneath a cover of darkness on November 22, 1910, at a railroad station in Hoboken, New Jersey. A delegation of the United States' leading financiers left in a sealed railroad car, with all blinds drawn, on a secret mission. Newspaper reporters who had gathered around for the purpose of observing and hopefully, conducting an interview got nothing. The destination was not revealed that night and for some time later.

The delegation was led by Senator Nelson Aldrich, head of the National Monetary Commission, which President Theodore Roosevelt had signed into law in 1908, hoping to permanently stabilize the national economy. Aldrich had just led the members of the commission on a two-year tour of Europe, casually spending some three hundred thousand dollars of tax payers' money. He had not yet made any report on the trip nor had he devised any hard plan for banking reform. [6]

Accompanying Senator Aldrich at the Hoboken station were his private secretary, Sheldon A. Piat Andrew, Assistant Secretary of the Treasury, and Special Assistant of the NMC, Frank Vanderlip; the President of the National City Bank of New York, one Henry P Davison; Morgan's personal emissary and senior partner of J.P. Morgan Company, Charles P. Norton, president of the First National Bank of New York, a bank also dominated by Morgan. At the last moment before train departure, in leaped Benjamin Strong, lieutenant of J.P. Morgan, followed at his heels by Paul Warburg, an immigrant from Germany who had joined the banking house of Kuhn, Loeb. According to Bertie Charles Forbes, six years later, Warburg was the link that bound the Aldrich system and the system of the time given in the statement (1916) together. In Forbes' own words, "He more than any one man, has made the system possible as a working reality."

Aldrich informed the others that his plan from that moment on was to keep them virtually imprisoned at Jekyll Island, a resort area in Georgia, until they had created a "scientific currency system" for the United States.

Reporters appeared to have been tipped off that something of interest was astir and were waiting at the station in Brunswick, Georgia. Henry P. Davison went out to address them, speaking only in generalities, never divulging any classified secrets. The cover for their true project was that they were going on a two-week duck hunt.

They commenced constructing a series of lavish mansions, which they called "cottages," for use by their families during their winter vacation. They called themselves "The Jekyll Island Hunt Club. "It has been said that one sixth of the entire world's wealth was represented by the members of the JIHC! Membership was exclusive only to family and by fact of blood inheritance, rather than any form of earned right.

Banking "reform" had been ordered by the National Monetary Commission. Here they set out to draft the plan for control of the money and the credit of the United States Government, and thus of the citizens, and all other national banking entities as well.

If true banking reform was what they really were after, they would have taken power away from the elitists by demanding a check on currency, demanding that the face value of banknotes issued be backed by an equal amount in gold or silver. But consolidation of power was their real goal: the ability to dictate the national direction, to the advantage of an elitist few.

In the end, their monetary "reform" plan was presented to Congress, billed as the work of the National Monetary Commission — not a bunch of big bankers. The taint of big money directly from Wall Street was concealed from public view.

Examine this direct quote from the primary source used in regard to the Jekyll Island meeting inside this work. The source used is *Jekyll Island, Secrets of the Federal Reserve*, by Eustace Mullins:

> It (the struggle against the centralized bank) had begun with Thomas Jefferson's fight against Alexander Hamilton's scheme for the First Bank of the United States, backed by James Rothschild. It had continued with President Andrew Jackson's successful war against Alexander Hamilton's scheme for the Second Bank of the United States, in which Nicholas Biddle was acting as the agent for James Rothschild of Paris. The result of that struggle was the creation of the Independent Sub-Treasury System, which supposedly had served to keep the funds of the United States out of the hands of the financiers. A study of the panics of 1873, 1893, and 1907 indicates that these panics

were the result of the international bankers' operations in London. The public was demanding in 1908 that Congress enact legislation to prevent the recurrence of artificially induced money panics. Such monetary reform now seemed inevitable. It was to head off and control such reform that the National Monetary Commission had been set up with Nelson Aldrich at its head, since he was majority leader of the Senate.

Note the references to the First Bank of the United States, and specifically who Alexander Hamilton's backer was: James Rothschild. We notice the President of the Second Bank of the United States was Nicholas Biddle. A very revealing detail is that Biddle was the acting agent for James Rothschild of Paris.

Now we know the reason for the ruthlessness of those supporting a central bank and currency, a means to guarantee their "right" to corrupt. Its financier was demanding payment, and all who were in collusion stood to gain by borrowing money, then forcing repayment of that debt back down upon the heads and backs of America's citizens!

The result of the war against the bank was the creation of a supposedly independent sub Treasury System, which gave the American public the impression that it served to keep federal funds out of the hands of self-serving financiers. But only insiders knew who the fund contributors were, and what amounts were in the fund on any occasion; so therefore the Treasury was wide open to the forces of corruption.

The public was demanding reform to head off artificially-induced financial panics by 1908/1909. But it appears that the purpose in this meeting on Jekyll Island, and supported by the National Monetary Commission, was in fact to head off efforts to reform the monetary system. Warburg even instructed that they avoid using the name "central bank." His proposal was to label this new center of American finance with the beguiling euphemism, the Federal Reserve System.

This de facto central bank would be owned by a small circle of huge banks, whose shareholders in turn were individuals who would profit immensely from the business. As a bank issuing funds, those in control would literally dictate the nation's money value and credit. The bank would give all appearances of being "controlled" by Congress. The US President himself would select the Federal Reserve Board of Governors, furthering the impression that the Federal Reserve was under US Government control. A majority of the directors would be appointed directly or indirectly by the banks in the Federal Reserve association. The real decisions made by the Board would be controlled by a Federal Advisory Council, meeting with these presidentially appointed governors. The FAC would be chosen by these directors of the twelve Federal Reserve Banks, who would always remain unknown, intentionally, by design of Warburg.

Now we are going back to the same time-honored struggle that had been with America since the days of the Washington administration: some voices sought safeguards against potential corruption, against the ever-present figures who are determined to take advantage where they can. The difference in this new round of the great battle is that now those most vocal in their concern no longer had any representatives in Congress to fight on behalf of the American public. The ones now demanding the hard check were the mass of citizens themselves appealing to their congressional representatives, whom they recognized were not representing their collective interests.

The potential for corruption continued, as the representative body could be induced to turn coat and betray the citizens who had voted them into office.

Further to mislead the public, the design of the Federal Reserve System included a regional reserve system, twelve branch reserve banks located in different sections of the nation, giving the impression of decentralization. Individuals outside of the banking world would be oblivious to the fact that America's currency and credit system was still highly concentrated in New York City alone.

The other deception was that rather than having the Board of Governors proposed by Congress, it would be proposed by the President himself. This arguably renders the Federal Reserve System proposal unconstitutional. The reason goes back to the same argument made by Jefferson and Jackson, as we may observe in article one, section eight, part five of the Constitution: "Congress shall have the power to coin money and regulate the value thereof."

The FRS was designed to be a bank of issue (issuing funds to finance the nation's work). Tyrants rule nations by controlling their currency; so therefore the founding fathers, primarily Jefferson and his backers, demanded that any issuance of funds first pass through Congress before being accepted. Warburg's proposal was an end-run around that, virtually allowing for an absolute authority to dictate the direction of the nation's financing, by placing the selection of the bank's leadership in the hands of the US President — an individual with his own self-serving interests and who could, in any event, be induced or compelled to serve other interests.

With the establishment of the Federal Reserve System, the banking cartel now truly did hold absolute power over the nation. The old authoritarian dream of reducing the population to an expendable resource was making great headway.

In the 21st century we can see how this is playing out. Our national debt is approaching $20 Trillion! — several times the annual GDP, and about

$167,000 per taxpayer.[1] the interest alone is more than half our gross national product, so that there is no prospect of ever paying it down. What do the facts of history suggest as the inevitable result?

The People Who Held the Vision

The perpetrators of this financial conquest were essentially the same forces that had conquered the Confederacy militarily, destroying those whose Representatives in Congress called for checks and balances on the money supply. When the military conquest had concluded, the Treasury and the Bank of New York only held approximately six months' worth of national funds.

So the de facto national bank of the day printed loads of non-specie backed banknotes, then known as "greenbacks," to create liquidity. But this cheap paper facilitated a financial collapse in 1870. The inflation of prices that resulted from this over printing, in combination from intentional currency value manipulation to the benefit of the elites in charge of the system by 1893, led to a series of economic crises in a thirty-eight-year period.

Pressed by the public to provide some stability, Washington saw the opportunity to undo the achievement of President Jackson who had done away with the National Bank. Now they moved forward to finalize their conquest. A new factor was the large number of powerful corporations that had evolved, all owned and controlled by the corporate, banking, and government collusion.

The following phases of the conquest would be implemented gradually. The first step was to seize resources held by individuals and families, then move to reduce these hard-working, enterprising people to a meek, docile workforce and an expendable resource.

Let us zoom in on the lives of the characters at Jekyll island back in November of 1910. Remember the supreme strategic maxim of war, "Know thy enemy and know thy true self."

(1) Nelson Aldrich

Aldrich was one of four Republicans who dominated the Senate by the 1890s. Aldrich held a chief position on the Senate Finance Committee. He was referred to by the public and the press alike as "General Manager of the Nation." He largely controlled tariff and monetary policies the first decade of the twentieth century.

Aldrich became immensely wealthy with investments in street railroads, sugar, rubber and banking. He married into the Rockefeller family and his

---

[1] According to http://www.usdebtclock.org/ (accessed Feb. 9, 2017).

descendants became powerful figures in American politics and banking. Aldrich was born in Rhode Island. His family descended from well noted English immigrants. Let's zoom in on them:

(a) John Winthrop

John Winthrop was a wealthy English puritan and one of the leading figures in the founding of the Massachusetts Bay Colony. Winthrop was born into an immensely wealthy landowning and merchant family. He was trained in law and became Lord of the Manor at Groton in Suffolk, England. He served 19 terms as governor.

He believed in an authoritarian rule of government. He ardently resisted attempts to broaden civil rights or to codify a body of laws that magistrates would be bound by. He called democracy "the meanest and worst of all forms of government." Winthrop's son was one of the founders of the Connecticut colony, and Winthrop himself wrote one of the historical accounts of the time period. His descendants include a long list of famous Americans, and his writings continue to influence politicians to this day.

(b) Roger Williams

Williams was a puritan minister. He was apprenticed under Sir Edward Coke, educated at Charterhouse, and also at Pembroke College, Cambridge. Williams began to view the Church of England as corrupt and false. He believed in freedom of religion and separation of church and state. Williams eventually arrived at the conclusion that no valid church existed; all were self-serving. Eventually he was banished from Salem, Massachusetts, for his beliefs regarding church and state. He and twelve followers moved outside of the Plymouth Land Grant territory and founded a colony he called "Providence." In time, Williams was sent by the colony back to England in order to found an official charter for the colony. Williams sealed the charter making him President of Rhode Island in 1654.

(c) William Wickenden

Wickenden was an early Anglo Baptist minister who co-founded the colony of Providence, Rhode Island. Although portrayed in the official history as a "poor cobbler with a large family," he was one of 39 signers to form an agreement that led to the formation of Providence government in 1640, and one of the 12 men who signed the "Providence Compact." He served in the Rhode Island legislature from 1648–1651, then again in 1664.

To summarize, Aldrich's ancestors held very powerful positions of leadership and wealth in both Britain and early colonial America. Aldrich served on the Rhode Island House of Representatives from 1875 through 1876, serving as Speaker of the House. He served in the US Senate for thirty years from 1881 to 1911. His tenure was beaten only by Claiborne Pell in the late twentieth century.

If there is anything to learn from looking at whom he served under, where he worked and where he placed his interests, it is simple to deduce that the needs and interests of the common man were not his primary concern.

(2) Arthur B. Sheldon

Sheldon appears to have been somewhat a maverick and a mystery. He was born around 1874 in Washington D.C. to Charles and Emma Sheldon. The record on his life does not pick up again until 1897, when Sheldon had become clerk of the Senate Finance Committee. We may presume that he had solid connections and was able to make a good impression. Aldrich became chair of the SFC in 1898, and sometime before 1901 Sheldon had worked as Aldrich's personal private secretary.

In 1908, Congress passed the Aldrich-Vreeland Act, which primarily created the National Monetary Commission, whose purpose and intent was to reform the US banking and financing system. Aldrich chaired the commission and Aldrich served as its secretary. In 1910, Sheldon was appointed clerk of a new customs appeals court that Congress created as part of the Payne-Aldrich Tariff Act of 1909.

Sheldon married Ann Latimer in 1899 and had a surviving son named Charles, who lived into old age. Sheldon died in 1954.

(3) Abram Piatt Andrew

Andrew was born in La Porte, Indiana, on February 12, 1873. He graduated Princeton College in 1893, presumably not as part of any affirmative action program. He studied at the Harvard Graduate School of Arts and Sciences, graduating with a Master's degree in 1895 and a Doctorate degree in 1900. Andrew later pursued post graduate studies in Universities of Halle, Berlin and Paris. In January 1907, Andrew published a paper that anticipated the economic Panic of 1907, occurring later that fall. On the strength of that paper as well as his strong education in economics, he was selected to serve on the National Monetary Commission, tasked with reforming the United States banking system.

He served as director of the US mint in 1909 and 1910, and the assistant Secretary of the Treasury from 1910 to 1912. He drafted Senator Robert Latham Owen's version of the Federal Reserve Bill in 1913. His version came the closest to the act eventually signed into law on December 1913.

Given Andrew's deep understanding of the mechanics of the economic process, during the meeting on Jekyll Island he would have been keenly aware of any loopholes in the process that could be arranged to benefit the Corporate-Banking elite, while simultaneously indenturing all of American society into serving this elite and their future personal financial ambitions. In other words, Senator Owen's bill quite likely contained a veiled intent to subordinate the entire financial system to the benefit of the banking families already noted as being behind US finances. The bill left no checks in place to safeguard the system and prevent an out-right exploitation of the people.

(4) Frank A. Vanderlip

Vanderlip, an American banker, was Assistant Secretary of the Treasury from 1897–1901. He was President of the National City Bank from 1909 to 1919. He created the Scarborough School at Briarcliff Manor in New York state and a California development known as Palos Verdes in 1913, the same year that the Federal Reserve System came into existence.

Schools are one of the straw-man entities that can be used as fronts, one form among countless others into which public funds may be funneled, concealed inside a daunting bureaucracy, and distributed back to the primary beneficiary; all done under the guise of benefiting the commoner and the community at large. No doubt some benefit does make it back to the community, but the price the public pays local and state tax, both direct and indirect.

It is interesting that he had gone to work at a lathe factory at age 16, then, after one year at the University of Illinois, Vanderlip became city editor at the Aurora Evening Post in 1885. That's a quick rise. Economist Joseph French Johnson took Vanderlip under his guidance, eventually allowing him to obtain a position at a financial investigative service for stock investors in Chicago in 1886. Let us observe specifically who Joseph French Johnson was in order to get better picture of what was going on at the time.

Johnson was an American economist, journalist, professor and dean of the School of Commerce, Accounts and Finance at New York University; he founded the Alexander Hamilton Institute in 1909, suggesting he was a supporter of Hamilton's financial philosophy including the lack of concern for checks and balances, all plebeian interests be damned. That same year Johnson was offered a position on the National Monetary Commission. Indirectly, it would appear, Alexander Hamilton influenced the development of the National Monetary Commission as well as influencing the Federal Reserve/clandestine US central bank.

Vanderlip Moves On

In 1889, Vanderlip secured work at the Chicago Tribune, first as a reporter, then financial editor. While at the Tribune, Vanderlip took a course in political economy at the University of Chicago. This allowed him to attract the attention of Lyman J. Gage, who became Secretary of the Treasury under President William McKinley in 1897. Gage brought Vanderlip with him to Washington as his private secretary. Six weeks later Gage promoted Vanderlip to Assistant Secretary of the Treasury. How did he court influence so readily? Was he a member of some elitist fraternal organization? Was Vanderlip a Mason? At least 15 US presidents were Freemasons, and so were many of the other most influential figures.

As directed by the War Revenue Act of 1898, Vanderlip was placed in charge of selling out the 200 million dollar bond issue to fund the Spanish-American War and procuring the subscriptions, with the smallest subscribers receiving the first issues, so that the public would feel invested in the fight. We should take special notice of the deceptive plan here. Vanderlip and his team of 700 clerks sold out the bond issue in just thirty days, closing out the bond drive on July 14, 1898.[7]

This astounding level of success brought him to the attention of James J. Stillman, president of the country's largest bank, National City Bank of New York. By 1902, Vanderlip had become vice president, and was president from 1909 until 1919. During the Panic of 1907, Vanderlip worked with other stable bankers led by JPMorgan, to stop the depositors' run on banks exacerbating the economic disaster. The Vanderlip alternative plan nearly derailed the plan promoted by President Wilson and the Democratic Party. A number of Vanderlip's ideas were incorporated into the final Federal Reserve Act drawn up on December 23, 1913.

(5) Henry P. Davison

Davison was born in Pennsylvania. After completing his education he became a bookkeeper in a bank managed by one of his relatives. At age 21, he gained employment at a bank in Bridgeport Connecticut. He and his wife, Kate Trubee, had two sons who later became men of importance: F. Trubee Davison became director of personnel for the Central Intelligence Agency. Henry Pomeroy Davison became director at Time Magazine and a Yale University graduate, and a member of the Skull And Crossbones Society.

These connections linking the new central bank with forces such as the CIA and the SACS are important notations.

Davison moved to New York City where he was employed by Astor Place Bank. He later became president of Liberty National Bank. He was markedly involved in the founding and formation of the Banker's Trust Company. After his involvement with the meeting on Jekyll Island, he helped expand the Red Cross internationally, distinguished himself in World War One, then died of a brain tumor in 1922, at age 54.

(6) Charles D. Norton

He was president of J.P. Morgan's First National Bank of New York; other than that, there is very little information on him.

(7) Paul Warburg

Warburg was born in Hamburg, Germany, into a banking dynasty with origins in Venice. After attending the Realgymnasium, he entered the employment of Simon Hauer, a Hamburg importer and exporter, to learn the fundamentals of business practice. He worked for Samuel Montague and Company, bankers in London 1889–90, then the Banque Russe pour le Commerce Etranger, in Paris, 1890–91.

In 1891 he entered the office of the family banking firm of M.M. Warburg and Company, which had been founded by his great-grandfather in 1798. He interrupted work there to take a world tour during the winter of 91–92. Warburg was admitted into a partnership with the family firm in 1895.

That October, Warburg married Nina J. Loeb, daughter of Solomon Loeb, founder of the New York investment firm, Kuhn, Loeb and Company. He was a member of Temple E-Manu-El, in New York City.

Warburg was elected a director of Wells Fargo in February 1910. He resigned on September 1914 following his appointment to the Federal Reserve Board, and Jacob Schiff was elected to replace him on the Wells Fargo board. Warburg went on, following his part in the meeting on Jekyll Island, to sit on the chief director boards of a number of important financial trusts and associations. Warburg, as we shall recall, was noted as the chief architect of the Federal Reserve Bank.

(8) Benjamin Strong

Strong was born in Fishkill, New York. His family were descendants of wealthy British merchants and bankers. Strong became a clerk at a Wall Street investment and financial management firm associated with his father's employer. Strong worked for a banking trust company, but at the time commercial banks viewed trusts as potential threats to their profit margin, since they could handle large financial accounts for corporations and provide the same services as a commercial bank.

Strong moved to Banker's Trust, a trust composed of commercial bankers acting as a single unit, with the agreement that they would not threaten the surrounding commercial banks. This trust also held the money for other Trusts, thus becoming the second largest US Trust Company and a dominant Wall Street institution.

The voting power was held by three associates of J.P. Morgan. Strong worked closely with J.P. Morgan to lend only to sound financial institutions. Strong later served as President of the Federal Reserve Bank of New York, because of his leadership skills. He was considered a primary force in US banking and monetary affairs.

(9) Col Edward House

House was either present at the meeting on Jekyll Island or, at the very least, his credentials indicate that he knew well of the proceedings. House was born on July 26, 1858, in Texas. His father had come from England and had become a very prominent business man making his fortune developing the city area, and serving a term as its mayor.

House attended a series of private schools, and returned to Texas during his third year of college to care for his sick father, who later died. Upon his return he sold the family's cotton plantations and invested heavily in banking. He was the founder of Trinity and Brazos Railway. He moved to New York City in 1902.

He helped make four men governor of Texas; James S Hogg, Charles A Culberson, Joseph D Sayers and S.W.T. Lanham. Hogg eventually assigned House the title of Colonel. He became an adviser, close friend and supporter of New Jersey Governor Woodrow Wilson in 1911.

Later on House attended the Paris Peace Conference as chief deputy to Wilson. He backed Franklin D. Roosevelt with the New Deal proposal, only to express disappointment with it later on. He is also noted for supporting the US inclusion into the League of Nations.

The Federal Reserve Act

"Let me issue and control a nation's money and I care not who writes the laws." Mayer Amschel Rothschild (1744–1812), founder of the House of Rothschild

"This [Federal Reserve Act] establishes the most gigantic trust on earth. When the President [Wilson] signs this bill, the invisible government of the monetary power will be legalized....the worst legislative crime of the ages is perpetrated by this banking and currency bill."— Charles A. Lindbergh, Sr., 1913

On December 23, 1913, the Federal Reserve Act was signed into law by President Woodrow Wilson. This law was an amalgamation of the proposals made at the secret Jekyll Island meeting of multimillionaire bankers and top end politicians. In a nutshell, the FRA established America's first officially recognized Central Bank since the days of Jackson and the SBOUS.

The difference in this bank primarily was that it would be clandestine in its design, with twelve satellite banks located throughout the nation, though highly central in their linking. This structure deceived the casual observer into thinking it was not simply a power center for the New York-centered industrial/banking clan of the Northeast.

The primary proposal came in the form of the Glass-Owen bill, which included many ideas taken from the Aldrich bill, but gave control over to an entity called the Federal Reserve Board. The new Federal Reserve Note, the new dollar, was to be an obligation of the Treasury, and nationally chartered member banks were under obligation to be included in the system.

Opposition to the bill echoed the arguments made by both Jefferson and Jackson many years earlier, primarily that the entity would serve the interests of only an elitist few at the expense of small producers, businesses, farmers and consumers, and that the economy could be destabilized to the advantage of this elite through speculation, intentional inflation and deflation. Critics asked *who*, who would govern the new centralized banking system?

The Federal government decided to have the US President appoint governors to the board. Now the Federal Government was married into the new Central Bank, which would wield so much power over the economic lives of US citizens. Essentially, the true rulers of both the FR board and the Federal government were now the international families holding the money out to supply the FR banking system.

In other words, the new Federal Reserve System was simply a front for these families to continue lending money to the government, while deceiving the working people into believing that the US Federal government was the originator of national funds, and that FR banks were nationwide, rather than centralized into a single location in New York City.

President Woodrow Wilson, who signed it into law, was himself among those who were horrified to see what it really was.

"I am a most unhappy man. I have unwittingly ruined my country. A great industrial nation is controlled by its system of credit. Our system of credit is concentrated. The growth of the nation, therefore, and all our activities are in the hands of a few men. We have come to be one of the worst ruled, one of the most completely controlled and dominated

Governments in the civilized world no longer a Government by free opinion, no longer a Government by conviction and the vote of the majority, but a Government by the opinion and duress of a small group of dominant men." —Woodrow Wilson

"From now on, depressions will be scientifically created."— Congressman Charles A. Lindbergh Sr., 1913

"We have, in this country, one of the most corrupt institutions the world has ever known. I refer to the Federal Reserve Board. This evil institution has impoverished the people of the United States and has practically bankrupted our government. It has done this through the corrupt practices of the moneyed vultures who control it."— Congressman Louis T. McFadden, 1932 (Rep. Pa)

The Next Step: The Revenue Act 1913

"By this means government may, secretly and unobserved, confiscate the wealth of the people, and not one man in a million will detect the theft."— British Lord John Maynard Keynes (in his book the *Economic Consequences of Peace*, 1920)

The Supreme Court had been debating the legality of an income tax ever since the Civil War. Progressives in Congress attached a provision for an income tax to a tariff bill in 1909. Conservatives, seeking to end the discussion once and for all, proposed amending the Constitution to implement the tax: then, as now, it was hard to believe that a Constitutional amendment could garner support from three-fourths of the states. They were shocked when the amendment was ratified by one state legislature after another. The 16th Amendment took effect on February 25, 1913. (Even so, at the time, exemptions and deductions spared 99% of the people of the tax, which was only 1% of net income. Few could have foreseen how this monster would evolve.)[1]

Read the amendment very carefully, then keep in mind that Congress had no more representatives to call for protections.

The Congress shall have power to lay and collect taxes on incomes, from whatever source derived, without apportionment among the several states, and without regard to any census or enumeration.

In other words, Congress can charge the people, regardless of income differences, demographic differences, or any other distinction that might be

---

[1] From https://www.ourdocuments.gov/doc.php?flash=true&doc=57 (accessed Jan. 29, 2017).

relevant, from one state to another. Take notice of the fact that no checks were established to determine where the line exists between a "legitimate" tax rate (say, 5 to 6% in total, without the addition of state tax) and outright extortion (any amount exceeding that).

With this law passed, the Federal government could now approach the Federal Reserve Board to demand whatever funds they could imagine, then charge the American people to repay the loan, plus interest.

And this was just in time to pay for the next war. Recall what happened when the charter for the FBOTUS was signed, and the loans that paid for the Revolutionary War were foisted off upon the states. Citizen property was confiscated when the states defaulted, not to mention the flagrant way that Revolutionary War veterans were defrauded of their pensions, when they needed funds to pay mortgages on land and purchase general supplies around the farm and home.

Another possibility also exists. The economy had improved by 1913 and stood to prosper for the future ten-year period. It seems possible that the CBCC feared that a new wave of entrepreneurial success could create a class of citizens who, once again, could support Representatives in Congress who would actually protect their interests, against the collusive cartel.

Consider the advancements in mechanization by 1913. Farmers could use machines rather than more field hands. The steam engine was replacing sail and water power; clay bricks, laboriously dug and transported, were about to be supplanted by Portland cement as a basic building material; new opportunities were changing the economic landscape. There were opportunities of many kinds newly opened to small producers who could generate enough profit to move up.

An income tax tactfully designed to increase incrementally, in proportion to any form of individual gain, would help to neutralize such efforts — and for all time to come. Citizens attempting to skirt the extortionist bill for the loans, in the looming future, would be fined at loan sharking interest rates, at risk of having their lawfully purchased property confiscated in direct violation of the Constitutionally guaranteed property rights.

The Four Primary Lords of America's Economy

According to online sources and others such as Eustace Mullins' work, *Secrets of the Federal Reserve*, four primary banks dominate the US economy. These banks are as follows: Bank of America, J.P. Morgan Chase, Citigroup and Wells Fargo. These banks are heavily invested into the four primary oil conglomerates that dominate the economies in virtually every nation on earth: ExxonMobil, Royal Dutch/Shell, B.P. and Chevron Texaco. It has been said that these entities rule not only US finances but the finances of the world.

According to J.W. McCallister, an oil insider with House of Saud connections, just eight families own 80% of the New York Federal Reserve Bank. Those eight families are the Goldman Sachs, Rockefellers, Lehmans and Kuhn Loebs of New York, the Rothschild family of Paris and London, the Warburgs of Hamburg, the Lazards of Paris and the Israel Moses Seifs of Rome. These same sources tell us that these four lords of banking are among the top ten stockholders of all the fortune 500 corporations.

So if the corporations get the funding they need to exist from the financiers/owners of these banks, then whom do they really serve, the top families or the common people? Whom do our US representatives truly represent, when they get their campaign funding from these corporations and other entities controlled by these families. Do the American people really continue to think that they actually have true representation in the halls of US Congress?

The House of Morgan

Both the Rockefeller Foundation and the Federal Reserve were born in 1913, the same year that John Pierpont Morgan died. The House of Morgan (HOM) presided over American finance, acting as the unofficial central bank since 1838, when George Peabody founded it in London. Peabody was a business associate of the Rothschild family.

According to Mullins, the Morgans were Rothschild agents. The Rothschild family, a Jewish dynasty deeply embedded in the finances of Europe as well as America, preferred to operate behind the House of Morgan, an Americanized front.

The House of Morgan spread internationally, opening up branches in Paris. The extended Rothschild family, the Lamberts, set up Drexel and Company in Philadelphia. The HOM worked with the Astors, the DuPont family, the Guggenheim family, and the Vanderbilt and the Rockefeller families.

Needless to say and very important to recall, the HOM financed corporations that we are all familiar with, among others AT&T, General Motors, General Electric and DuPont. Like their main source, the Rothschild family in Europe, the HOM eventually wound its way into government and the power structure of America itself. By 1890 the HOM was lending money to the Egyptian central bank, Russia and Brazil, and even funding government-backed projects as far away as Argentina.

Economic downturns suited the bankers as much as upticks. The year 1890 was a period of panic for the US economy, only to be supported by a shipment of Rothschild gold worth an astounding $62 million dollars, to be repaid with interest.

The HOM financed development of the American West through voting trusts. According to Mullins, Cornelius Vanderbilt's Morgan financed the New York Central Railroad and gave preferential shipping rates to John D. Rockefeller's Standard Oil monopoly. This act welded the bond between the Rockefeller and Morgan entities, serving to pass control of the HOM over to the Rockefeller and Rothschild families.

Kuhn Loeb controlled the railroad industry, while Lehman, Goldman Sachs and Lazard joined the Rockefeller family in controlling the US industrial base. These same families had very close ties with European royalty, who also needed financial support. The 1913 creation of the Federal Reserve fused the power of these international banking families to the military and the US government.

By 1895, the HOM controlled the flow of gold in and out of the US. The industries that we are all familiar with from that era of time — Standard oil, US Steel, Harriman's railroads — all were financed by Jacob Schiff at Kuhn Loeb, closely linked with the Rothschild family.

The US government eventually attempted to sever the influence of old European money, spearheaded by none other than Teddy Roosevelt himself. This unwelcome in initiative by TR may have been at least one of the most direct reasons behind the deceptive design of the FR in the first place.

The House of Rockefeller

The most powerful bank on earth is the Bank of International Settlements (BIS) headquartered in Switzerland. This sole bank is in actuality the central bank for the eight families described, who control the private central banks of all Western and developing nations. It "controls most of the transferable money in the world. It uses that money to draw national governments into debt for the IMF."[1] the first president of the BIS was Rockefeller banker Gates McGarrah, an official of both Chase Manhattan and the Federal Reserve. McGarrah was the grandfather of former CIA director Richard Helms.

This link to Richard Helms is of vital importance in understanding future events in US history.

Some writers, such as Carroll Quigley, have theorized that the BIS was part of an international plan to create a world system of financial control held in private hands to dominate the political system of each country and the world economy itself. The US government attempted to lobby the BIS out of existence at the 1944 Bretton Woods Conference. Needless to say,

---

[1] http://www.bilderberg.org/bis.htm (accessed Jan. 15, 2017).

their efforts failed. The result was that power for the eight families was dramatically increased.

Manifestations of the vastly increased power came with an appearance of the International Monetary Fund and the World Bank. The BIS in Switzerland holds 10% of monetary reserves for 80 of the world's central banks. It serves as financial agent for international agreements, gathers data on the so called global economy, and holds itself out in an effort to neutralize global financial collapse, when doing so becomes necessary. The BIS has other characteristics that are certain to be of future interest to readers of this volume, as we shall observe later on.

In Summary

This section has described in brief how the same centralized banking interests (married with the interests of the corporation and funded by the Morgans via the Rothschild family) that won the Civil War went on to force a centralized currency and banknotes upon the masses — and the liberated individual enterprise economy that supported them — and then regrouped forty-five years later to form a central bank rather misleadingly called the Federal Reserve. The delay of forty-five years may be due primarily to the fact that the US Civil War had nearly bankrupted the Treasury and the de facto national bank of the day. [8]

The bankers dealt with that situation by printing huge numbers of banknotes that were not backed by gold or silver, and that therefore were subject to manipulation. While the average family was on hard times, corporations sponsored and owned by the bank of Morgan were able to purchase huge tracts of Western land at extraordinarily low rates. In a series of back-to-back economic depressions, foreclosures and property confiscations by the bank further dispossessed the populace while concentrating assets in the "hands" of the corporate and banking cartel. In other words, life for the rank and file, from 1870 on down to 1908, was essentially life under collapsed/severely depressed economic conditions, while the great corporate monopolies or Trusts expanded, that later called for the "Trust-busting" measures sponsored by Theodore Roosevelt.

It was in response to cries for relief from the average family, as a result of this failure to stabilize the currency and the economic situation, that the banking families all united with the US government to meet at Jekyll Island, Georgia, giving birth to what would become the Federal Reserve three years later.

Once President Woodrow Wilson had signed the bill into law, three years later the Sixteenth Amendment was added to the Constitution that allowed Congress to take on any amount of debt. There was no provision for questioning the necessity of doing so or for regulating how the borrowed money was spent, and the bill would be paid at whatever interest rate the cartel desired, by the American taxpayer.

It was of little or no concern to the top families if this evolved, by our times, into an unstoppable repressive tyranny.

As we have discussed earlier, the Thirteenth Amendment did not outlaw slavery! the Thirteenth Amendment only outlawed the individual person's right to own slaves, while preserving the concept for the government and the corporation. As we shall recall, a false safeguard was put in place, that being that a court of law could still force individuals into slavery. Given the current creeping increase in warrantless and unwarranted searches and seizure, "pre-emptive" confiscation of personal property that can quickly render a person penniless, incarceration for minor infractions, and so forth, the trend is pretty clear. In cases of wrongful arrest, which are not uncommon, the risk is even more frightening.

Today, the real rate of unemployment and underemployment in the US is close to 25%, if we include those forced to work part-time because they cannot find full-time employment,[1] and young people are affected disproportionately, making it impossible to start life and form a family. Now, consider the increasingly possible scenario if the job base further declines due to outsourcing and automation, until an overwhelming majority of the population loses access to earned income. When the rank and file citizen can no longer pay his property tax and mortgage, he loses his home. But besides that, anyone who is given a traffic fine or other minor penalty can be hit with fees for public defenders, prosecutors, court administration, jail operation, and probation supervision. "And when the defendants fall behind on their payments, courts order them arrested and jailed without even a hearing to determine their ability to pay." [9]

Income tax, and recurring term property tax (which means you never actually own the property you've "bought"), are unconstitutional/illegal, since they rob citizens of their Constitutional right to own property. Although the Sixteenth Amendment was established as a fig leaf, we must keep in mind that it was done without any solid representative body in place to demand a check preserving the interests of the citizens who would be affected.

With this income tax imposed, the national debt can be raised to any level, regardless of the nation's ability to ever pay it off. If the bill for that debt, per citizen, consumed more than half of the citizen's income, whose fault is that? When the citizens cannot pay, will their property be confiscated? Will

---

[1] From Shadow Government Statistics, http://www.shadowstats.com/alternate_data/unemployment-charts (accessed January 15, 2017).

they be condemned as guilty and sent into a corporate-owned prison? Will they, in fact, wake up homeless?

This runs contrary to the official history that has been virtually hammered into the consciousness of every American citizen for the last 150 years, by what in time amounted to a nation-state owned and controlled system of education. The same message is constantly reinforced by Washington and the media. That doesn't make it true.

In the last sixty years this effort to deceive has increased dramatically, not to mention the fact that this perverted history has been hammered in conjunction with an endless barrage of appeal to emotion [10] serving not only to conceal facts, but to sharpen divisions already intentionally created by the Federal government during the US Civil War. By emphasizing emotional arguments rather than reason, they excite people and make it difficult to discuss serious issues. Instead they should be reminding, or educating, Americans about their own Constitutional past, and most importantly reminding them about the constant pressure exerted by these banking families and US government insiders. The mass media serve the CBCC who seek to weaken all citizens' rights, regardless of the individual's hair color, shoe size, or favorite pet — setting us against each other and keeping us focused on petty issues.

The Mafioso In Brief

To what extent is the CBCC, the corporate/banking/colluding government insiders, a type of mafia? the model may help explain how the CBCC operates. A "mafia" is a type of organized crime syndicate, whose activities include extortion for "protection" against threats that would not exist if the racket did not exist, and racketeering — running illegal businesses such as gambling, loan sharking, drug trafficking, arms smuggling, and fraud, and using legitimate organizations to embezzle funds or commit other crimes.

It seems that certain branches of the Italian Mafia got their start working as private clandestine armies of the banking families that controlled various Italian provinces during feudal times. These banking families took over an area by purchasing the raw land outright. Any person who wished to own or occupy the land were required to utilize the financial services of the banking family. Loans were made at interest rates set as high as the economy would allow them to go, with of course, special allowances made for those with inside connections.

The Sicilian Mafia

Under feudalism, the nobility owned a majority of the land and enforced law and order through their own private armies. After 1812, the feudal barons sold off or rented their lands back to the working populace. Land could no longer be seized to settle debts. One fifth of the land was to fall under the ownership of the people. [11]

Following the annexation of Sicily in 1860 by Italy, a large portion of Church and state held land was given to the public, and the numbers of landowners jumped from 2,000 to 20,000. [12]

More landowners meant more competing enterprises, and people were not always honest in their dealings, business like or otherwise. More disputes needed settling, contracts needed enforcing, transactions required oversight, and one had to protect one's property from other forces within the local community.

The new state authorities could not provide these services, and the feudal barons had dissolved their standing armies in wake of the annexation. Some entire towns were left completely exposed to criminal elements, strikingly resembling the situation inside the Southern and Western states from the last year of the Civil War on down through Reconstruction, and arguably on down until the economy improved in 1908.

Property owners turned to extralegal arbitrators and protectors. In other words, a type of paramilitary organization, again strikingly resembling the response in Southern and Western states due to the same motivation. These extralegal paramilitary organizations would soon organize themselves into the first Mafioso families or clans.

Later on these families or clans influenced politics, intimidated voters into voting for the candidates that their clan supported. The superior Mafia family could use their influence in government to avoid prosecution, and condemn their less well-connected rival clans for crimes that they themselves committed. Certain clans obtained vast wealth and influence due to their business activities and political associations. [13] These clans maintained funds to support the families of imprisoned members and for the purpose of hiring defense lawyers, and of course, to buy "favors." Meanwhile, the "earnings" from their activities was poured into front businesses that served for money laundering.

This type of network has long since gone international, comprising an invisible private enforcement army to ensure compliance with the demands of huge national and even international banks. The great clandestine army terrorizes kings, prime ministers, and presidents alike. There is even a theory that the Iraq war was started in part to prevent Hussein from pricing oil in Euros rather than dollars. [14]

Social Effects

In many ways, the CBCC now operates like a mafia, with the Godfather providing certain benefits while keeping the threat ever present. Think of Obamacare. We are obliged to pay for our own protection, whether we believe we need it or not. The State obliges us to hand over our money to the corporations, every month, without fail. That is on top of federal, state, and local taxes. That is on top of home insurance. Fall behind on student loans or any of these other obligations, and we may lose everything.

More dramatically, explosive scandals come to light showing that the financiers handling our billions of dollars are literally laundering money for the drug trade, arms, pornography, you name it. Is it credible that just a "few bad apples" can do this on their own, without anyone at the Federal Reserve and the big banking families being involved?

Charles Lindbergh Sr.

Charles August Lindbergh studied law at the University of Michigan. He graduated in 1883 and was admitted to the bar. Lindbergh served as prosecuting attorney for Morrison County, Minnesota, 1891–93. He was elected to the US House of Representatives in 1906 as a Republican, serving four terms. In 1916 he unsuccessfully campaigned for a seat in the US Senate.

Lindbergh was highly against the Federal Reserve Act and creation of the Federal Reserve. Since the economy was seemingly picking back up again, people were looking forward to the opportunity of working their way up the economic and social ladder. For the reason of preserving that right of unsuppressed prosperity, a decentralized bank was favored by the masses.

Lindbergh and the American public felt that the prior negative economic situation on the ground was the fault of Wall Street bankers who had simply flooded the market with worthless banknotes in an attempt to fill their own pockets. Congress had pretended to address these concerns in 1912–13 in a series of hearings, finding that there was too much "camaraderie" among Wall Street tycoons. We must recall, however, that the secret meeting on Jekyll Island, Georgia, had already taken place by then, and introduced the drafted plan for what was actually a centralized bank.

Lindbergh and Wisconsin Senator Lafollette, making very forceful speeches, attacked the Aldrich initiative as a "Wall Street Plan." Their speeches attracted attention of the people on the ground and led to the Pujo Committee Hearings, which launched an investigation of New York bankers (which neither Lafollette nor Lindbergh was invited to attend).

The heated debates in regard to the Federal Reserve being established gave us a number of famous quotes:

"This [Federal Reserve Act] establishes the most gigantic trust on earth. When the President [Woodrow Wilson] signs this bill, the invisible government of the monetary power will be legalized....the worst legislative crime of the ages is perpetrated by this banking and currency bill."

——Charles A Lindbergh Sr., "On the Economic Pinch"

"The conspiracy here is to usurp the powers of Congress, and do as little for the people as it is thought the people will accept. I have been fighting the caucus system and the secret meeting of committees ever since I came to Congress." —— Charles August Lindbergh Sr.

Lindbergh stated in Congress that the conspiracy was "to make the people believe that the trusts are opposed to the very thing that the trusts favor. It is assumed that the people will favor what the trusts openly claim to be against. Smoothly the Money Trust has played a game of fake opposition."

In fact one of Lindbergh's most revealing statements came as he resigned from office, and it applies to this work. It involved the issue that neither political party represented the interests of the citizens on the ground, but only those interests of the greed-intoxicated banking cartel in collusion with US government. The Democratic Party, who once stood strong in demanding a check on the interests of the banking cartel, had been rendered entirely impotent since it had no choice but to bow down before the interest of the banking cartel, to receive the financial support necessary to facilitate any supporting representative body.

The Democratic Party existed in 1913 as only a state-based party, rather than one of any solid national platform. Any idea by now that the Democratic Party was still aligned with the concerns of the man in the street, at the national level, was only a heartless deception. Both political parties by now were in fact, married into a single representative body who served only the interests of the CBCC. The people of America by then had no check what-so-ever in the halls of government to secure their interests and concerns, as is still true in this present day. Let us examine the definitive Lindbergh quote:

"The plain truth is that neither of these great parties, as at present led and manipulated by an 'invisible government,' is fit to manage the destinies of a great people, and this fact is well understood by all who have had the time and have used it to investigate."

Response to Lindbergh's Gallant Stand

When the debates had concluded, the forces of the CBCC ruled the day; the quote below leaving us with more suggestions of possibility to consider.

In 1913 he published "Banking, Currency, and the Money Trust." By 1917, the third year of the Great War, Lindbergh's son was aged 16, which meant that the possibility of conscription was creeping closer. He wrote a polite anti-war polemic entitled, "Why is Your Country at War?"

Hot off the press, it was rushed to distribution. Wilson ordered the confiscation of all possible copies. Agents carrying out this order found pallets of the lead plates used for printing, which were melted in a refiner's fire. This insult to the Lindbergh family is one basis for the original opposition of his son to U.S. participation in World War II. Eustace Mullins documents that plates of this book were confiscated and destroyed. [15]

But to ensure no one else with a public platform became emboldened to question the direction taken, an overt political attack and a heartless kidnapping made the Lindbergh family an example to all. There are many narratives of the kidnapping of the Lindbergh baby. In view of the events her told, it appears that the Lindbergh family was the target of a vendetta of the banking cartel. Attacking Lindbergh Sr. directly would have been too obvious, revealing their true motivations to the masses and making Lindbergh Sr. a martyr for his words of warning and prophesies of doom.

There again, in striking similarity to General Lee's situation, the terror was directed toward Lindbergh's son, with the end result revealing the ice cold callousness of the cartel collusion of wealth, power and influence in charge of US affairs.

A national campaign was raised, as well, to destroy Lindbergh. The Nonpartisan League, which he associated with, was denied the right to assemble. Street mobs were aroused by associates of the banking cartel, making provoking emotion by claiming that his observations were nothing more than worthless "conspiracy theories" intending to destroy the nation. The raging mobs in the streets hanged him in effigy and burned his figure.

Some even claimed that he was aligned with the enemy, since he was against US involvement in World War One, viewing it more as war for profit than a war for positive humane intentions. In 1924 he would be dead, ending his effort to fight for plebeian interests and give fair warning to the masses concerning who the master of the puppet really was, that ruled completely unchallenged in the White House throne so high above them.

Charles Lindbergh Jr.

Charles Lindbergh Jr is an interesting personality all of his own right. We are all familiar with his solo flight around the world and his high profile celebrity lifestyle. Fewer people are aware that his father was a high profile politician, with direct access to the President himself. Even fewer people are aware of his father's hard line stance against the Federal Reserve.

In addition, Lindbergh realized that the looming European battle campaign was more a banker's war than any struggle for the positive benefit of mankind. His hard line stance against both the influence/dictation of unchecked banking in US government and the daily choices of American citizens, as well as in the direction of international policy, naturally made him a target by these same forces.

There was an early attempt, it seems, to silence the Lindberghs. While flying his father to a campaign stop during his run for the US senate, Lindbergh's plane lurched and then landed in a ditch on a farm, either on take-off or landing. It seems that someone had tampered with the plane's rudder, which would indicate an attempt to eliminate both the Junior and Senior Lindbergh, while conveying a message to intimidate anyone else.

In 1926, Lindbergh was hired to serve as a mail carrier flying between St. Louis and Chicago. In mid-February 1927, he left for San Diego to oversee construction of the Spirit of St. Louis, the plane that he would bring him both fame and fortune.

During the time that Lindbergh flew the SOSL, he toured a vast area, including flying for the first time from New York to Paris, France. In 1927 the Orteig Prize of $25,000 ($347,222 today) was offered to the first pilot who could make the first non-stop flight from New York to Paris. Lindbergh was an unknown as an aviator at the time, but we all know how the story played out. On May 20–21, 1927, Lindbergh successfully made the non-stop New York to Paris flight. A mob of 150,000 spectators was there to greet him. He had achieved instant lifelong fame.

He soon met and married Ann Morrow, who became a talented and successful author.

Ann Morrow

Ann Morrow's father Dwight Morrow was a Wall Street banker and partner in J.P. Morgan and Company, who would later become US ambassador to Mexico.

Ann and Lindbergh were married in a private ceremony on May 7, 1929, at the home of her parents in Englewood, New Jersey. After the attack on Pearl Harbor, Lindbergh became involved in combat as a civilian with the military. This assignment would keep him away from home for long periods of time, we should presume. During this time Anne Morrow Lindbergh met the famous French writer, poet and pioneering aviator, Antoine de Saint-Exupéry, author of the famous novella the *Little Prince*, and the two had a secret affair. In the 1950s she had a three-year affair with her personal doctor. The Lindbergh family would go on to have five children in spite of this.

The Lindbergh family, in conjunction with Pan American World Airways, evolved an interest in developing a great circle air route over Alaska, Siberia, China and Japan. In the summer of 1931, Lindbergh and his wife flew the route, which was not available for commercial flight until after World War Two, since the US was at war with Japan and the US government had not officially recognized Japan. While in Japan, the Lindberghs volunteered to help out in a relief effort resulting from the central China flood of 1931.

Dwight Morrow

Morrow was born in West Virginia. The family moved to Allegheny, Pennsylvania in 1875. His father was principal of Marshall College. Morrow studied law at Columbia Law school and began practicing at the law firm Simpson, Thacher and Bartlett in New York City. He married Elizabeth Reeve Cutter, his college sweetheart, with whom he would have four children.

In 1913, he was a partner at J.P. Morgan and Company, the largest and most powerful commercial bank in the US during this period. JP Morgan financially backed industrial giants such as General Motors. Morrow sat on the leadership boards as director in many corporate and financial firms.

With the outbreak of World War One, the bank of Morgan lent huge sums of money to Britain and France. Morrow served as director for the National War Savings Committee for the state of New Jersey when the United States entered into the war. During this same time period, he also served as adviser to the Allied Maritime Transport Council and as a member of the Military Board of Allied Supply, in what appears to be the capacity of a civilian aide. Once he had proven himself with his leadership abilities in the area of finance and logistics, he was transferred to France, and made a civilian aide to General John J Pershing.

In 1925 Morrow was called upon by President Calvin Coolidge, an old college friend, to head the Morrow Board which consisted of military, political and civilian aviation experts, whose assignment was to inquire into all aspects of American aviation. The recommendation they made led to the creation of an Air Corps within the army and the eventual creation of the US Army Air Corps in July 1926.

With Morrow's partnership at JP Morgan and Company and his appointment as Ambassador to Mexico, we observe evidence of the connections typical of the CBCC, from school days to finance to corporations to the halls of government.

Morrow was appointed US Ambassador to Mexico by Coolidge from 1927 to 1930. The Mexican government had expected a return to dollar diplomacy, and we know that indeed, the oil firms expected a hard line approach in view of the great land dispute between the Mexican government and US oil corporations. Morrow, so it appears, took a very different approach, apparently attempting to court the Mexican government rather than forcing them into an agreement.

Morrow diplomatically changed the sign on the Embassy from "American Embassy" to "United States Embassy." Morrow also hosted a series of breakfast meetings with President Plutarco Elias Calles, in which he discussed a number of contentious issues from religion to big oil, and irrigation. While he was hailed as a success on many fronts, it is possible that he made enemies at the same time.

The oil industry at large was not completely contented with Morrow, and he also appears to have been disturbed over the fact that the oil companies obviously desired an unconditional victory over Mexican interests rather than any sort of diplomatic negotiation concession.

Morrow believed that long-range Mexican stability would be achieved only by the complete financial reorganization of the Mexican nation. The Sterett-Davis report commissioned by the International Committee reinforced this conviction, although not everyone concerned was happy about the conclusion. In essence, what Morrow was advocating was a consolidation of the entire Mexican national debt and a balanced budget that would allow Mexico to make payments to provide funds for essential government functions.

In other words, the approach would originate from the standpoint of a government dealing with a bankrupt corporation, and the desire was to allow the Mexican government to file for bankruptcy, but with a modified repayment package somewhat resembling the new American civilian personal bankruptcy plans of today.

Thomas W. Lamont did not agree with this, since he was being pressured by huge corporate bond holders to negotiate an effective repayment plan on their investments. He complied with the concerns of Morrow from late 1928 through early 1929. In silence he appears to have only been placating Morrow, hoping that he would cooperate with any revised agreement between the International Committee and the Mexican Government.

Vernon Monroe, a Morgan executive, attempted to neutralize what he anticipated would be a negative situation between investors, Morrow and Lamont. A meeting had been arranged between Legorreta, a high end Mexican official, and General Palmer Pierce of Standard Oil Company. The ideal was to negotiate a deal between Mexican government and the oil executives in regard to the situation of Mexican debt, since corporate bond investors stood to lose a multiplicity of millions in dollars, should Mexico default or be allowed navigation around their debt responsibilities. He sent a professionally written letter explicitly detailing all of this dire matter in clear notation to Morrow.

We observe evidence of this concern when we view that the interests of bondholders were represented by the International Committee rather than governments. These bond holders at once demanded that a new agreement be arranged to secure the fact of payment on their investments. Morrow, on the other hand, believed that any series of unconditional settlements would completely destroy Mexican finances. Apparently, Morrow had assumed more of a humanitarian position on the engagements, rather than a finance centered position of unconditional negotiation on behalf of corporate investors.

Thomas W. Lamont overrode Morrow's opposition and negotiated a revised agreement with the Mexican government in July 1930. The Mexican Congress, however, refused to ratify the Lamont-Montes de Oca agreement. Lamont appears to have simply removed himself from the scene of events, at least for the time being.

So the debt issue to the bondholders was not resolved, although it appears that Morrow kept the peace between the US and Mexican governments. This does not mean that the hatchet was buried. We must recall that big money interests were at stake and would have to be satisfied. The message had to be delivered loud and clear.

Certain powers inside Mexico were no more pleased with the state of affairs than the big oil corporate investors were. These oil conglomerates were all virtually owned by JP Morgan/Rockefeller Bank (as they still are).

It appears that a plot was hatched, perhaps by Mexican radicals, to neutralize Morrow, possibly with support from various power centers. The plan, it seems, was initially to kidnap Morrow by a group of anarchists who accused Morrow of representing only Wall Street interests. [16] We observe this fact in an anonymous message delivered to the US embassy on September 1928. They accused Morrow of desiring a change in the Mexican Constitution that would accommodate US properties (owned by US firms) and force Mexico into a state of dependency on the United States government. Behind these accusing voices were the oil conglomerates.

A group of anarchists who called themselves the Cristeros were going to carry out the deed. On his way to Cuernavaca, Mexico, Morrow was nearly struck by a bullet. Morrow narrowly escaped death.

Thomas W Lamont

We already know that Thomas W Lamont was both a colleague and friend to Morrow. He had superb connections. Lamont may not have directly been involved in any scheme to harm Morrow, but perhaps someone with whom he associated may have been. Lamont caught the attention of Henry P. Davison, who asked Lamont to join the newly developed Bankers Trust. He moved up, eventually becoming Vice President and then Director. There again, we shall vividly recall what the Bankers Trust organization was and who controlled it. Later Lamont rose to the position of Vice President of the National Bank itself.

On January 1, 1911, he followed Davison and became a partner with JP Morgan and Company. During the 1919 Paris negotiations leading up to the Treaty of Versailles, Lamont was selected as one of two representative of the US Department of Treasury on the American delegation; he was a member of the Council of Foreign Relations; and he played many other leadership roles.

Since his associates knew of Morrow's negotiations with the Mexicans, and since at least a few of these associates were bond investors in the oil corporation's plans to invest in Mexico anticipating a windfall profit, there would have been powerful motivation to "put the scare" into Morrow.

Lamont was also a member of the notorious Jekyll Island Club, along with JP. Morgan Jr.

Enter Again, Lindbergh

We have established the link between Lamont, the banking families, and Morrow. Morrow failed to help the bankers, the oil corporations, and bond investors to profit in Mexico. We also observe the connections with Lindbergh and the same banking families of the Federal Reserve through the stand that Lindbergh Senior made to contest development of the FR.

By the time Morrow's tour of duty in Mexico ended in 1930, Lindbergh was a major celebrity. When he married Ann Morrow, we have a bond between two elements who had insulted/disrespected the interests of the banking cartel.

Morrow went on to fill a position in the US Senate, but he died in October, 1931, only 58 years old.

Lindbergh became more public with his anti-war stance as a spokesperson for the America First Committee, pushing for neutrality. The Bank of Morgan already had big plans for making a fortune by investing first with the Axis powers, then with the allied powers. Some of the greatest fortunes in banking are made during times of war.

The banking cartel was not about to lose another round to virtually the same brood of trouble makers.

At 2000 hours on March 1, 1932, the Lindbergh family nurse put baby Charles to bed in his crib. He was only one year and eight months old. He was abducted under circumstances that were never fully clarified, and a man with a German name was eventually convicted on dubious grounds.

Research related in a book entitled the *Lindbergh Baby Kidnap Conspiracy*, by Professor Alan Marlis, suggests that James P. Warburg, the son of Paul Warburg, chief architect of the Federal Reserve, was behind the kidnapping. There is a whole body of literature exploring various theories about the crime and many puzzling details.

Sins That Betray A Dark Intent

> For nothing is hidden that will not be made manifest, nor is anything secret that will not be known and come to light. —Luke 8:17

At this point in the story, we have an independent cartel banking organization that has sat in absolute authority in the throne above America now for over fifty years. This banking cartel has eliminated all opposition.

What if, after the war, these same villains were to turn on the entire citizen base of America, reducing all of them down into an expendable resource for their own gain? Who then is left to stop them? What would their reign of terror look like to the people on the ground?

We shall begin by examining which corporations the banking cartel actually owns, and what their record indicates in regard to what they have supported financially. The House of Morgan financed both sides during the first two World Wars. Paul Warburg's family sat on the board of directors for I.G. Farben.

We have observed that a number of other banking families with immense wealth also invested heavily in this very profitable government enterprise called Fascism, [17] where the people are reduced to a commercial resource, right along with all other resources extracted from the earth itself. We must always recall that Fascism is only corrupted capitalism. For capitalism to work effectively on all levels involved in the enterprise effort, there emphatically must exist a system of hard checks and balances, no matter what our authoritarian critics such as the current governor of South Carolina, Haley, may choose to have us believe!

A huge corporation does not function in the same manner as a small individual enterprise, where poor decisions may jeopardize the whole business. When there are many experienced people pooling their knowledge and their instincts, gross blunders are rare; small businesses are more at risk.

Now we have reviewed the context; what can we observe about the CBCC's true intent for US citizens and the nation itself. The House of Morgan is only a deceptive front for the Rothschild banking dynasty of Europe. It is the HOM married with the Rockefeller family that primarily rules America financially, so we shall begin by focusing there.

What specific corporations are financed/owned by the House of Morgan? What role did they play in events of the past? Who are their allies, what are their secrets, and what should give us most concern for the future?

Chase Manhattan Bank

Chase Manhattan was founded by Aaron Burr on September 1, 1799. We may all recall that Aaron Burr was the winner of the famous duel with Alexander Hamilton. From 1799 to 1959, it was called the Bank of Manhattan Company.

Later called the Chase National Bank, it acquired a number of smaller banks in the 1920s, most importantly the Equitable Trust Company of New York, in 1930. The largest stockholder was John D. Rockefeller Jr. This last acquisition made Chase the largest bank in America and the entire world. They have financed clients such as General Electric and the entire US oil industry, holding longstanding connections with the board of directors in such companies as Standard Oil and ExxonMobil, which are Rockefeller holdings.

And who were John D. Rockefeller and JDR Jr.?

John D. Rockefeller

Rockefeller was the co-founder of Standard Oil Company, which dominated the oil industry and was the first great US business trust. He revolutionized the petroleum business, running Standard Oil until he retired in 1897. Upon his death in 1937, his fortune was the equivalent of $336 billion, more than 1.5% of the entire national economy, making him the wealthiest person in US History!

The facts are really astounding. Rockefeller co-founded the University of Chicago and Rockefeller University. Rockefeller believed in capitalism by right of social Darwinism, which as we shall recall, means simply "survival of the fittest."

Primarily, Rockefeller was an oil tycoon. Obviously his enterprises were funded by Chase Bank, so it is here that we make our connection. We shall also be reminded that Rockefeller representatives sat in on the meeting at Jekyll Island. We shall recall as well, that the House of Rockefeller is one of the families that dominate the Federal Reserve Bank, even into this very day. The House of Rockefeller is united with the House of Morgan, both families standing as Lords over the Federal Reserve.

Chase Bank, in Paris under German occupation, handled accounts for the German embassy and German businesses operating in France. Chase operated with the Nazis to raise money from US sympathizers, doing so up six months from US involvement in the war. In direct quote from Higham, in the book, *Trading With the Enemy*, (our primary source on this subject):

> The Chase Bank in Paris was the focus of substantial financing of the Nazi embassy's activities throughout World War II with the full knowledge of Chase Headquarters New York. In order to assure the Germans of its loyalty to the Nazi cause... The Vichy branch of Chase at Châteauneuf-sur-Cher were strenuous in enforcing restrictions against Jewish property, even going so far as to refuse to release funds belonging to Jews because they anticipated a Nazi decree with retroactive provisions prohibiting such a release.

The details reveal the extent of direct collaboration, betraying an overt disregard for the condition of plebeians in the name of increasing corporate profits. Financing immoral policy is unjustifiable, but direct participation is beyond our comprehension.

General Motors

The DuPont family, close associates with J.P. Morgan and Company, controlled General Motors. The DuPont family owned 80% of the stock in Opel AG, which produced 20% of Germany's passenger cars during the 1930s and early 40s. Opel earned GM $36 million in the ten years preceding World War Two.

GM reinvested into other German firms. Some $20 million were invested into corporations owned or controlled by Nazi officials. According to our source listed above, when the blitzkrieg thundered into France and Eastern Europe, the Nazis were riding Opel trucks. Had the tide turned, transforming the House of Rockefeller into the category of weakness, we may only wonder if there would have been any love remaining for this ideology of social Darwinism then.

According to Higham, GM representatives met with Baron Manfred Von Killinger, Germany's west coast chief of espionage at the time, and Baron Von Tippelskirch, Germany's consul general and Gestapo leader, in Boston on November 23, 1937. They signed an agreement showing total commitment to the German cause, proclaiming that in view of Roosevelt's attitude toward Germany, every effort must be made to have him defeated in the next election.

The GM rep even proclaimed that a leader of unconditional loyalty to the Fuhrer must be transposed into the throne of the US White House, such as Senator Burton Wheeler from Montana. Although the idea and effort was to keep the meeting secret, Senator John M. Coffee of Washington found out and had the entire text of the agreement printed into the Congressional Record in August 1942.

Henry Ford [18]

From all appearances, Ford bankrolled Hitler at least from 1939 onward, and probably earlier. It appears that Henry Ford strongly agreed with many of Hitler's views. Henry Ford is the only American mentioned in Hitler's manifesto, *Mein Kampf*. Hitler even borrowed passages from Ford's work, *The International Jew*, for use in *Mein Kampf*.

During the reign of Hitler, the German Ford operation, Ford-Werke, made use of slave labor and built equipment used by the German army. The president of the company at the time was Robert Schmidt. No charges were ever filed nor did any company executive ever object to Schmidt being rehired in 1950, only five years following conclusion of the war. [19] Schmidt was reinstated as Ford's technical director in 1950.

Elsa Iwanowa, who had once been one of Ford's slaves, filed a class action lawsuit in US District Court against Ford Motor Company on March 4, 1998. In 1999 the court dismissed her suit. At the age of 16 Iwanowa had been abducted from her home in the southern Russian city of Rostov by German soldiers in 1942, with hundreds of other women. They were housed in barracks, in miserable conditions. According to Iwanowa, the only reason that they survived was that they were all young and very fit.

According to the Ford spokesman, Spelich, the US branch of Ford Motor Company did not have any form of control over its German branch. Spelich even went as far as to claim that Ford Motor Company did not profit from its operations in the city of Cologne at that time, where Iwanowa and hundreds more were held captive. The US District Court allowed Spelich and Ford Motor Company to get away with their ridiculous excuses, as well as their attempts to justify their crimes by "putting on the poor mouth." Most importantly, we always hold in mind that this trial occurred in 1998, not all that long ago. And in this case, as in a multitude of others, the victims were not Jewish but Russian. [20]

Ford was eager to demand compensation for losses due to US bomb damage to its German plants, which suggest they had other plants also using forced labor. Allow us to be reminded once again that at conclusion of the

US Civil War, the legal right to own slaves was simply transferred from the individual to the corporations.

Curtis-Wright Aviation Company

When the blitzkrieg raged through the heart of Europe and the chimneys of Auschwitz and many others of similar nature belched their sweet smelling stench, American employees taught flying techniques to the German Luftwaffe.

According to the section "Helping Hitler," in *Trading With the Enemy*, the US Navy had demanded that the techniques be kept classified, these flying techniques having been developed years before Hitler, but the CWAC discovered a method of subverting the classified order. The Germans then mistakenly demonstrated their "newly developed" warbird flight maneuvering techniques in a number of air shows across Europe, which prompted government official observers to ask for a US senate investigation into the matter.

Standard Oil Company

One of the most important connections is that of Standard Oil and its support of the Nazi government, plus its connection with I.G. Farben in its synthetic fuel partnership program.

The founding Father of Standard Oil was John D. Rockefeller, who was a leader at the secret meeting on Jekyll Island, helping to design the Federal Reserve system. The family also owned/owns the Jekyll Island Club House mansion. Paul Warburg was the chief architect in the design of the Federal Reserve. The Warburg family also sat on the board of directors at I.G. Farben.

The Warburgs backed off from the organization during the late 1930s. Strong suggestive evidence tells us otherwise. I.G. Farben owned Auschwitz and manufactured the infamous chemical known as Zyklon B. Germany was forced to import 85% of its fuel. Using a process developed by Standard Oil Company and I.G. Farben together, it found a way to convert its huge coal reserves into synthetic diesel. SOC taught IG Farben how to add tetraethyl-lead to gasoline to make leaded gasoline, so necessary for mechanized warfare. By their own public statements, German representatives announced that they did not have to struggle with development and would presently go directly to the business of war, since the Americans had done all of the work of developing the process for them.

Standard Oil also assisted with the $20 million production of aircraft fuel intended to be stockpiled for future war. Brown Brothers Harriman was the Wall Street investment firm that arranged for the tetrahedral-lead loan to the Luftwaffe, and Prescott Bush, the father of George H. W. Bush, was a senior managing partner of the firm.

IBM

IBM (International Business Machines Corporation) was a huge supporter of Hitler and his system of joining government and corporate interest. Most agreements were made orally, so that there would be no paper trail to haunt anyone later on. IBM specialized in producing the alphabetizing cards used to organize the roundups. These were precursors to the mainframe computers that were driving big businesses soon thereafter. In the war period, thousands were killed, including at least as many gentiles as Jews, especially Russians and Poles, those who were weak or disabled, minorities and social nonconformists. [21]

IBM Chairman Thomas Watson approved the opening of the school for Hollerith technicians in Berlin. He approved the opening of a subsidiary plant in German-occupied Poland that same month as well, with a printing press across from the street of the Warsaw Ghetto at 6 Rymarska street. This facility produced 15 million punch cards at that location, a major client being the railroad.

Watson and IBM employees designed the paper forms and the punch card systems for every specific purpose. These forms and cards counted concentration camp prisoners, confiscated bank accounts, coordinated the transport trains, even facilitated the death-by-labor campaigns. Every occurrence on the ground had coordination that the Hollerith office agreed with. Code one meant "released," code two "transferred," code three "natural death," etc.

All the money and machinery was claimed by IBM as legitimate business following the war. The company managed to recover all its bank accounts and machinery through deep contacts in the US State Department and the Pentagon, and the US government facilitated it; just like they facilitate outright corporate theft of worker retirement plans when corporate operations close down here in the US today.

Kodak

It is reported that Kodak-German branches used forced labor from concentration camps. Many of the European subsidiaries routinely did business with the Nazis. One of Hitler's top economic advisers, Wilhelm Kepler, had solid ties in Kodak. Kodak continued doing business after the US and its allies entered the war. The office in New York exercised direct control over the offices in Switzerland, an officially neutral nation. Control was also dictated in Spain and Portugal, where it also directed sales of product and trades in foreign currency.

Kodak paid 72,000 Swiss francs to wartime Germany for photographic supplies, paid 24,000 Swiss francs to purchase photographic supplies from occupied France, and paid 272,000 Swiss francs to agents in Hungary for photographic supplies. Kodak branches in Spain purchased products from Germany totaling 17,000 Reich-marks. Kodak was never penalized for any of it's trading with the enemy.

Coca Cola

CC sold drinks to both the allies and the axis soldiers, according to the best information. The demand appears to have begun when Luftwaffe pilots landed in the once-American controlled areas, discovering caches of coke in bottles, but no ice. Their own solution was to wrap the coke bottles up in a wet cloth, tie them to the wings of their planes and allow the coolness of the high altitudes along with the wind to drop the temperature of the valuable liquid. News of these activities soon reached high command, and through contacts, that demand was destined to be filled. Eventually the demand even led to a new drink formula, named Fanta, to circumvent embargos in Fascist Germany.

We have an interesting quote here from the US ambassador to Germany, William Dodd, in a note to FDR from Berlin, October 1936:

> Much as I believe in peace as our best policy, I cannot avoid the fears which Wilson emphasized more than once in conversations with me, August 15, 1915 and later: the breakdown of democracy in all Europe will be a disaster to the people. But what can you do? At the present moment more than a hundred American corporations have subsidiaries here or cooperative understandings. The DuPonts have three allies in Germany that are aiding in the armament business. Their chief ally is the I. G. Farben Company, a part of the Government which gives 200,000 marks a year to one propaganda organization operating on American opinion. Standard Oil Company (New Jersey sub-company) sent $2,000,000 here in December 1933 and has made $500,000 a year helping Germans make Ersatz gas for war purposes; but Standard Oil cannot take any of its earnings out of the country except in goods.

> They do little of this, report their earnings at home, but do not explain the facts. The International Harvester Company president told me their business here in Germany rose 33% a year (arms manufacture, I believe), but they could take nothing out. Even our airplanes people have secret arrangement with Krupps. General Motor Company and

Ford do enormous businesses here through their subsidiaries and take no profits out. I mention these facts because they complicate things and add to war dangers.[1]

He also wrote,

A clique of U.S. industrialists is hell-bent to bring a fascist state to supplant our democratic government, and is working closely with the fascist regime in Germany and Italy. I have had plenty of opportunity in my post in Berlin to witness how close some of our American ruling families are to the Nazi regime...

The truth is that while the nation of Germany was defeated in World War Two, Nazism never was, and neither was Fascism. Nazi Germany was a corporate enterprise, where upon the corporations seized control of the entire nation.

The overall idea of this system is that everything is geared to the benefit of the corporate/state partnership, with all other interests subordinated. The people and the land would all be reduced down into an expendable exploitable resource for corporate profit; with the exception of an elitist group who would be charged with running this suppressive corporate enterprise system.

At this point in our study, our most pervasive question still yet remains. Where did the others who performed the organizational hands-on skill of designing and operating the system go? In these individuals would be found fresh talent in any new ruling design; that skill in logistical organization being even more refined in view of experiencing the systemic failure in Germany upon losing the war.

The Rat Lines

There was essentially an underground railroad for ex-Nazis desiring to escape Europe in the aftermath of World War Two. The individuals most eager to escape were those who were most notorious for their criminal deeds. For those individuals, the most convenient time for escape would have been during the chaos found inside the last year of the fighting, and the tangle of immense chaos immediately following the aftermath of the war.

Before the war had ended, it was clear to many that Germany was destined to lose, and a series of escape routes were devised. One route was penciled in by a German priest, Anton Weber, the head of Rome-based Society of Saint Raphael. He first traveled to Portugal, then to Argentina, to lay the groundwork for a future "Catholic" immigration. This would be known on the streets as "The Vatican Ratline."

---

[1] http://reformed-theology.org/html/books/wall_street/introduction.htm

Spain appears to be the first center of ratline activity. Bishop Alois Hudal obtained a position to minister unto German war captives and used this position to assist ex-Fascists escape justice. Some officials were hidden inside internment camps using false names and being without papers. Other ex-Nazis were hiding out in Italy, where word arrived in regard to the services of Bishop Hudal, and these individuals sought out his assistance in formulating an escape plan as well. He assisted with money, false identity documents, and general organizational specifics involved with the plan of escape. It appears that personal contacts inside the International Red Cross issued the false passports.

They were sent to havens in South America such as Argentina, Paraguay, Brazil, Chile, and Bolivia, Great Britain, Canada, the Middle East... and the United States.. Funds were appropriated via business donations from wealthy persons, such as those employed by or invested with I.G. Farben, for example. The Catholic Church and the International Red Cross assisted with transport and movement across borders.

A Time of Exuberant Jubilation

When World War Two ended, there was no question that the United States was the most splendid economy left on the face of the earth. The destruction caused by the war created great opportunity for corporations that specialized in rebuilding what had been ravished. And the production and movement of wartime materials had generated a new explosion of industrious activity inside the heartland of America.

With the Marshall Plan came more contracts for corporations. The general mood of the American people was one of exploding patriotism. Evil on earth had been conquered; most certainly so many claimed, the allied nations were entering the reign of a new millennium ushered in by a heavenly endorsed veil of prosperity, especially inside US borders. The air of self-satisfaction and prosperity, after the Depression and the War, with the "boys" all home again, served as the perfect distraction to keep people from worrying much. The masses were intoxicated with the air of neo-modernism and progress.

A perfect distraction would be facilitated by an overwhelming sense of patriotism, where anyone who merely questions is to be overtly condemned, if not attacked outright by philosophical, if not physical violence. Such actions must never be rushed, however, instructed the master propagandists employed by the same financial forces in absolute control of US government; and just like the Wicked Witch of the West intimated in Frank Baum's classic tale, the Wizard of Oz, as she gazed forward into her huge crystal ball; "such endeavors must be made delicately," so that the few who are observant and wise will not alarm the majority; who is continuing to relish their own intoxication by the air of complacency and the feeling of timeless prosperity, perfectly combined with a sense of conquest and eternal liquidation by all that is positive, over that which was corrupt to an astonishingly extraordinary extent, and vile beyond even the limitations of gifted human imagination.

A new work of laborious research has emerged on the market today, offering explicit details to verify the claim that shockingly large numbers of high ranking specialized Nazi officials were recruited into the United States and offered amnesty for their talents and assistance. One of the latest works is called *Operation Paperclip: the Secret Intelligence Program That Brought Nazi Scientist To the United States*, by Annie Jacobsen. Jacobsen claims that the US government brought more than 1500 of these people over and was still hiding many more. [22] Many of these were doctors and scientists who were close collaborators. Untold numbers of these men were acquitted of war crimes, never standing trial for their crimes against humanity. Many German officials tried at Nuremberg were already employed by the US, either in Occupied Germany or stateside on US soil.

New methods of assassination and mass human immobilization were endlessly debated and heavily researched, according to Jacobsen. The US military and the CIA utilized and engaged these techniques on a massive scale, according to the literature. Completely new weapon systems were devised, including VX and Agent Orange, the chemical so heavily utilized in Vietnam that is responsible for untold mass incidences of citizen birth defects to this very day.[23] Nazi officials were even placed in charge of NASA, revealing a US military quest to position weapons in outer space, quite possibly suggesting the true intent later on for the US exploratory trip to the moon in 1969, if indeed such an event really even occurred.

In other words, bringing these criminals into the US facilitated a dawning powerful industrial military complex that would one day be responsible for inaugurating the New World Order. The German chief had splendidly accomplished in Germany within a mere twelve years what the corporations and centralized bank designed to do for a hundred years inside US borders. The only event that halted their dark plans was the Great Stand For Plebeian Liberty made by those resilient, most determined people of the South, contrary to the presumptions of the Federal government at the time.

It appears that the American Federation of Scientist urged the US government to end this practice of employing ex-Fascists in high positions. Albert Einstein himself was one of those who protested the loudest. Hans Bethe asked President Truman directly in statement:

"Did the fact that the Germans might save the nation millions of dollars imply that permanent residence and citizenship could be bought? Could the United States count on [the German scientists] to work for peace when their indoctrinated hatred against the Russians might contribute to increase the divergence between the great powers? Had the war been fought to allow Nazi ideology to creep into our educational and scientific institutions by the back door? Do we want science at any price?"

The response from Truman was to give birth to the CIA, the organization supreme of the industrial military complex. The US Chemical Warfare Service had taken up study of the German chemical warfare machine, seeking to continue the massive profit generating business of war for a long time to come.

A new world order was being planned and one of the key seats in this new type of Fascist empire was destined to be located in the heartland of America. The corporate industrialists were in great need of individuals who had experience in running a profitable Fascist enterprise, and with the business end of an international war machine complex.

The Second Dark Step Downward

> Oh, how kind it is, that someone left an apple half on this metal tray,
> saith the ole 'possum to the pretty little blue jay.
> —The author

Warning! Hard, bloody truth and cold reason ahead. Any reader with sensitivities, beware.

One of the principal themes of this work is that the public has been intentionally divided — most visibly during last two years of the American Civil War — and is being manipulated, one against the other, to this very day.

The appeal to emotion is one of the sharpest tools for cleaving apart our society. The appeal to emotion is reinforced in every facet of daily life, exacerbating divisions and motivating entire demographic sectors to support alien ideologies that sound good — appearing to benefit one specific group or individual — but that in fact weaken and impoverish the population at large.

Examples of this attempt at deepening divisions and appealing to emotion can be seen in mandates drawn up by state government under dictation by the Federal authorities (in direct violation of the tenth amendment) to deprive school districts of freedom of choice; and college admissions policies that make special allowances for certain constituencies under the guise of assisting unproductive elements who fall under the euphemistic label of "disadvantaged"; the continual comparisons between demographic groups, where those who are in fact given subsidies of various kinds are hailed nonetheless as "disadvantaged," while the demographic segment that pays the most tax serves under the label of political scapegoat for the propagandists employed by those who would keep us at each other's throats rather than working together for the common good.

The appeal to emotion is used to sell tax payers on housing laws, public welfare laws, Federally-mandated hiring policies, all sorts of policies regarding the public schools, laws regulating social environments by removing all freedom of choice in public service from property owners. In some cases, even worship services are controlled by Federal authoritarians and compelled to diverge from teachings that are in line with the local mainstream, and even the national majority, lest they offend someone!

In short, all US social policy is overtly mandated/dictated by Federal design, making heavy use of appeal to emotion in both directions: an appeal to self-serving sentimentality for all those metaphorical victims of history, and appeal to sympathy toward those allegorical victims of history.

In other words, the US system makes extensive use of the tactic of placating specific groups with special treatment, by appearing to offer gifts, [24] suggesting favoritism intended to correct something that was done in the past to other individuals, in the propagandistic effort to misdirect blame for past crimes committed by the corporate and banking elite.

What results is a clash of ideologies and personal belief systems; in other words, an outstanding method of diverting attention from the intention of complete systemic domination and a flagrant pillaging of the privately-held resource base; in combination with a virtual enslavement of the entire population base as the process of institutionalized theft proceeds to unfold before the very eyes of the masses; though in their minds the citizens persist in denying that-which-is-self-evident by its manifestation on the ground.

By utilizing a process of gradual entrapment, the present day Fascist-collectivist system of the United States metaphorically takes on the form of a flesh-consuming leaf known as the Venus Fly Trap. The citizens continue to live their lives, embracing the illusion of liberty, without realizing that each of us has been reduced to a common house fly.

While the ex-Fascists were being smuggled into the United States by the thousands to serve the purpose of instructing United States officials in the specifics of running a hard core Fascist system, Americans had come to know a liberty such as none that had ever existed before. When the instructions for the new US/World Order were given, those in offices of leadership, per command of the Federal Reserve, were lending ear. In fact, many may not have like it, but they had no choice but bow down to the banking cartel.

What occurred to facilitate this movement of US economic policy in an alien direction? Why did Americans not catch on to the deception? Where was the attention of the American people while the events at home were materializing?

The best place to search for answers might be found in one glance in the opposite direction, maybe far across the big pond, toward Russia! What was the Cold War about, after all? The Soviet Union was never a threat to take over the US, per se; it had neither the manpower nor the ambition to do so. However, it did indeed rival the capitalist system. In the context of capitalist exploitation of workers, the Soviet socialist model certainly had some appeal, maybe not so much I the US, but for people around the world. The well-to-do in the United States and other Western nations had no intention of losing their wealth and privileges by allowing the socialist/communist idea of income leveling to take hold here. What would these people do, if they could no longer make millions simply though their monopoly of profits?

In other words, Russia and the United States were in a competition, but were nowhere near any overt act of warfare between the two, least of all not a nuclear war. The fear of an impending thermonuclear calamity was instilled in the citizens of the land of America, creating a terrifying myth and inserting into the minds of Americans the belief that the Russians were enemies seeking our destruction. This went hand in hand with fostering and magnifying the assumption that the US government was highly against Communism because of their supposed ideology of suppressing liberty; thus convincing people unquestionably that the United States government was the only qualified guarantor of liberty and the eternal guardians thereof, both worldwide and at home.

What were the Russians doing in respect to the nations of Eastern Europe? Not as much as the US was doing in the West. We have military bases all over Europe and the rest of the world. From Russia's perspective, Eastern Europe was a necessary buffer zone between them and the West; European armies have invaded Russia many times. In World War II, it was Russia who bore the brunt of the Nazi onslaught and they who did most to defeat the Axis powers. When the Nazis had taken over all the countries on Russia's western border, the US was still providing them with fuel and other supplies.[1] The top shareholders and leaders of the major corporations involved were precisely those highly connected corporate/banker/government insiders, the moneyed class, who keep the rest of the populace in its place.

Thus, setting up the notion that a Russian attack was a real threat to the US, the propaganda machine set emotions aflame and kept them burning for decades, so that no one could imagine that the threat might be stronger the other way around. This tended to reinforce ideas of extreme patriotism already present inside the minds of Americans after the War and during the Cold War that followed. This prevailing belief in combination with the public conviction that the US political and economic system at large was

---

[1] "How the Allied multinationals supplied Nazi Germany throughout World War II." Ibcom.org, at https://libcom.org/library/allied-multinationals-supply-nazi-germany-world-war-2.

the bastion of individual liberty effectively neutralized anyone who dared ask questions.

If a second step was indeed taken on the stairway to tyranny, then what would it have looked like? How are we, the children of the future, to ever know?

Demagogues of Subversion

Grundy County, Tennessee, in 1932, is a handy (albeit far from obvious) place to start our search. This was in the midst of Great Depression following the stock market collapse of 1929. The need for a great transformation, economically and socially, hung heavily in the air about this rural county. Work reform was needed desperately. Ben Bernanke himself has said that "At all times, the Federal Reserve had the power and the knowledge to have stopped [the further crashes during the 1930s]."[25] Far more workers were unemployed than the available jobs could satisfy. Corporations were taking advantage of the situation by lowering wages sharply, and job security was nonexistent.

The people soon came to realize that they desperately needed either the government to provide a safeguard, in the form of a disinterested regulatory body, or a defense from the bottom up, which we mostly recognize in the form of a Labor Union.

The only possible third form of safeguard for the interests of workers would be inside the corporate body, in the form of an inviolable legal contract ensuring certain workers' rights. The problem is that when unions call for higher wages, or any other check is imposed that gives the workforce a bit larger share of the pie, that means that the corporate profit is reduced. The shareholders don't like that. Often, due to employee tension over wages and the brute determination of the corporate resistance, the situations turned violent.[26] A virtual combat situation materialized in quite a few instances.[27]

Individuals in positions of authority who were astute observers recognized the public hunger for the minimal amount of security that could provide a bit of personal liberty, allow him to build a bit of a nest egg, and benefit the broad spectrum of the population rather than simply cater to a wealthy elite.

Individuals in power positions also were quick to recognize an opportunity for a self-serving agenda under the mask of an intended positive correction in the system. One name stands out, reverberating across the ages, demonstrating the ease and effectiveness with which a freeborn population may be completely subdued (and perhaps, later, eradicated if it is of no further use).

Myles Horton

Horton was the son of a poor farm laborer from West Tennessee. He attended Union Theological Seminary in New York City under Reinhold Niebuhr. Niebuhr appears to have been an instructor and philosopher at the same time. Along with "educator" Don West, and Methodist minister James Dubrowski of New Orleans, he founded the Highlander Folk School And Education Center in Monteagle, Tennessee, in 1932.

This so called "school" supposedly specialized in maintaining traditional Appalachian folk arts, but before many years had passed, it had transformed into a virtual bastion for radical elements in US society. The underlying concept of the school was that "an oppressed people collectively hold strategies for liberation that are lost to its individuals."

The school's purpose was to offer how-to instruction regarding strategies of subversion. It aimed to "educate" and "empower" adults for social change, through the economic-societal system of Socialism. The famous authority Google defines socialism as "a political and economic theory of social organization that advocates that the means of production, distribution, and exchange should be owned or regulated by the community as a whole." In other words, instead of a handful of super-rich stockholders raking in the profits, the money made would be used for the public benefit: salaries, housing, healthcare and education for workers and their families, and so forth. Like capitalism, it sounds great on paper. And like capitalism, how rigid or how flexible it is depends on who is in charge. Most of today's developed nations, from Europe to Taiwan, operate on the basis of a mixed capitalist/socialist system.

Socialism was starting to gain considerable appeal as folks heard about the progress being made in the Soviet Union, where the basic necessities, like housing, were assured, at precisely the time when so many Americans were losing their homes. (The darker aspects of the authoritarian way the Soviet system was operating did not become clear until later.)

The Situation As A Front

Before we return to the person of Myles Horton, consider the atmosphere that remained in the South. Here is an excerpt from the book, *Rape And Justice In the Civil War*, by Crystal N Feimster. President Lincoln's General Orders No. 100, also known as the Lieber Code of 1863, set clear rules for engaging with enemy combatants. But the code also clarified how Union soldiers should treat civilians, and in particular women. Largely forgotten today, the Lieber Code established strict laws regarding an issue that was everywhere and nowhere in the consciousness of the Civil War: wartime rape.

Three articles under Section II declared that soldiers would "acknowledge and protect, in hostile countries occupied by them, religion and morality; strictly private property; the persons of the inhabitants, especially those of women" (Article 37); that "all robbery, all pillage or sacking, even after taking a place by main force, all rape, wounding, maiming, or killing of such inhabitants, are prohibited under the penalty of death" (Article 44); and that "crimes punishable by all penal codes, such as ... rape, if committed by an American soldier in a hostile country against its inhabitants, are not only punishable as at home, but in all cases in which death is not inflicted the severer punishment shall be preferred" (Article 47).

Together the articles conceived and defined rape in women-specific terms as a crime against property, as a crime of troop discipline, and as a crime against family honor. Most significantly, the articles codified the precepts of modern war on the protection of women against rape that set the stage for a century of humanitarian and international law.

Such explicit prohibition was necessary, because even after the code was in place, sexual violence was common to the wartime experience of Southern women, white and black, as it is common in most wars. Union military courts prosecuted at least 450 cases involving sexual crimes. In North Carolina during the spring of 1865, Pvt. James Preble "did by physical force and violence commit rape upon the person of one Miss Letitia Craft." When Perry Holland of the 1st Missouri Infantry confessed to the rape of Julia Anderson, a white woman in Tennessee, he was sentenced to be shot, but his sentence was later commuted. Catherine Farmer, also of Tennessee, testified that Lt. Harvey John of the 49th Ohio Infantry dragged her into the bushes and told her he would kill her if she did not "give it to him." He tore her dress, broke her hoops and "put his private parts into her," for which he was sentenced to 10 years in prison.

In the aftermath, a simmering vendetta went on for generations as Southerners had no way to avenge the dishonorable crimes that came on top of lost homes, businesses, family members and loved ones.

Back To Horton's School

The Highlander Folk School and Education Center advocated correcting present-day societal wrongs by subverting the ideal of capitalist enterprise whereby the owner collects all the profit generated by his employees in favor of Social-Communism.

Many now famous radicals, elevated into the position of virtual icon, attended the school seeking instruction. These leaders include Martin Luther King Jr., Rosa Parks, John Lewis, James Bevel, Bernard Lafayette, and Ralph Abernathy. A few of these iconic leaders recognized the fact that they were being utilized as pawns in a manipulative game that suddenly did not appear as playing out to their own advantage in the large picture of events.

Horton left home at the age of fifteen. He graduated from Cumberland University, the University of Chicago and the Union Theological Seminary, where he studied social gospel philosophy: *the process in which the prevailing society could be challenged and transformed by use of education/indoctrination as a weapon.*

Reinhold Niebuhr

Karl Paul Reinhold Niebuhr was an American theologian, ethicist, public intellectual, commentator on politics and public affairs, and professor at Union Theological Seminary for thirty years. He is known for authoring the Serenity Prayer. He received the Presidential Medal of Freedom in 1964, under the administration of Lyndon Baines Johnson, a very important notation for future reference. His most influential books include *Moral Man And Immoral Society*, and *Nature And Destiny of Man*.

He began as a minister with the working class, holding sympathies with the labor class. He gradually worked his way up into the ideology of *Theological Pacifism* and *Neo-Orthodox Realist Theology*.

He was founder of the group *Americans For Democratic Action (ADA)*, which was attacked by McCarthy for being a Communist entity on American soil, which the group denied. However, in those days any movement that suggested there was a lack of social justice in the system was already suspect. Niebuhr himself was accused of being Communist, but always denied it. The ADA defines its vision and its values as being: "an America that works fairly for all." They helped get the Federal minimum wage increased in 2007. This is the sort of thing that helps individual workers — but corporations and investors don't like it.

Other founding members worthy of note are former Senator and Vice President Hubert Humphrey, Ronald Reagan, Eleanor Roosevelt and the economist Kenneth Galbraith, whom we shall discuss in more elaborated detail. Galbraith served under the Kennedy and the Johnson Administration, and earlier under FDR and Harry S. Truman. Without a doubt his hand played a tremendous part in shaping the socio-economic system that followed.

Galbraith's literary work *The Affluent Society* argued that corporations virtually inflate and dictate prices, and push the public to spend in excess through advertising, while taking no responsibility for public development so that we wind up with polluted parks (or no parks at all), underfunded schools and widespread poverty. The method by which modern society has addressed such realities is through taxes on market activity. But is the tax collected sufficient to cover the social costs? The radioactive nuclear waste byproduct and a tax on the corporation for the cost of cleanup might be a good example for testing that proposition. In any event, most corporations manage to evade paying their taxes anyway. Galbraith also omits the fact that the system tends to corruption, and the costs of corporate tax are foisted off upon the citizen public anyway, in the form of higher prices, and then we pay payroll tax, real-estate tax and all the rest as well.

He also argued for a tax on land values. The tax works well when the unlimited wealth of corporations is footing the bills, but it when it applies to mere homeowners and small businesses, being taxed every year for something you've already paid for is a good way to find your property confiscated. Sometimes, people will miss their payments. Then their land is sold out from under them at a tax sale. And banks, insurance companies, etc. buy up the land at a great discount, to sell it later on for a profit.

One problem in balancing capitalist and socialist measures is that people get used to being protected, and they also ask for more and more help, so that they can quickly end up as wards of the state. Whatever the intention of policies of the Kennedy Administration and especially Johnson, Welfare and the other "safety-net" programs created some misguided incentives so that single parents received more than families that stayed together, and other quirks and loopholes ended up causing great societal damage of their own.

Galbraith believed that corporations and government should work together to maintain social stability among the population. With a system of adequate checks and balances, the process should move along smoothly to affect people's lives in a manner that facilitates the very best that productive, civilized society has to offer. How to do that remains a puzzle yet to be solved. Some checks are needed to prevent abuse by the citizens, and even more so, if the government is given more control over people's lives, checks are needed to prevent the corporate/government collusion from becoming a totalitarian force that restricts citizens' independence and individuality, what is casually called *fascism*.

It is the view of this author that such checks were removed when elements of welfare socialism were implemented in America, with the intent being to subdue the individual and remove the incentive, indeed, the opportunity, to take responsibility for our own economic advancement.

The influence of Fascist elements from Germany were being manifested in US government throughout the 1950s, and by 1960 "welfare socialism" being observed by its influence in programs such as the New Frontier and the War On Poverty. For the purpose of facilitating overall corporate Fascism, some degree of Welfare Socialism would make Fascism acceptable. Without it we would only have 19th century predatory capitalism.

Other Interesting Notes

Ronald Reagan: While most are well aware of Reagan's past as Republican California governor and US President, few are aware that he began life as a liberal Democrat. This platform changed in 1964. We may presume that this transformation was due to the overt Socialist stance of the Johnson Administration, but this author makes other distinct notations that bear more suggestions of a clandestine intention on part of big money and the central bank in absolute power.

In the 1950s, Reagan worked as a motivational speaker for General Electric. *The New Yorker* says, "his theme—the threat of an encroaching, expanding government—did not vary. It was less a speech than a sermon, as Reagan himself understood—a malediction against the evils of income taxes, federal spending, central planning, godless Communism, and government controls on commerce and freedom. 'We'll preserve for our children this, the last best hope of man on Earth, or we'll sentence them to take the last step into a thousand years of darkness...'[1] Note the call to emotion, and the confounding of the corporation's interest in restricting government versus the workers' interest in being protected and served through government planning and spending — who else was going to build schools, roads and post offices?

Hubert Humphrey: Humphrey sponsored the clause of the *McCarran Act (Subversive Activities Control Act of 1950)* that threatened concentration camps for "subversives!" This act actually legalizes the coming persecution soon to unfold. Anyone labeled as a "subversive" can legally be delivered into the concentration camps, suggesting as well the existence of a clandestine program for constructing such facilities on American soil.

But he also authored the Civil Rights Act of 1964, which outlaws discrimination and segregation based on race, color, religion, gender, or national origin in voter registration, schools, at work and in public facilities. Is it possible to be a populist and a totalitarian at the same time? That is the risk.

The first question that we must ask is *who, who* are the subversives? *How* is that determination made as to just *who* it is that will fall underneath the label of subversive, making them ripe for persecution? Will it be American citizens who protest efforts to confiscate guns, audaciously violating the second amendment of the US Constitution? Or will it only include those who are angered and protest government confiscation of bank accounts and

---

[1] *The New Yorker*, Oct. 29, 2014, http://www.newyorker.com/news/news-desk/caught-reagan-trap

retirement accounts? Parts of the Act were repealed, but parts of it are still lurking, and how broadly it can be applied is not even clear.[1]

Joseph P. Lash: From 1930 until 1937, Lash was a member of the Socialist Party of America. He worked for the League of Industrial Democracy, officially labeled as a Socialist organization, but in this author's humble opinion, the name smacks more of clandestine Fascism. He also worked for the Communist Party USA.

Walter Philip Reuther: Reuther was an American union leader, who made the United Automobile Workers a major force in the Democratic Party and the Congress of Industrial Organizations. He was an overt Socialist. His goal was to give the union a strong voice in the Democratic Party; thus we may conclude that the Democratic Party began its great switch from being a Party seeking to protect the people by securing a check on the national currency and by protecting the individual's Constitutional right to earn his way up, to installing centralized mechanisms to shape society.

Keep in mind that the Democratic Party had, for all practical purposes, been rendered impotent from the end of the Civil War until the 1930s since Democratic Congressional representatives had traditionally been funded by the South, whose economic base was destroyed. The transformation from having its zone of influence as a state-based organization upholding the rights of individuals to the best of its ability, into one of national importance, feigning support for the interests of the common man, is one of immense importance.

Author M Schlesinger: Schlesinger was an intelligence agent at the Office of Strategic Services, a precursor to the CIA. During the Kennedy Administration, he was Assistant Secretary of State for Cultural Relations, an innocent-sounding office for creating influence abroad). He also closely assisted the UN Security Council. We may conclude that he assisted in propagandizing the new government as its conditions were being imposed on the masses at large.

Wilson Wyatt: Wyatt, a lawyer, worked closely with the new Democratic Party.

Summarizing the Specifics

As we may observe, Socialist policy of the ADA meshed with the Democratic party, eventually constituting itself with internal national policy all together. Virtually all of the founding fathers of the ADA, aka the

---

[1] In 2004, "The Supreme Court...took the case of Rumsfeld v. Padilla to decide the question of whether Congress's Authorization for Use of Military Force authorized the President to detain a U.S. citizen, but did not give an answer, instead ruling that the case had been improperly filed." Wikipedia, https://en.wikipedia.org/wiki/Non-Detention_Act

new Democratic party, were indeed flagrant Socialists or adhered to Social-Communist ideology. As we may recall in the person of Schlesinger, Socialist adherents had even infiltrated a precursor to the CIA, so we may conclude that those infiltrations continued with the birth of the CIA that we know today.

In the eye of the public, the CIA was adamantly against any sort of Socialist/Communist demagoguery; but it is noteworthy how many times appearances are designed to deceive, especially in agencies having double agents and double-doubles! What's even worse, as indicated above, even policies that in one way help the average person to maximize his accomplishments may, in other ways, inhibit his liberties. Furthermore, recent statistics show that, in fact, welfare and other subsidy program actually discourage people from working.[1]

So, to resume in brief, by the last year of World War Two, we had German ex-Fascists being smuggled into the US (and the UK) by the thousands. Officially, they were brought in to give the US the benefit of their scientific/technological innovations. America's corporations were among the strongest financial supporters of Fascism, so one may wonder whether the US government and corporations were also perhaps interested in having access to individuals experienced in the science of purloining the population's privately-held resources and acclimating the citizens to serving as an expendable resource for the purpose of profit maximization.

At the same time, we have the rise of strong advocates for a socialist-type government, who eventually send two Presidential candidates into office back to back. Inside of five years, aspects of socialism could be seen in all areas, in ways that most people were not aware of at the time, and never noticed until they were compelled to interact socially with demographic groups vastly different from their own, and with some who had traditionally been their bitter enemies. In these compelled interactions, we may always find the great distraction that heralds the next step downward into the raging purgatory of tyranny.

---

[1] "Another interesting observation from the report concerned the Earned Income Tax Credit, which is supposed to provide incentives to work for the lowest income brackets by relieving them of tax burdens for their meager income. Instead, the report found that "EITC explains 71 percent of the decline in low-educated married mothers' desire to work between 1988–1993 and 1994–2010." The authors theorize this happened because EITC "raised family income and reduced secondary earners' (typically women) incentives to work. Overall, the report found that "changes in the provision of welfare and social insurance explain about 60 percent of the decline in desire to work among prime-age females." Daniel Mitchell, https://danieljmitchell.wordpress.com/2015/04/27/dependency-work-incentives-and-the-growing-welfare-state/ cited at Breitbart, http://www.breitbart.com/big-government/2015/04/27/the-science-is-settled-welfare-discourages-work/.

Students of the school were trained and instructed to be subversive, for the purpose of generating support for, and implementing, the new order. With the power of appeals to emotion serving as a distraction, and sympathy for the metaphorical oppressed as justification, any stance contrary to the prevailing system would appear justified to the misled majority. History was twisted to label as villains the descendants of those who had possessed the fortitude to stand up to the banking cartel, and who were the chief opponents of the new social engineering. Talk about purloining individual liberty: we see the snowballing effect today, when we are bombarded by images suggesting there's something wrong with us, if we feel most comfortable among people we grew up with or whose backgrounds are similar to our own. That is human nature, no matter how much the public may be psychologically manipulated.

Back To Reinhold Niebuhr

The thoughts and opinions of Niebuhr have had a dramatic impact on the political agenda of the US and the world in general, past, present and, unfortunately, for a newly dawning future. Apparently Niebuhr not only espoused a socialist agenda, but specifically one ruled by an ideological absolute authority who would supervise a redistribution of resources, using whatever means necessary to enforce this policy.

As we observed, what the DP began to advocate in 1948 was the clandestine formation of a "socialist" looking government selling itself to the masses as a party dedicated to serving their interests, while concealing the Democratic Party's marriage with interests of the banking cartel by feigning the correction of exaggerated historical wrongs inside the system and among the citizen base at large. Appeal to emotion would be the psychological tactic that history had proven most effective in luring the masses into going along.

We may also recall that the Republican party was/is a direct descendant of the old Federalist party, whose majority were against any checks and balances being placed on the banknotes/currency or government insiders working in collusion with corporate interests. In recent years it has become inescapably clear that the two parties operate essentially as one. There seems to have been a mid-night marriage between the two parties, since the DP could only gain influence in the national government by embracing corporate interests, rather than standing hard to oppose them, as they did before the War.

Thus it seems that labels such as Republican, Democrat, fascist and socialist are far from reliable, and can be used or misused, one can be used to mask the other, or elements of different systems can be combined; or one can be used as dust in the eyes of the public while the opposite policies are prepared.

The point is that Niebuhr's sphere of influence went from the Highlander Folk School to the Democratic party, all the way up to the President himself. Not only that, his opinions, and the need to respond to propaganda from other systems, including both fascist and socialist, transformed American government future. What is revealed by a careful study of his work is that in theory, he foresaw a carefully crafted and well-presented form of socially responsible government that, *with solid checks and balances may have actually worked* relatively well in real world application — the problem is that no such checks or balances were ever developed. Over time, what began as a positive possibility was corrupted in the absence of checks, deteriorating into undemocratic collectivism.

What is most astounding about this study is that the American public was never alert to the transformation on the ground, to the point that only a minority were motivated to contest the new developments, on the streets, as they emerged. This resistance was neutralized at the start by labeling it as a historical villain, while constantly drumming up sympathy for the oppressed. The Cold War and the possibility of nuclear war certainly created a distraction, but we are also aware of public dissension along old demographic rifts that were revealing themselves at the same time. The question that we must dare ask ourselves is: was there anything else, even more direct, that could have served as a mass distraction, seeking to agitate the public along demographic rifts for the purpose of creating tension between two opposing groups?

In 1829, even as President Jackson was taking office, the appeal to emotion was generated by Abolitionist propaganda designed to incite hatred of the plantation system and to change the way society viewed the institution of slavery. Up until about that time, slavery was commonplace throughout the Caribbean and Latin America, and to some degree also in the northern United States. But rising up and pointing a finger of blame at the South, certain interests began disseminating propaganda throughout most of the nation, with the intention of arousing the public along political and demographic lines.

Not only that, the intention was to provoke violence. A prime example is the incident at Harper's Ferry, where an abolitionist leader literally attacked the opposition, seeking to provoke the spread of violence. This message of incitement was then magnified by other agents.

Was there any situation on the ground, that would have effectively served the same purpose in the time period around 1948, when the Democratic Party changed direction and appeared to become the party of socialism, through the decade of the 1950s, into the early years of the 1960s?

The Inflaming Appeal To Emotion

To find the answer to our question we must again consult our oracle; at first there appears to be a cloudy haze, but then it suddenly clears. What is revealed is an apparently comfortable scene in a slow-paced agricultural town called *Money, Mississippi*, and the year is August 24, 1955.

In the heart of town there is a small community market store, known locally by name as *Bryant's Meat And Grocery*. The day was Sunday. Bryant, who was twenty-four years old at the time, was also a truck driver. He had gone away to the Texas waterfront that day for the purpose of hauling a load of shrimp, and would not return until August 27.

At the store all alone was his young wife *Carol Bryant*, who was working in the store taking care of paperwork and placing packages on the shelves. Her sister-in-law was in the back watching the children. The front door was left wide open since the climate was very humid and warm, with crime seldom being a problem in this small town at the time. The moment was one that had been repeated far too many times in the past for recollection. By the time the sun went down on this day, however, not only would the lives of the couple be transformed for all time, so would the direction of the entire nation at large.

According to the official record, Carol's husband had left a loaded pistol for her underneath the front passenger car seat. She had neglected to even carry the pistol inside, since the town was small and the people all knew each other very well.

Specific details remain unclear, but the official information published made the story one that suited *national leaders who were in search of an event they could distort and magnify*, to further enflame divisions already made deep within the population during the time of the Civil War.

A distraction close at home was most necessary, so that the population of America would never notice what was going on. The identical process followed, with some of the same groups designated as the historical *victim*, and the same group designated as the *scapegoat* that was politically acceptable to condemn.

The facts remain somewhat unclear, but the official historical account of the incident can be summarized very briefly. A black youth named Emmett Till went into the store, on a dare from his buddies, to speak to Carolyn Bryant. Many of the details are disputed. She maintained that Till grabbed her around the waist and said highly inappropriate things; but what is certain is that Mrs. Bryant became sufficiently alarmed she ran out to get the gun. The youths left the store. But three days later when Carolyn's husband got home, Emmett was brutally murdered. Mr. Bryant and his half-brother were tried for murder but not convicted; they later gave a sensational story to *Look* magazine, which may have been exaggerated in a bid to get attention. However, even their friends concluded that if any part of the story was true, it was abominable, and the men were universally reviled for the crime.

Of course, with scant reliable information, this shocking incident can easily be portrayed or perceived one way or another, and is bound to enrage people either way, much like the killing of Rodney King. No one came out of this incident unscathed. The case made the international news and was kept aflame for a long, long time.

The Civil Rights Act of 1957

Examine closely the official record of what the CRAO1957 is defined as by our online source, Wikipedia:

> The goal of the 1957 Civil Rights Act was to ensure that all Americans could exercise their right to vote. By 1957, only about 20% of African Americans were registered to vote. Despite comprising the majority population in numerous counties and Congressional districts in the South, most blacks had been effectively disfranchised by discriminatory voter registration rules and laws in those states since the late 19th and early 20th centuries. Civil rights organizations had collected evidence of discriminatory practices, such as administration of literacy and comprehension tests, poll taxes and other means. While the states had the right to establish rules for voter registration and elections, the federal government found an oversight role in ensuring that citizens could exercise the constitutional right to vote for federal officers, such as the president, vice president, and Congress.

> The Democratic Senate Majority Leader, Lyndon Baines Johnson of Texas, realized that the bill and its journey through Congress could tear apart his party, whose southern bloc was opposed to civil rights, while northern members were more favorable toward them. Southern senators occupied chairs of numerous important committees because of their long seniority. Johnson sent the bill to the judiciary committee, led by Senator James Eastland of Mississippi, who proceeded to drastically alter the bill. Senator Richard Russell of Georgia had denounced the bill as an example of the federal government seeking to impose its laws on states. Johnson sought recognition from civil rights advocates for passing the bill, while also receiving recognition from the mostly southern anti-civil rights Democrats for reducing it so much as to kill it.

We may also review the outcome from the new proposals inside the halls of congress, farther pushing the appeal to emotion in search of justification for the dawning government of US socialism. There again, our source is found on Wikipedia:

> Although passage of the Civil Rights Act of 1957 seemed to indicate a growing federal commitment to the cause of civil rights, the legislation was limited. Because of the ways in which it had been changed, the government had difficulty enforcing it. By 1960, black voting had increased 3%. Passage of the bill showed the willingness of national leaders to support, to varying degrees, the cause of civil rights.

> At the time, Reverend Martin Luther King, Jr. was 28 years old and a developing leader in the civil rights movement; he spoke out against white supremacists. Segregationists had burned African-American churches, centers of education and organizing related to voter registration, and physically attacked African Americans, including women, who were activists. King sent a telegram to President Eisenhower to make a speech to the South, asking him to use "the weight of your great office to point out to the people of the South the moral nature of the problem". Eisenhower responded, "I don't know what another speech would do about the thing right now."

> Disappointed, King sent another telegram to the President, stating that Eisenhower's comments were "a profound disappointment to the millions of Americans of goodwill, north and south, who earnestly are looking to you for leadership and guidance in this period of inevitable social change". He tried to set up a meeting with President Eisenhower, but was given a meeting with Vice President Richard Nixon, which lasted two hours. Nixon was reported to have been impressed with King and told the president that he might enjoy meeting with him in the future.

Thus we see that the Federal government was already making use of the "*race issue*" to impose its demands on states, whose majority populations on both sides of the fence were not very open to it at the time. Yet the government dragged its feet instead of robustly addressing the situation — in order to exacerbate the rising emotions.

The issue of race was also used as an excuse to probe deeply into the business and private lives of individual American citizens, especially as time moved forward. The excuse was a desire to facilitate or, rather, impose, integration, in hiring practices as well as personal choice in living accommodation, and in numerous other areas of social interaction.

The true intent was to violate a citizen's Constitutional right to make decisions regarding personal interactive space, freedom of choice socially —

to choose with whom one wishes to associate — and financial privacy, while secretly intending a massive future confiscation of wealth (from the middle class, not the truly wealthy and powerful, of course) through taxation and other policies that result in a systematic redistribution: a distorted form of socialist policy. A huge distraction was caused by the ensuing social chaos and resistance to the imposition of integration and compelled interaction between two entirely different groups, people with little in common, raised within totally distinct cultural realms, with different social values at large; would nearly guarantee that the friction would continue for years to come into the future, allowing just enough time for the eventual absolute rule of Fascist law to become established above all, to replace rule of the Constitutional law that had set out to protect the rights of the individual.

The violence that resulted was deplorable; that is not in dispute. But we must inquire, at this point, what caused it, who provoked it, and why? As we have already observed, the *Highland Folk School And Education Center* specialized in offering instruction on how to incite the public in order to enroll them in subverting the public order and social stability by calling for elements of a socialist or communist system. This should be compared to the last two decades or more of Color Revolutions, the instigation of Arab Springs and coups like the one in Ukraine, all sponsored and organized behind the scenes by democratic-sounding nonprofit organizations, the "NGOs", sponsored by George Soros and others, the majority of which start by promising a better deal for the man in the street and end up creating a massive national breakdown, privatizing the national assets that were held for the benefit of the general public and handing them over to the private benefit of wealthy investors — a disaster for the society as a whole, but great for the international capitalists.

While we may all agree that social wrongs should indeed be corrected promptly, in a society founded on the rights of the individual we have to be careful what measures are taken to make those corrections. All theories aside, most models of socialist or communist systems that have been created in reality bear worrying characteristics of totalitarian control. Fascism need not even be discussed. Rectifying unfair economic conditions inevitably implies opinionated moralist concerns; but who has the right to impose which morals on whom?

If indeed it be true that this movement of incitement was pushed by a visionary champion, whose human face would our crystal modem reveal to us? Who was the rogue puppet master in those days?

Stanley Levison

The Communist Party USA had joined with the Democratic Party of America to steer the Democrats toward a more and more socialist agenda by 1950, and behind the scenes one of the most active figures was Stanley Levison.

Levison was a businessman from New York, with law degree from St. John's University. He was chief adviser to Martin Luther King Jr. He wrote King's speeches and organized the marching events. In some circles he has been labeled as the mastermind of the entire so called *"revolutionary"* movement.

Levison was in the leadership of the Communist Party USA. King had been introduced to Levison by co-party member Bayard Ruskin. It has been said that King offered to pay him a salary for helping out so greatly, but Levison refused, declaring that it was an honor to assist in a movement of what he tactfully labeled as a great "liberation"; but his true intent as time was destined to reveal, was to use the blossoming Civil Rights movement as a cover to impose a Socialist/Communist agenda on the citizens of America.

Even J. Edgar Hoover feared Levison's capacity to incite mass political unrest. Think of Occupy Wall Street and Black Lives Matter combined. Levison took over the fundraising effort of the Southern Christian Leadership Conference; here again we are reminded of the fact that repressive government organizations in the US tend to hide behind the Christian Church and the educational establishment, in an effort to downplay the true intent of their efforts to dominate in the absolute. The SCLC was the clandestine body in charge of facilitating the intent to incite, a front-line force, to simplify the description. Who then was Bayard Rustin, the man who introduced Levison to King?

Bayard Rustin

In 1936, Rustin joined the Communist League at City College, New York. Charged with draft dodging, Bayard went to prison for two years in 1944. On January 23, 1953, the *Los Angeles Times* reported that he was convicted of lewd conduct, coexisting with homosexual perversion, and was sentenced to jail again for sixty days.

Rustin attended the 16th Convention of the Communist Party, USA in 1957. He and King together founded the SCLC one month later, with Dr. King as President. The Vice President was Reverend Fred Shuttlesworth, who was also President of another component of the movement called the Southern Conference Educational Fund.

The field director of the SCEF, Carl Braden, was also a national sponsor of the Fair Play for Cuba Committee. The Program director of the SCEF, Reverend Andrew Young, was also Jimmy Carter's ambassador to the UN. Young was trained at the Highlander Folk School, in Tennessee. Rustin eventually was replaced in 1961 by one Jack O'Dell, who was also a devoted member of the National Committee of the Communist Party, and had been so since 1956.

Dr. Martin Luther King Jr.

The chief mouthpiece of this new inflammatory movement soaked in appeal to emotion and sympathy for the downtrodden in America was none other than the Reverend Martin Luther King Jr. While in all probability, most Americans have never heard of the others mentioned in this new effort of the banking cartel to distract, deceive and divide by appealing to emotion, virtually every American has heard of MLK. The nation has established a holiday named after him. There are roads and streets named after him all over the country, not to mention statues bearing his image standing on many US college campuses.

King held strong Communist sentiments, but there were also *other specific details* concerning the person of King that our mainstream media had rather the citizens of America never knew, and that the nation's state indoctrinated schoolchildren never found out.

The book *The FBI and Martin Luther King Jr.* by David G. Garrow, gives a great deal of pertinent information. The Federal Bureau of Investigation had for many years been aware of Stanley Levison's Communist activities. It was Levison's close association with King that turned the FBI's interest to Reverend King.

In charge of the FBI's probe of King was Assistant Director William C. Sullivan. Sullivan described himself as a liberal, saying that initially "I was one hundred per cent for King...because I saw him as an effective and badly needed leader for the oppressed people in their desire for civil rights." But the probe of King not only confirmed their suspicions about King's Communist beliefs and associations, it revealed other secrets that many wished to keep sealed. According to Sullivan, who had direct access to the surveillance files on King which are denied the American people, King had embezzled or misapplied substantial amounts of money contributed to the "civil rights" movement to pay for liquor, sex parties, and other activities. In fact, the National Civil Rights Museum in Memphis, Tennessee, which is putting on display the two bedrooms from the Lorraine Motel where King stayed the night before he was shot, has declined to depict in any way the "occupants" of those rooms. That, according to exhibit designer Gerard Eisterhold, would be "close to blasphemy." Why? Apparently Dr. Martin Luther King Jr. did not spend his last night on Earth with his wife. Sullivan also stated that King had alienated the affections of numerous married women.

Violence almost invariably attended King's supposedly "non-violent" marches. Often, that sort of thing can be attributed to provocateurs sent to discredit a movement; but Sullivan's probe revealed a very different King from the carefully-crafted public image. King welcomed members of many different groups as members of his SCLC, many of them advocates and practitioners of violence. King's only admonition on the subject was that they should embrace "tactical nonviolence."

Sullivan also relates an incident in which King met in a financial conference with Communist Party representatives, not knowing that one of the participants was an infiltrator working for the FBI. J. Edgar Hoover personally saw to it that documented information on King's Communist connections was provided to the President and to Congress. Conclusive information from FBI files was also provided to major newspapers and news wire services, but virtually none of this information passed back down into the hands of the American people.

In Summary of the times

The great divisive distraction was on. The specifics of the movement, the moralistic considerations, are covered in other books; here, we are looking at specifically what was going inside the halls of US government. We have discussed that ex-Fascists were transported to the US by the thousands throughout the late 1940s and through the 1950s. We have discussed that the official explanation was to benefit from their scientific knowledge. However, some of these people also had knowledge in regard to how to run a Fascist system, where privately owned assets are expropriated and the resources of a nation are controlled in the absolute, while the people of the land are reduced to expendable resources. Don't forget that one of the first successes of the Nazis was to destroy the labor unions in Germany, to the benefit of the corporations.

The clandestine central bank of the US, the Federal Reserve, had big plans. Since before the US Civil War, the true intention of the cartel including the bank, the corporations and their government connections, was to gain control over the nation in a likewise fashion. At the time of Hitler's rise to the German Chancellery, the banking cartel of America saw and supported the first effort of its kind on the world scene, and knew that billions in profits could be generated from such a system.

When World War Two ended, the same individuals who had operated this machine inside the German nation were being smuggled into America.

The US government was being transformed. Many of the philosophical leaders in the US at the time, nearly all of whom were avowed socialists and communists, actually embraced a fascist system, as self-contradictory as that may be.

Links That Reach Back to the Great Banking Cartel

Interestingly enough, generous support was coming from Nelson Rockefeller, then governor of New York State. Rockefeller and even the famous Chase Manhattan Bank were donating large amounts to the incendiary movement and its Socialist/Fascist ambitions. This dark connection with the banking cartel and Martin Luther King Jr., the SCLC, is noted in the King Encyclopedia put together by Stanford University: [28]

> Rockefeller used his position to advocate civil rights in the South. When King was arrested at a sit-in demonstration in Atlanta in October 1960, Rockefeller used the pulpit of a Brooklyn, New York, church to applaud King's ideals: "We've got to make love a reality in our own country. When the great spiritual leader, the Rev. Dr. Martin Luther King, finds himself in jail today because he had the courage to love, we have a long way to go in America" (Dales, "Governor Turns to Lay Preaching").

> In early 1962, Rockefeller offered to help King set up a New York office of the Southern Christian Leadership Conference (SCLC)....

> After King's assassination, Rockefeller asked the New York legislature to pass "a series of measures vitally affecting the lives of all our Negro citizens: jobs and health, housing, education, and training" (Witkin, "Rockefeller Asks 'Memorial' Laws").

The highly socialist organization called the Democratic Party of America soon merged with the official Democratic Party, giving it a new national prominence, while selling to the people as a party centered around their concerns. The transformation was astonishingly quick, about seven years, from 1948 until 1955.

At the same time, the center for socialist subversion in Tennessee was becoming a gathering place for radical dissidents from all over America. Some of these radicals have become American icons. From that school a great inflammatory movement emerged, effectively dividing the American people and pitting two primary vastly different cultures against each other — "Divide and rule," as the maxim says. Behind closed doors, the entire economic system of America was being transformed. The real opponent of the people was the CBCC, the collusion between the moneyed interests and the government, and a once great nation took its second step down this stairway into corporate-sponsored tyranny.

The 1960s

A major societal shift shook the US in the 1960s. There were race riots, marches for "women's liberation," and protests against the escalating war in Vietnam, on the one hand, and socialist gestures like the institution of new government programs including Welfare, giving subsidies (redistribution of wealth, that is, property) paid by the tax-payers — those in the work force — to those who were deemed to be disadvantaged.

Note that the very wealthy do not make most of their riches through salaries but through capital gains on investments (taxed at a lower rate than wage & salary income) and inheritance (also taxed at a lower rate).

Simultaneously, young men leaving high school were being swept up into what would become the major trauma of their lives. In the beginning days of the Vietnam conflict, the official figure of the dead returning home in body bags was 300 a day. The average age of the American soldier in Vietnam was nineteen, to the best that we may determine. Like the Korean War in the early 1950s, this war was sold to the public as a necessary effort to halt the Communist advance into Southeast Asia.

The problem is that, while claiming to be fighting Communist for decades, the US was actually implementing socialistic provisions at home.

In other words, the intent was to establish the idea in the minds of American civilians and citizens at large, that the US government was forcefully protecting them against the kind of "regime" that could confiscate property and share it out among the rest of the population, while in fact taking larger bites out of the average family's income in order to do just that. By provoking empathy for those who were designated victims of past discrimination — non-whites, women, etc. — these became emotional issues, difficult to assess in a rational way.

Television was now in every home, and it brought images of US forces incinerating villages in Vietnam. The anti-war fervor became high-pitched, matched by passionate patriots spouting slogans like, "America – love it or leave it." Emotions again.

Agent Orange

Vietnam also served as a testing ground for some of the new technologies garnered from the ex-German scientists, including infrared night vision and innovations in nuclear technology and rocket propulsion. A case in point would be the relatively new discovery of the chemical Agent Orange.

Agent Orange was developed primarily by Monsanto Corporation and Dow Chemical Corporation, for military purposes. We are forced to remind ourselves that these corporations were collaborators with I.G. Farben, which had committed such crimes during World War Two, but they in union with Farben are directly linked back to the banking cartel. We may also recall that implementing such policies offers huge profit potential for these chemical giants.

Herbicides like Agent Orange are used to destroy crops and forests, the food supply and cover for any enemy fighters, and, of course, for the local population. However, the herbicide is highly toxic. Concentration in the soil and waterways of Vietnam were hundreds of times greater than the levels considered safe by the US Environmental Protection Agency.

In other words, we may conclude here that Vietnam was a huge open air lab for testing of this chemical and possibly many more. The entire population, plus American soldiers, were the human victims of these experiments. The success of the experiment, however, meant millions of dollars or more to Monsanto and Dow Chemical Corporation in military contracts.

According to the Vietnamese Government, four million of its citizens were exposed to AO and over three million have suffered dearly from this exposure. People who live in the mountainous areas of highest exposure are also noted as having unusually high incidences of genetic diseases, even to this very day. This poison still affects Vietnam by entering the food chain, causing skin diseases and numerous kinds of cancer, as well as a multiplicity of other diseases.

More Plebeian Victims

American vets are also suffering in untold numbers. While the fighting was going on, the military, per high command's instructions — influenced by the corporate/banking cartel, were told "not to worry" about the situation of the chemicals being used, that these agents were virtually harmless. [29] Upon returning home many vets suddenly began experiencing ill health, while numerous others had wives that experienced a high number of miscarriages or worse yet, children born with varying bizarre birth defects. The vets who were suffering, knowing on the inside that the culprit of their misery was the Agent Orange that they were exposed to, began to file for disability, as well as making other medical claims. The CBCC-owned American government categorically denied their claims. As late as 1993, the Department of Veteran Affairs had only compensated 486 claims out of 39,419 filed by US servicemen who had been exposed while serving in Vietnam during the time of the war [30]

The People On the Home Front

For the first time in history, scenes of warfare were brought home daily, and the impression was not that of brave and honorable conduct by our valiant fighting forces. The vision suddenly emerged of grown men shooting villagers in grass huts, including children and adolescents. Young or old, male or female, anyone who could pull a trigger or throw a grenade, or walk up with explosives under their shirt, might be one's killer; but to see our men waging war this way was heartbreaking.

The soldiers were conscripted; it wasn't their decision to put themselves in such situations. No wonder so many people decided that evading the draft was no loss of honor. In addition, the inflow of body bags, many times containing the corpses of friends, neighbors and close family members, was increasing dramatically. People began to question what we were fighting for. No real battle objective was obvious. In reaction, response of a sizeable portion of the citizenry was to embrace the peace movement and everything that sounded more fair, more moral, and more just.

The critics were on target when they deduced that a major impetus for the unjustified mass slaughter was to serve corporate interests, the same interests primarily who had supported making profit out of mass slaughter in the past. Even President Eisenhower, a general, was deeply concerned about the forces of the CBCC influencing decisions made in Congress, sacrificing the lives of US citizens and others on the altar of corporate profit. Just read Eisenhower's Farewell Address To the Nation given in 1961:

> A vital element in keeping the peace is our military establishment. Our arms must be mighty, ready for instant action, so that no potential aggressor may be tempted to risk his own destruction...
>
> This conjunction of an immense military establishment and a large arms industry is new in the American experience. The total influence — economic, political, even spiritual — is felt in every city, every statehouse, every office of the federal government. We recognize the imperative need for this development. Yet we must not fail to comprehend its grave implications. Our toil, resources and livelihood are all involved; so is the very structure of our society. In the councils of government, we must guard against the acquisition of unwarranted influence, whether sought or unsought, by the military-industrial complex. The potential for the disastrous rise of misplaced power exists, and will persist. We must never let the weight of this combination endanger our liberties or democratic processes. We should take nothing for granted. Only an alert and knowledgeable citizenry can compel the proper meshing of the huge industrial and

military machinery of defense with our peaceful methods and goals so that security and liberty may prosper together.

Manifestation of the People's Response

In the end, the people *en masse* boldly demanded a change. Young people especially — always the more revolutionary, and idealistic, portion of a society, and in this case also the next in line to be sent to the front — exercised their Constitutional right to protest decisions of the government. The demonstrators were not welcome, and the path of protest in those days was not an easy one to walk. We of the future should vividly recall the response of authoritarians, backed by the interests of the CBCC.

However, this same sentiment, which evolved into a movement for social justice and a rejection of the capitalist model at large, made it possible to pass legislation that mandated wealth re-distribution and damaged individuals' rights to the fruit of their labor. When emotions are running high, it is easy to be bamboozled.

The socialist-communist movement inside the United States had been simmering since 1948, but now it had reached the population in general. Up until the war in Vietnam, the general population had embraced the declared values of a capitalist society at large. The generation born during the years immediately following World War Two had grown up during the times of the Civil Rights movement, the terrible Korean War, and the beginning of the war in Vietnam; they were inclined to doubt their parents' unblinking belief that America was infallible. When they heard the claims of socialist rhetoric from leaders of the Civil Rights Movement, they idealistically wished that peace and plenty could be bestowed upon everyone. And due to the Baby Boom, these young people constituted a *majority* of the national population.

Visions of utopian ideology saturated the intellect of these masses, since it appeared that their own world was falling apart at the seams. Ideas of communal living, sharing resources, disregarding the need to be productive simply to access the basic necessities of life, a wish for egalitarian society, and free love representing an overt rejection of the established moral system — these were openly embraced by this new and inexperienced majority.

This embrace was so distinctly in line with the National Socialist direction already present in the US government suggests strongly that they were manipulated into, or powerfully helped along, as a well calculated and planned initiative by both the US government and the exploitative CBCC.

Other suggestions of this clandestine intent from the cartel are found in the additional doors opened in American society that had never before been opened on such a mass scale. These intentions are primarily that of generating new lines for immense profit and a type of social experimentation very similar in its destructive profiteering ideology to that which occurred on the battlefields of Vietnam.

The doorway to use of illegal drugs was opened wide during the so-called American counter culture movement. There was immense wealth to be made, directly from the drug trade, but also from the policing and security complex that would be built to control (but not kill) it, as well as that from the incarceration industry, the legal system, the pharmaceutical companies participating in rehabilitation programs, and most of all, the intelligence agencies who actually ran most of the drug trade (and still do).[31]

Another door that was opened wide during the time was that of pornography.[32] Its expanded acceptance quickly grew this into a multi-billion dollar business, one that is still growing rapidly and reaching all the way up into the coffers of the banking cartel, even into both houses of Congress.

Again, not only do we observe the banking cartel's lust for profit at all cost, but we see a blatant disregard for societal morality, health and human life, even to the point of destroying society in the name of generating a profit.

Simultaneous Alterations of America's Belief System

There are many other developments, some weirder than others, that came to distract the public around this time. Starting in the early 1950s we observe the UFO phenomenon being deeply inserted into the belief system of the mainstream populace. And laws were passed to facilitate a rejection of the moral compass that had guided most of the nation in favor of a new "moral" guidance.[33] Who gets to decide when to case off elements of the established moral code that our society has accepted for centuries, and what to replace it with? There have been continual assaults on religion in the US, a country that once was united by the Christian beliefs o most of the inhabitants. Tolerance for other religions is fine; but mandating that religion be removed from society and relegated to obscure corners is troubling. It also leaves room for speculation that someone wants to an effort to introduce some newly made up "world religion" as yet another tool for manipulating the public, to gradually impose a new state-endorsed, all-inclusive politically-correct religion?[34] Isn't that the most profound affront possible to those citizens who were guaranteed a right to their own beliefs?

The Assassination of President Kennedy

It is worthy of notation here that the assassination of Kennedy has been the source of hundreds or more books, film documentaries and movies, each claiming different reasons for the assassination and different details as to how it may have been carried out; and by whom. Let's add one reason for the murder.

As we intimated earlier, when the capitalist system possesses an effective set of firm checks and balances against the certain possibility of corruption, there is a chance that the result could be the best of life that modern day industrialized society has to offer. The problem is that the US system as it presently stands has hardly any such checks in place. We are left with a quasi-authoritarian state, bearing the imprint of corrupt capitalism.

It is the contention of this author, based on hard historical facts already covered, that just such corruption *was a part of the original calculation.* And the goal can be reached by many different paths, including via a form of socialism, when it is used as the first step in the process of seizing a country's privately-held resource base.

Kennedy appears to have had the concerns of the people at large in mind when he embraced the ideology of socialism for what he perceived to be a better American nation, with programs facilitated by US government for the benefit of the public. Whether that was good or bad also depends on how it was carried out, with what kinds of limits and checks to stop abuse by either the aid recipients, the bureaucracy managing it, and the forces that always ty to expand such programs. For our purposes, though, let's focus on his Executive Order against the Federal Reserve.

Executive Order 11110

This order reveals that Kennedy was aware of the Federal Reserve's negative influence and the large corporations that were in line with Federal Reserve, and their tendency to fix prices, as well as engage in other corrupt ventures.

In simplified version, this order appears to grant the US Treasury authority to strip the Federal Reserve of its power to lend money to the United States Federal Government at interest.[35]

The privately owned bank would then either have its profit vastly reduced or would be out of business altogether, as far as in dealing with the USFG is concerned. It appears, judging from my research, that the order may still be valid to this day, yet never enforced.

If, like Thomas Jefferson, Kennedy had his eyes wide open to the corruption of the centralized bank, and if he decided to utilize his Presidential authority for the purpose of neutralizing it, then we can imagine they in turn had a hand in neutralizing him. Even though Kennedy actively embraced Socialist ideology because of the few positives that the concept has to offer, he appears to have been set on establishing limitations on the corruption of the system. Just as Jefferson and Jackson had done years before, he publicly called for checks, and by his actions he sought to provide those checks on the CBCC to protect the American people.

Socialism usually suppresses economic growth, due to rigid regulation (since programs of financial support must be funded at the expense of those who are productive).

This order turned the Constitutional ability to create and issue currency back over to the US Federal government and specifically, the Treasury Department. For every ounce of silver or gold inside the vault of the US Treasury, the UST could issue new currency based on that value. The Federal Reserve, in circulating its own "legal tender," was going against the US Constitution, which young Kennedy must surely have been aware of. Just as soon as Kennedy was assassinated, his United State Notes were removed from circulation. Our footnoted source claims that by 1999, 99% of all US paper currency were Federal Reserve Notes.

More than four million dollars of new "United States banknotes" were brought into circulation in $2 and $5 bills. The $10 and $20 bills were being printed when Kennedy was assassinated only five months after the passage of Order 11110. Our source claims that if any other US president since had chosen to enforce the order drafted by Kennedy, the US would not be in debt to the tune of trillions in dollars today. By being forced to go through the Federal Reserve, the USFG is charged interest on that debt, applying the force of Kennedy's order would have eliminated that interest. We may therefore, conclude that Kennedy was virtually martyred for his actions to liberate citizens from the dawning tyranny that he silently knew would one day manifest itself.

Kennedy did what our military, fire and police personnel must do: he stood strong to face the forces of evil in our midst. Above all else, he should be remembered for all time to come. The details of who shot him, and who arranged it directly, are almost irrelevant. If we continue to simply follow the money trail, and see whose interests were served and whose were threatened at each turning point, that will lead us all into the utopia of truth, and indicate which powers were behind the whole crime.

Beginning in 1957, Senator John Little McClean launched an all-out attack on organized crime known as the Valachi Hearings. He specifically mentioned going after Hoffa and Sam Giancana of Chicago. In spite of the attack, Hoffa managed to remain clear. Kennedy appointed as attorney general his younger brother Robert, who had been frustrated at the failure of earlier attempts at nailing the chief crime leaders. Once appointed Attorney General, Robert Kennedy launched the greatest attack on organized crime that had ever been witnessed in America.

Likely, the Kennedys' dogged pursuit of organized crime in 1961, and their persecution of corrupting agents inside certain specific FR-invested corporations, in combination with Executive Order 11110 intended to neutralize corruption in America's financing, drove the Federal Reserve to contact the highest ranking crime bosses of the day to contract a hit on Kennedy.

Robert Kennedy also worked tirelessly with his brother to prosecute the executives of US Steel. A strong contender for US President in his own turn, who very closely resembled his brother in both appearance and conviction, RFK lay dead in a pool of his own blood by assassins a mere five years after the death of his brother.

Third Dark Step Downward

What followed the Civil War, as we shall recall, was a series of economic depressions that appeared to the rank and file as an ongoing economic collapse from 1870 until 1908. Toward the end of that phase, the people on the ground had commenced in earnest to appeal for relief to authoritarian forces high up in the big house on the hill. What followed was an order from the US Congress to the banking establishment, to stabilize the currency, since the US economy had apparently strengthened and was viewed as heading only upward from that time forward.

These banking forces primarily consisted of entities represented by the family of J.P. Morgan and the Rockefeller Family, along with a Federal Representative backing. The virtual brains of the new clandestine central bank was Paul Warburg, of the Warburg family that dominated finance in Germany and intermarried with the famous Rothschild family. In this intermarriage we see the ties that bind to give absolute advantage over the US economic infrastructure and consequently the citizen population.

In 1910, on Jekyll Island, Georgia, a clandestine meeting of those banking efforts met to design a new central bank. To gain popular acceptance for this controversial initiative, the institution was labeled "Federal," as if it were controlled by the federal government, not by a consortium of private banks and, in the lead, the old Bank of New York, which had always been the central bank either in actuality or in de-facto.

The father of famous aviator Charles Lindbergh stood strong against the Federal Reserve. He called the FR out for what it was, a banking conspiracy designing to rob all liberty and wealth from the people of America. Lindbergh's son also publicly criticized the banking/corporate war machine and he suffered the consequences. The unspoken message was that nobody, no matter how high and powerful, should dare to stand in their way.

Endless distractions were served up to the public for the rest of the 20th century, keeping the focus off this slinking power grab and ongoing centralization of forces. From McCarthyism to Cold War scares of imminent nuclear destruction, to the civil unrest of the 1960s, shocking assassinations and hedonistic appeals to sex and drugs and rock n roll, there was enough to keep young and old pre-occupied with other matters than watching the Central Bank.

When Kennedy was killed, Johnson seized the controls and the first move he made was to allow the Federal Reserve to keep on printing unbacked banknotes, terminating Kennedy's initiative to have the US Treasury print real money for the nation, backed with a stated face value in silver or gold.

The second move that he made was to announce unto all the earth that he was embracing Kennedy's social welfare programs in America, under the unassailable title of "The War On Poverty." For such a lofty goal with all the emotions it inspires, any level of national debt would be justifiable, wouldn't it? By 1966 came a new round of tax increases to facilitate this dawning era of Big Government.

For the next twenty years the system moved in gradual increments, allowing the citizens to adjust, getting used to increasing regulation and the ever-increasing loss of personal liberty due to regulations on business, individual enterprise, and every aspect of life. Part of the purpose was to generate tax and fee revenue to feed the newly imposed social agenda, among other forms of corruption, and part of it was to get people used to having a fire marshal, code inspector, accountant and lawyer involved in everything they tried to do: some for additional fees, and some with a responsibility to ensure you are abiding by every possible limiting regulation.

By the mid-1970s most Americans had even come to believe that the tax-payer supported "social safety net" was more important and more "progressive" than personal responsibility, despite the coincident loss of personal individual liberty; while corporate interests were allowed to swallow up smaller businesses.

By 1981, a new era had arrived. It was not an era of individual citizen progress, but an era of regress, if not outright oppression of the individual in the name of freeing corporations from any responsibility to land, nation, employees and the citizen base at large.

This too was implemented gradually, and at first only applied to certain areas of the economy, to certain numerical minorities inside the system, and it was construed that losses incurred by these citizens were justified by their own lack of education and qualification, broadly speaking, as well as their general failure to adapt to changing environments.

The clandestine central bank and its minions inside Capitol Hill capitalized on the basic instinct of the average American citizen, who generally paid more attention to what was happening to his own family more than any negative impact on his fellow citizens. The majority did not realize that they were heading toward a potential loss of the entire nation, as they were being conquered piece by piece, sector by sector. Travel this road to its logical conclusion, and one day soon they would all find themselves homeless, landless and very vulnerable to a new, ruthlessly exploitative master, ruling the blessed land that their fathers before them had labored to develop.

Conditions On the American Work Floor

To review developments since the Civil War, corporate America expanded into the Western states. The workers continued to experience an economic depression, but there was expansion of the US corporate entity. When the forces of banking and the corporation won the war in the end, the treasury and the de facto central bank of New York/Pennsylvania mass produced non-backed banknotes now known as "greenbacks," allowing the railroad corporations and some others to invest in government-held land to the West. The idea was that the success of the corporation would produce value, which would support these virtually worthless notes, and the financial success would "trickle down" to the citizens at large.

This notion was echoed later in Ronald Reagan's "trickle-down economics" theory in the 1980s. The problem is that it doesn't work right away, and it doesn't trickle down to American workers at all if one imports Chinese laborers to build the Trans Continental Railway or, as today, the corporation moves its factories abroad altogether. At home, we are left with an economic crash.

In any event, at the first sign that some crumbs are, actually, arriving in the laps of the less wealthy, people are encouraged to buy a home, since real-estate tends to hold value. This is then used as a weapon especially against those enterprising and hard-working individuals ambitious to work their way up the ladder. With little experience of these matters, they are easily led to invest in property they can hardly afford. Any brief period of unemployment or other set back, and they miss making payments. Their property is subject to bank foreclosure or is sold out from under them at tax sales. Meanwhile, mortgage rates (and in our times, credit card lending rates go up), and those who were making their payments may find their bills increasing anyway. They are trapped in debt. The trickle down now flows back up, and quickly.

In any era, steadily deteriorating work conditions are the result when there is a ready supply of willing workers who can replace any employee who is not satisfied with deteriorating conditions and plummeting pay. Contrary to popular criticism, skill level was irrelevant, since the supply for virtually any skill outstripped the demand, and what the people on the ground were left with was a saturated employment base. Meanwhile, the corporations make more profit for their shareholders by taking advantage of their employees. This was certainly the case between 1970 and 1940.

Families were pushed to employ every person in the household, including children, out of basic necessity. Today we have laws to limit this, but of course there are abuses.[36] And, since 2008, several states have allowed high school students to work longer and longer hours, raising the question of how much focus is put on education when the job is more important and a young person cannot get enough sleep?

In previous times, children were subject to flagrant verbal, physical, and even sexual abuse from their supervisors. They could be forced to labor in an unsafe environment against their will, for substandard wages, and basically endure whatever harassment their supervisors decided to deal out to them. There are recorded cases where many children perished from abuse and overwork.[37]

The women of the house were forced to work as textile mill workers, telegraph decoders, maids for the wealthy, nurses, teachers and others — which on the surface may not appear to be all that negative. The problem was that they were nearly as vulnerable as the children, in many respects. They could be sexually harassed by male employees, and made to work for almost nothing.

There were no safety measures in place, and no requirement to pay overtime — although people were being forced to labor twelve hour days, six days a week and sometimes more. There was no such thing as holiday pay, paid vacation, paid sick leave, retirement plan, or guarantee that you would still have a job tomorrow. And there was no one to appeal to, if the situation got out of hand.

One hair-raising accident is known to history as the Triangle Shirtwaist Factory incident, which took place in Manhattan, in 1911.[38] The building is now called the Brown Building and is part of New York University.

The incident began when a bin filled with fabric scraps on the 8th floor burst into flames, quickly engulfing the floors above. The factory floors were over-crowded, the doors could not be opened, and the terrified teenaged workers — Italian and Jewish immigrants — were trapped. More than 50 died by jumping to the sidewalk below.

In the aftermath, the city and state of New York passed regulations to try to minimize future incidents. Let it be stated here, however, that astonishingly similar tragedies have occurred in recent decades, including chicken processing plant fires in North Carolina and Arkansas.[39] Even laws cannot secure the rights of the general population if they are not enforced.

By the early 1900s, there were many labor unions and some had well over a million members. By banding together, workers sought to provide a barrier between themselves and the management to create some standards, or checks on abuses, to safeguard employee interests. Corporations resisted the formation of unions, but they needed workers. Without that worker base, the enterprise was doomed to fail.

Simply having a job does not keep the bills paid. What does pay the bills is a salary commensurate with the skill, effort or service provided, and benefits that allow workers to access basic necessities of life. When corporate interests are united in treating workers like disposable machines, so that employees have no alternatives, the employees are forced to unite among themselves to see to their own interests.

Reasonable wages were one key demand. Some degree of job security, and the opportunity to settle disputes in a mediated discussion was another. Assurances were sought that only qualified workers would be allowed on the work floor. This was facilitated by the creation of union-approved apprenticeship programs.

Corporations resisted the call for a check by making use of threats, intimidation of union employees and outright violence. There are records of riots erupting on company grounds when management refused to negotiate; and corporate-hired militia would fire directly into the crowds.

Still, corporations have always found ways to undermine the workforce by bringing in foreign workers (skilled as well as unskilled) to compete for jobs, thus lowering the wage anyone can expect to be paid. When that is not enough to feed the coffers of the corporate shareholders, they send the jobs out to low-paying countries wholesale.

But the last century was a series of dramas showing just how welcome unions were. In response to unionization, and at the same time proving the need for unions to protect workers, here are just a few of the most shocking incidents, in brief. These are well worth reading about in detail.

The Pullman Strike

Workers at the Pullman rail car factory walked out in protest when they were required to work 12-hour days and take a cut in pay, joined by the

American Railway Union, for a total of perhaps 250,000 protesters. There were major disruptions of rail traffic.

Millions of dollars in corporate revenue was being lost by the day. President Grover Cleveland sent in Federal troops to crack down.

The Ludlow Massacre

The Colorado Fuel & Iron Company came to the rescue of the Colorado national guard, "saving" them from a tent colony of 1,200 striking coal miners and their families. Some two dozen people were slaughtered. The principal owner of the mine was John D. Rockefeller himself.

The Battle of Blair Mountain

The largest labor uprising and best organized armed conflict on American soil since the Civil War was dubbed the Battle of Blair Mountain. The confrontation in the West Virginia coalfields had been boiling since early 1920 and exploded at the end of summer 1921. Some 10,000 armed coal miners confronted 3,000 police and strikebreakers hired by coal mining operators. More than one million rounds were fired.

President Warren Harding sent in the US military, and the union leaders had to send their men home to avoid a greater slaughter.

Corporate Checks

By the end of World War Two, America could afford to offer employees a better deal. There was no significant competition left standing, in industry, banking, or the service businesses. In this era we see the beginnings of company pension plans for all employees, and a wide spectrum of benefits offered. Today, the global situation has changed, and so have the relations between corporation and employee.

To safeguard the employee at the expense of the corporation by truly threatening its profit margin would be counter-productive. But wiser heads realized that contented employees make far more productive employees, and they sought that balance of maximum efficiency that reaped the highest reward for both sides.

Possible Exception to the Rules?

Let's remember that "the workforce" is the same people as the "national population" and the "voters." Now, what kind of relationship should the corporations that dominate the nation's economic resources establish with those people?

Present day corporate policy toward employees seems to indicate that when competition increases, they are willing to disregards the factor of humanity in the name of preserving their own profit margin. However, even under these hostile, self-centered conditions, management on any level should be able to apply its analytical ability to anticipate potential problems, conceive solutions, and determine both where and how to apply them.

Otherwise under such situations, human labor and human bodies are seen and treated as "products," or as organisms that consume resources. The individuals with power are allowed to assume the status of product consumers; the remainder of humanity are relegated to the level of organisms that provide both labor and actual products derived from their personal property, and that provide the dead bodies that inevitably are part of any war.

In other words, the most valuable thing that persons relegated into this group have is their intellectual output and labor. If these targeted individuals cannot provide labor or any other service valued by the corporate elites for profit or personal pleasure, then their rate of consumption may appear to exceed their value as living, breathing organisms.

This sounds like we are venturing into a creepy, evil sci-fi scene, but examples of it are played out every day. Don't forget, organ harvesting and human trafficking are happening today. People are already being used as products, nonhumans, and apparently the trend is spreading and growing rapidly.

What Fascism represents is a marriage between unregulated government and corporate interests to facilitate this corruption,[40] so that both entities can profit at the expense of the rank and file folks who are only viewed as an expendable resource. As we have observed, government simply removes the controls and regulations, then turns a blind eye.

There are specific facts explaining corruption at the highest levels in government that eventually facilitate the development of fascist tendencies even in our present time. [41]

How is it possible? The pull of propaganda often lures people into going along with things that are hard for outsiders to believe. Such emotional and psychological notions as patriotism, civic duty or religious respect can be aligned with a nationalist agenda, or any other notions that we have learned not to question; then we simply act to fulfill our so called "national obligations" like all our neighbors, whatever that may require.

Those who refuse to do so are labeled unpatriotic, retrograde, complainers, people in search of a hand-out rather than those who take action to improve their personal situations. Much worse labels are the broad category of "extremist" and the new, increasingly imposed, but intentionally broad, label "terrorist."

Just as those who dared to criticize the Fascist entity were liable to be persecuted, negatively labeled and promptly condemned without benefit of trial, so today many nonconformists are automatically branded "pro-Russian" or "racist" or "homophobic." Anyone who fails to enthusiastically endorse policies that our parents and grandparents would have recognized as "un-American" or "immoral" may now be liable to ridicule and harassment, at the very least.

The same trend can be seen in the persecution of those who have determined to live outside of municipal influence. Congress has been moving, for years already, to demand that everyone possess a passport or national ID simply to move from one US state into another, as has already been mentioned.

Travel on the highways already puts an innocent person at risk of losing his life savings at the whim of the State. Through programs like "asset forfeiture," if an officer "suspects" your possessions or cash could be related to a crime, he can confiscate it. And you can go to court to try to get it back.[1]

What these authorities are searching for is hard cash; guns; and even "stockpiles" of food — anything they can claim seems "suspicious," and even if the owner has a legitimate explanation. Thus, any individual person relocating his personal resource base in general will be in danger of having his possessions confiscated, since some underhanded motive can always be imputed. This happens more often to people of limited resources, and the confiscation may take all their life savings. So much for freedom and liberty for all.

Warning Signs of A Seriously Corrupting Government

Using history and a number of online guides,[42] this author has deduced the primary signs of government heading into a serious state of corruption. According to the research, governments worldwide can be categorized according to fourteen basic signs suggesting the apex of corruption in any capitalist system, Fascism. This author will mention only those that apply to the United States at the time of this writing, notating the facts extracted from our source, yet recorded primarily in his own wording. These signs read as the following:

> Patriotic mottos, slogans, symbols and songs are widely seen and heard. Flags are displayed everywhere, on clothes with symbols and in

---

[1]   https://www.google.com/search?client=opera&q=tsa+confiscation&sourceid=opera&ie=UTF-8&oe=UTF-8#q=asset+forfeiture&*

public displays. The air about appears to be charged with a powerful sense of nationalism.[43]

Human rights may be allowed to fall by the wayside because of a perception of being under threat. The general public will accept incidents of torture, assassination, detention without charges, and extended incarcerations of prisoners in disregard for any facts.[44]

Certain groups are identified as enemies/scapegoats for the purpose of unifying the population toward a single cause, to eliminate a specific threat or to deflect attention from the real threat. The nature of these threats can be Christian or non-Christians, conservatives, gun owners, survivalists; those who have been transformed into history's villains by an intentionally twisted history, any symbols, historical or otherwise may be attacked, that these individuals possess as a group.[45]

The military is held up as supreme, even when the domestic problems are rampant. The greatest share of government funding, 57%, goes to the military industrial war machine. Soldiers are given honors and placating gifts at the expense of the general population, even though it was their choice to join the military since the draft was ended years before.[46]

Government or a portion of controls the media, either directly or indirectly.[47] Certain types of censorship may be fairly common, especially that which carries the age-old appeal to emotion already mentioned. [48] [49]

Corporate power is protected at all costs. The industrial and business aristocracy of corrupting nations tend to be the ones who put government leaders into the position of power, creating a mutually beneficial business/government relationship and power elite. [50]

Labor unionization is suppressed, and any collective well-organized formation of the ordinary population is viewed as a threat to (a corrupted) government. [51] [52]

Police are given unlimited power. Police abuses are overlooked in the name of patriotism and protection from a magnified threat. Basic civil liberties are cast aside in the name of security. A national police force is present or is one in the making, that has or will have unlimited power. [53] [54]

Elections fraud may be noticeable. In other instances elections tend to be overshadowed by smear campaigns or even assassinations against political opponents. Voting numbers, political district boundaries or manipulation of the media virtually dictates the flow of elections through use of legislation.

Corporate Deregulation under Reagan

Since we can see some of these traits in our own environment, we are now forced to ask ourselves: to what extent has America become a fascist state? We see the "domestics' socialism" in the form of measures to placate various minorities and the "underprivileged" —— like the billionaire letting his cook take home the leftovers —measures that keep them onboard and full of patriotism. On the other hand, we see a dismantling of the checks and safeguards that maintain some modicum of balance between what's good for the employer and what's good for the workforce (the rest of the nation).

We have seen that President Ronald Reagan, who was a liberal Democrat before he switched to the "conservative" side in the year 1964, had served as chief spokesman for General Electric for many years. General Electric is one of the US corporations that supported Fascist Germany during the 1930s and 1940s.

Is it possible that he played a role in creating a solid union between Corporation and Government, to the detriment of the freeborn citizens of America, while keeping the media and public attention focused on other angles?

His most outspoken critics were expected to accuse him of switching sides because of Civil Rights. He masqueraded as a traditional US conservative, appealing to the American people's sense of traditional puritanical ethics found in hard work, thrift and unquestioning dedication, combined with a positive historical pioneer spirit of entrepreneurship. If he could attach the issues of deregulation to those personal senses of tradition and patriotism, then he could sell the measure of corporate liberty covering the increasing loss of individual freedom.

The majority of America cheered his promise to reduce the welfare system, taken in by his publicly sworn vow to reduce taxes. As for reducing regulations on corporations, regulations that were intended to safeguard the public, Reagan attempted to appease the populace by claiming that with less regulation on business in general, then individuals would be encouraged to engage their own creative efforts to employ themselves.

With all welfare programs eliminated, what other choice would the individual citizen possess, but to try and put themselves back to work? Only, this time, individual citizens would find it harder to set up shop as time went by. The 1986 tax reform bill was one major blow. [55]

Reagan was true to his word in slashing benefits. He slashed the college lending funds, he slashed unemployment benefits, and dozens more in programs that honest hard-working citizens received — and were due, in view of the taxes that were paid out by middle-classed citizens. While he did not expand individual welfare to any noticeable amount, he never bothered to cut it. He claimed that he was going to slash taxes following any cut on welfare; but in fact with the onset of the 1986 tax reform bills, he raised taxes to a higher level than they had ever been before. [56]

If the citizens of America were not going to benefit from paying taxes, through public assistance programs, then who was and how?

The Presidency of Ronald Reagan represents another step down toward the manifestation of authoritarianism in America, dismantling all checks on the corporation, [57] allowing it to function in complete liberty at the expense of the general employee base.

Think of Dick Cheney, who sat as a director on the board of Halliburton/ Kellogg, Brown and Root, one of the largest military, industrial, security and construction firms in the world. They are in oilfield equipment, military technology, you name it. Cheney was able to bear influence in far ranging places, both at home in the US and around the entire globe; hence corporate policy could be enforced covering a huge range of areas.

We may also observe examples of flagrant corporate theft from employees on an increasingly rampant scale later that was facilitated by government allowing corporations to loot employee pension funds,[58] retirement accounts and general employee stock accounts by simply just declaring that they had invested in stock accounts which suddenly went broke. [59]

In more than a few cases, corporations were allowed to move offshore, only to loot their employees' complete retirement accounts as they made their way out;[60] while both the Federal and state governments turned a blind eye.[61]

Meanwhile, a more intellectual plebeian concern was that the college/ university system had gravitated from being an institution offering an education for true personal enrichment into a commercialized entity that would enable one to pass through a government/corporate gatekeeper on the road to success, sitting just over the horizon. As a direct consequence of taking on college loans and struggling to complete the coursework, unlimited economic opportunity was certain to appear magically. The truth was that the university system would crash if huge numbers of students failed to sign up for class each semester, so efforts were made to ensure that it kept growing.

As for the corporations who remained stateside, they declared that they could not compete with off-shoring US corporations that used foreign labor at near-slave pay levels, and in innumerable instances, labor held in virtual bondage.[62] Reagan said he was going to subsidize those remaining corporations with public funds (national tax dollars). Thus Reagan could claim that his efforts encouraged corporate enterprise, yet these efforts were financed on the backs of America's citizens.

Now the truth regarding a huge portion of the present day US debt/citizen tax margin is revealed. US tax margins are so high in part because the citizen base is compelled to subsidize corporations who remain on US soil.

Reaganomics

Deregulation of corporations coincided with the freeze in minimum wage, and acts of government mentioned earlier serving to neutralize the labor unions. The ideology of Fast Tract served to hasten the corporate offshoring with the advent of the North American Free Trade Agreement.

Corporations intending to close down at a later date were issued no legal requirement to relay the information to their employees or to assist them in any manner for the impending disruption of their financial and daily lives. The only sign that could be seen that foreshadowed such an impending event was when these entities ceased hiring.

And unemployment grew massively. Hundreds of thousands of people who thought that they had a secure job and a comfortable retirement ahead could find themselves unable to make their final mortgage payments. That is one of Reagan's greatest achievements through deregulation of the corporations.

Reagan deregulated controls on oil and gas, cable television and long distance phone calling services. He deregulated interstate bus service and ocean shipping. His most famous deregulation was on banking. Then the Garn-St Germain Depository Institutions Act was passed in 1982. This act removed restrictions on loan-to-value ratios and for Savings and Loan banks. The Federal Home Loan Board also had its regulatory staff reduced. This deregulation allowed banks to apply funds in virtually any direction that they chose, facilitating flagrant corruption via risky real-estate venture loans. This deregulation, and unmanageable budget cuts, contributed heavily to the Savings And Loan crisis of 1989, which cost American taxpayers more than $150 billion to clean up. It has been said that Reagan and his corrupted vision of economics contributed more to our present day unstable business climate than any other President before him.

With the Fannie Mae program, Wall Street brokerage firms deceived the American public into making very risky mortgage investments. Virtually all investment interests of the public were ignored. Some economic commentaries have even claimed that Reaganomics lead to the 2008 economic crisis.[63]

Reagan's policies caused the United States government to go into greater amounts of debt than virtually any President before him. His policies actually tripled the Gross Federal Debt from $900 billion to $2.7 trillion! He tripled it!

Ronald Reagan's policies were a huge failure for the nation of America and its citizens. With such intelligent, skilled and experienced economic advisers, why was this disease of debt and corruption allowed to spread?

If there was no real hard line effort to halt the corrupt, downward slide, then it must have been intentional. Why and for what purpose? Is it not possible that some parts of the CBCC still operate from the premise that corporations would be allowed to extract all resources from the land and, in the act, reduce the people themselves into a resource?

While most Americans are comfortable in applying this logic to other nations that have been chosen as scapegoats and labeled as "totalitarian regimes," such as Nazi Germany, Mao's China and Stalin's Russia, as well as a number of nations in Latin America, very few in the US, will tolerate even a well-organized intellectual conversation exploring that question.

Most people are very attached to the tactfully distorted history we were taught, combined with a heartening dose of patriotism. They do not want to be talked out of their self-confidence and pride, but will stand up in defense of the magisterial entity of the United States of regardless of any facts. The most powerful forms of persuasion are appeal to emotion, sympathy, and pride.

What Future Can America Hope For?

Reagan facilitated the dismantling of checks in the post-World War Two system; his true achievement was to apply on a nationwide basis the exploitation of the average man that once characterized the Reconstruction South. Increasingly, the corporation, working hand in hand with government, would own every town and every segment of real-estate.

The entire freeborn American economic system could then be dismantled piece by well-calculated piece. First the tax rates would go increasingly higher, even though wages would essentially drop, since the highest paying employment opportunities were being outsourced onto foreign soil, or insourced by making use of skilled foreign employees for a fraction of the standard US wage rate that a specific skill or service demands. At the same time technology is being developed that would eventually allow for an overwhelming majority of the work force to be replaced by computers and robotics.

Since the first expense that financially oppressed people tend to drop is insurance, mandates have been put in place to force the public to purchase both car and health insurance. Young men and women just exiting high school are driven to attend colleges and rack up huge debts, even if the added education does nothing to really prepare the individual for existing employment assignments.

Corporations, unlike craftsmen of old, have eliminated entry level hiring opportunities and apprentice level training. Instead, they demand that the employment seeker pay for all his own education and preparation, and show up when he is ready to provide a journeyman quality standard service or product — while being compensated at an apprentice level range in salary. The colleges and universities where he is expected to get his preparation are allowed to take complete advantage of him by demanding extortionist rates imposing a virtual lifetime indenture for their educational services.

In these circumstances, unemployed individuals will accept any offer that would appear to alleviate his most pressing financial needs, including part-time work with no benefits.[1] Very soon he would find himself relegated into the position of permanent bondage with no way to ever climb out, just as the workers of earlier times did in the mines, railroad towns and textile mills. Keep in mind that in our present time there are very few systems in place anywhere across the land to provide a hard check between the employee and the corporation. [64]

---

[1] http://www.skilledup.com/insights/longer-just-temp-rise-contingent-worker

The Fourth Dark Step Downward

1:254–255

> The mind is its own place, and in itself
> Can make a heav'n of hell, a hell of heav'n.
> —— Milton: Paradise Lost

To put the matter in simple terms, the middle class in America is being starved out, with no way to avoid slipping to the lowest economic class, relegating them into a Third World standard of living. To force Americans to accept this poverty, millions of immigrants have been allowed to invade by crossing poorly patrolled borders. Often discussed in the media and elsewhere in the same breath with "refugees" fleeing war-torn homes and in need of help, these are mainly people who hail from areas where the usual pay is just a few dollars a day. The US minimum wage looks good to them, and they have plenty of opportunity here since virtually the entire employment base is gradually converting to this minimum wage. In addition they were allowed to go on public assistance getting free healthcare for the whole family, and free education.

The government response, so far, was to feign efforts at controlling the invasion, while the they still continued allowing it to occur unabated. Allowing this influx accomplished two purposes: to raise the numbers of workers willing to accept a minimum/reduced/falling wage, and to flood the electoral districts with new voters who would support the policies that got them here.

Note that the well-educated from these areas know better than to try living where their business interests would be repressed through intense regulation, with taxes that would absorb nearly fifty percent of their profit. [65] The US is attracting a lower and lower percentage of educated and professional immigrants. Some who come to work choose to visit on very finite terms. The author has personally known many individual examples. One was in the States on a year-long work contract. He declared aloud that Americans were slaves, and that he would never go into debt. When his contract ended, he went back to Colombia, his homeland.

The additional purpose of allowing this huge influx of illegal aliens is to displace those citizens of colonial heritage who possessed a thorough comprehension of Constitution, Constitutional rights and individual liberty; with those who hold no concept of that ideal, who are used to blind submission to authority, especially to a corporate employer.

As a final step, all that the government authority has to do would be to simply placate the majority with some more or less symbolic concessions, manipulating them into going along with whatever loss of liberty might go with it.

Truly no other government on earth, past or present, has bamboozled its own population to such a degree or accomplished as much in the line of propaganda. The only problem is that Americans have yet to bear witness to the worst intentions being planned by this well calculated program of mass deception.

Astonishingly, people ae getting comfortable with the idea of changing or abolishing the present Constitution. When the issue of the Second Amendment is mentioned, [66] it's primarily hunters and outdoorsmen who balk. The idea that Americans reserved for themselves the right to bear arms, as such, seems to be more and more alien to today's citizens.

Any person who attempts to point out specific details suggesting an eminent emergence of tyranny here is seen as a nut, even in casual conversation; or, if taken seriously at all, as a conspiracy possessed radical. [67] The media make sure to perpetuate this as the only possible response; that there could be some worrying evidence is simply not to be considered for a moment.

The belief that tyranny in American is impossible is fostered by the media, but is based on the outdated, misguided notion that the US Government is limited by checks that serve to prevent such possibilities. Once upon a time the US government was subject to solid checks to prevent tyrannical takeover, [68] although as we saw in the presidency of Lincoln, such was still allowed to occur, since when push came to shove, it was shown that citizen voters in states do *not* have the right to divorce from the union, regardless of what the law says. We shall see whether the movement for Cal Exit is just a comedic interlude, a drama or a real tragedy.

The fact is that special allowances are granted by the Constitution to the US Presidency during times of national duress and emergency. Once any opposing representative body is effectively removed, anything goes.

The banking cartel never gave up on its original intent to totally dominate the land and the people of America. We have pondered steps taken in this direction immediately following World War Two, and again under Presidents Kennedy and Johnson. The Reagan Administration played its part. The two US political parties by this time appeared to be socialistic, on the one hand, talking about issues of concern to the recipients of government subsidies, and the other party promoting the interests of the unchecked Corporatist. The middle class majority actually have no political party or representation in the halls of US Congress right now to represent their interests.

Here in 2017, the plan appears to be to fleece the middle class and impoverish it until it is reduced to an impotent slave class, grateful for any role the government can play in relieving the distress. And you have to conform, to get your benefits.

But increasing the breadth of the government's role means increasing government's say. As Rand Paul has said, the level of economic freedom is inversely related to the size of government, which grew significantly under Obama.

In 1880, isolated pockets throughout America hinted at a totalitarian future beyond even the fascism we use as a reference point. In company towns, use of cash was banned; transactions were made using company script. Travelers passing through the town might have to pause at the local exchange and trade hard cash for company script, at a dollar's worth of cash for seventy cents value of script, and exchange it back at the same losing rate. Workers were forced to sign up for a 90-day supply of company script upon being hired. The company owned the entire town and the surrounding landscape.

Since the script was automatically subtracted from the employee's pay voucher in the form of a monthly bill plus interest, in fairly short order his debt exceeded his paycheck, indenturing him into a type of perpetual bondage with the corporate owned estate.

Company script was necessary to access housing owned by the corporation, food from company owned supply stores, supplies and all necessities of life, up to and including entertainment. The individual owned or controlled nothing, nor was he allowed to. His complete life was only an environment of totally dedicated service to the corporate entity. [1]

Corporations took over services once owned and run by enterprising individuals, who had worked their way up since before the American Civil War. With the right to accomplish this upward climb abolished, only the corporations now held the liberty to do business and achieve abundance.

The only time that any court responded was when the individual tried to fight back. If he tried to resign his employment, he was ordered to pay up in full on the debts owed in company script, or at a dollar rate in cash on every seventy cents in script. Failure to do so was equated to theft and condemned one to a chain gang labor farm; a form of American styled concentration camp.

While the incarceration might be listed for a finite period, any "infraction" could easily be fabricated and the detainee would be in for a penalty of extended time inside the fence. The individual had no way to contest any of the charges; and because of this reality, his stay of ninety days for speaking aloud in criticism of management, for example, could easily be transformed into years.

Today, people are losing their homes and banking corporations are buying them at bargain rates, eventually selling them back to people who take out mortgages with the banks. In many ways, thee game is set to help corporations literally purchase the entire real-estate base in the course of time. Then every town and city in today's America would be like a mining town, the local company-owned towns of the past.

And just like the workers of the past, the people of this dawning future would be permanently indentured to the corporation. Because of the transformations needed in the US Constitution to facilitate this complete takeover of the US resource base, and the potential of citizens to resist, the need for an absolute authority becomes apparent. It might not be that difficult: any time there is chaos, the people call for law and order, even if it comes to their own detriment.

Has any event in much more recent history occurred that might suggest this day is coming closer?

To achieve total dominance entails certain logistical problems. The first and most immediate observation is that many people do have resources such as land, retirement and savings accounts, food production equipment, and many other examples.[2] The Constitution preserves this right of private

---

[1] http://www.zerohedge.com/news/2015-02-28/most-americans-are-slaves-and-they-dont-even-know-it

[2] The government is certainly taking away our food independence already. http://govtslaves.info/government-cracks-down-on-gardening-as-self-sufficiency-becomes-illegal/

ownership. Labor is demanded to be rewarded by an agreed upon rate of exchange, between the laborer and the employer in a majority number of cases. Finally, the individual is allowed to keep and bear arms and ammunition.

Prior to this sort of scenario occurring, we would observe a number of heralding events. The first herald would be an attack on the Second Amendment. The second herald might be a strategic placement of military personnel inside US borders. These maneuvers would be clandestine in nature, so as not to alarm the population. What, in fact, is Homeland Security? Why do they have military equipment hidden in our towns? What was Jade Helm, a massive military exercise on US territory? [69]

Another herald may be a general over-reach and intrusion into personal choice on the part of local, state and Federal governments, including mandates that insult the basic fabric of American society[70] and the freedom of choice preserved by the US Constitutional law.

Such mandates are made, then observed very closely by elites, to record the details of any resistance to these authoritarian orders. Areas where they encounter the most resistance may be noted, and specifically who it is that will most likely resist the coming takeover.

Martial law has been declared in the US before, during times of major disturbances and a breakdown of the normal structure of authority. Martial law[71] means the Constitution is suspended, as are all Constitutional rights, including the precious right to trial by court of law. Citizens can be rounded up, the government could then sell the entire real-estate holding to some sort of corporate entity. [72]

In the same twinkling of an eye all savings accounts, retirement accounts and financial holdings would be in possession of the US government. That would be more than enough funds to pay off the US debt to China, for example,[73] but not the entire national debt. What martial law would look like is impossible to predict, but what we can do is keep looking for signs.

9/11/2001

Like the assassination of JFK, every individual American citizen (and many others) old enough to have witnessed the events remembers exactly where he was and what he was doing on 9/11.

Many were in disbelief. Questions floated about in the air. How could hijackers have managed to seize control of the planes? Who were the hijackers? Why did these people attack innocent American citizens? And how was the situation to be addressed?

At the time of the event, the author of this work had close contacts with airport personnel and was working for a traveling maintenance company that carried him virtually all over the United States, often working at airports in four-month stints.

During the time of the 9/11 attack, the author also worked as a representative for a major national charity. This charity solicited funds from business entities, including airports and maintenance companies, and held a very positive standing. Employees who were also representatives had no problems getting leave time to attend mandatory charity conventions.

On the day of the attack, the author was at one of these conventions. The group was being addressed concerning a forthcoming change in procedures. After a quick break with a breakfast snack of fried ham, biscuits and coffee, another speaker rose. After speaking for some thirty minutes he abruptly paused, making the announcement that something really huge had just occurred. He was not sure as to the specifics, but he had been notified by his hip monitor that something horrific had occurred somewhere inside national boundaries.

The author's mind drifted back some six months to another location, where all personnel on site at the airport were required to attend a meeting hosted by a CIA terror expert. This expert had made the announcement that something really big and bad was about to happen inside America, and that somehow it involved airports. No person could determine specifically when, where, or how, but they all knew that it would be really big and bad from international radio transmissions that were being picked up, he said. Many deaths were anticipated. That meeting included a how-to instruction for recognizing suspicious activity at airports.

For some reason, perhaps a premonition, the author did not want to go to work on the day of the attack, and had a heavy feeling of foreboding.

The speaker continued for approximately thirty minutes, then suddenly paused, appearing a bit choked up. He picked his hip monitor up, stepping to the side briefly. Two or three other supervisors raced up, pausing in consultation with him, then our speaker resumed his position before the podium and the microphone. He adjusted the mic', which rang sharply, then silenced just as quickly.

"I have an announcement to make," he spoke into the mic' with an air of foreboding anticipation.

"Something really big has happened, as I stated earlier. As a matter of fact, this incident is so large and dramatic that we have determined to cancel our meeting for today. We do not know all of the details as of yet, but it appears that a jet airliner has just crashed into one of the twin towers at the World Trade Center in New York City.

Allow me to repeat this announcement... It appears that a Boeing 747 has just crashed into one of the twin towers in New York City. The scene is one of astonishing horror that words just cannot describe at this time. This meeting is adjourned for the day!"

The general scene was one of astonishment and disbelief at the same time. The people moving briskly about with an audible hum that buzzed high above all other sounds in the meeting room. In the upper level television viewing room, we saw that the second tower had been struck, and both towers now roared with flames. The scene that bled into our faces was the one of a dozen or more people leaping from the towers and the flames to their deaths onto the pavement far below. The feeling that prevailed was one of heartbreak and wincing, when the level of terror from the smoke and flames experienced by the tower occupants was imagined by everyone present in the room.

The author then loaded back up into his company truck, making his way back toward the front gate on the airport grounds only a few miles away. Upon his arrival, the scene was certainly one of anxiety and tension, conjugated with a force of raw authority.

The regular police, in 9-man units, were supplemented by the military police who were highly visible at every exit and entry point, as well as doing regular patrols throughout the premises. They were fully armed and ready for confrontation. Security was so high that this author's supervisor was told to keep all personnel under his specific guard, at all times, or face arrest.

On a daily basis from then on, all employees were to chart their every move, handing this chart over to their immediate supervisors at the day's end. Several personnel were interrogated on an individual basis by security officials. A mere week before the attack, these individuals claimed to have discovered a large of portrait of Osama Bin Laden leaning against a wall in the hallway.

All flights on US soil were grounded for the next thirty to ninety days, except mail, emergency and security flights. The days consisted of general equipment maintenance, maintaining the grounds and simply making our way through the course of the day. During the time, since all airport personnel were basically grounded and available for assisting inside the general terminal area, their job was to rearrange the seats and general equipment of the facility.

Then some odd things happened. One day, all airport personnel were called out onto the runway grounds. According to the security officials present, thirty incoming soldiers had reported that a mysterious small plane had flown over the grounds, or possibly a hang glider. Radar in the air tower had failed to pick the suspected subject up.

According to the report, a parachutist had appeared, glided down to the airfield, folded up his chute, raced across the yard, leaped the fence, took out a folded motorized scooter and buzzed off down the highway. We were requested to search for clues and confirm or deny the report. Most of the people present simply laughed at the request, although very reputable and respected management officials appeared to confirm that the sighting was fact.

Unusual tracks were discovered by the author and his accomplices, but dead ended at the fence. A thorough check on the outside of the fence beside the highway revealed nothing. Most individuals present thought it was a hoax designed to test reaction time and the effectiveness of investigative efforts.

Reaction time and clarity of eyewitness accounts were being monitored. Alertness capabilities of employees was also of consideration, up to and including questions of why, when subjects were noted as failing the test.

Another interesting incident occurred that consumed half a day, if not slightly more. All airport personnel including those employed by independent contractors were requested to participate. We were requested to pretend that a mass terror attack had just occurred. We were all assigned specific wounds listed on a placard that was colored red, blue, or green. Red was critical, blue was serious and green was mild. The wound of this author was listed as a gaping chest wound. We were asked to simply lie down on the ground, and allow emergency personnel to respond.

We lay there for more than an hour. The emergency personnel arrived at long last. Then began a long day of loading casualties onto stretchers, stabilizing medical equipment, racing all of us to the local medical facility, surgeons quickly reviewing operating procedures, tools, and equipment, then finally reloading us and returning us back to the airport grounds.

What Exactly Occurred?

The most difficult part about understanding 9/11 is sifting through all of the information to determine specifically what occurred. Of course, the official story is full of holes, and many books have been published analyzing how much evidence was covered up, or faked, and offering possible interpretations.

In 2008 the author took a trip to New York City around Christmastime. Festive as it was, my wife and I were both struck by the obvious signs of deterioration all over the metropolis since we had spent several months downtown during the 1980s, when the general scene was strikingly different.

Immediately we suspected that the huge insurance drain from the attacks on the World Trade Center must have seriously damaged the financial capacity of the municipality at large. We started asking questions.

We began with some relatives on Long Island, who confirmed our suspicions; indeed, the city had been hurt financially by the attacks on the World Trade Center towers. As the towers collapsed into the gaping earth below, a house of cards collapsed with it — made up of insurance companies, life insurance policies, company medical policies and other considerations far too numerous to list. The result was that the city had no choice but to pony up.

Later on we spoke with other friends, who had wanted to view the scene of the tragedy in our company. As we all stood behind the metal railing surrounding the site, which at the time was only a huge gaping hole with the surrounding structures still under repair, I asked,

"How many people perished?"

An immediate but very tart reply was 5,000 people! Later on, I checked the figure from several other unrelated people and received the same response.

This figure, I was told, contrasted the official notation of 3,000 at most, because the official figure only included direct employees of the World Trade Center. The other unmentioned deaths included repairmen, flower delivery drivers, food delivery people, temporary maintenance personnel, elevator repairmen, mail delivery people, tourists who dropped by on the wrong day and at the wrong time, and the list goes on and on. All that I could do was to pause and glare at the massive hole in shock.

The next question that I asked was why the other deaths were not included in the official figure? The answers were a bit varied, but most people felt that the government did not want to disturb people with such massive death figures. Then I wondered, *What if other information has been intentionally distorted or withheld?*

No Iraqis were among the hijackers, were there? The terrorist hijackers were said to be primarily from Saudi Arabia; if we may recall correctly, a nation known to sponsor terrorism. Why did the US then invade Iraq? The US government offered as justification "a search for *weapons of mass destruction,*" although there was no clear definition given as to what specifically fell underneath that label.

Based on newspaper accounts, a sawed off shotgun constitutes a *weapon of mass destruction.*

A new revelation should be very obvious by now, that something else was going on. We should also be well aware that vast wealth lies in both war and oil, and Iraq was in possession of huge oil stocks long before the attack involving the World Trade Center and the US invasion of Iraq.

As we shall recall, Standard Oil, a massive oil conglomerate, is a company financed by the banking cartel of the Federal Reserve, as is Kellogg, Brown and Root, a massive security and construction firm. *What else could have possibly been going on here?*

In the introduction to David Chandler's work, *Why I Am Convinced That 9-11 Was An Inside Job*, Mike Cook enumerates many of the specific bits of evidence that any viewer can see on recordings and contrast with the official story, which simply cannot stand in the face of basic science. Just for starters, he says,

> My personal questioning of the events of 9/11 began a few years later...
>
> Several videos of the collapse of both towers show waves of horizontal mass ejections that race down the faces of the buildings, nearly keeping pace with material falling outside the building, well below the zone of destruction itself. (YouTube: South Tower Coming Down and Race with Gravity.) The ejections appear to come from many floors at the same time, which is inconsistent with the idea that the ejections consisted of debris blown out floor-by-floor as the floors pancaked together. In addition to the massive waves of ejections there are many photographs and videos showing individual, focused, high-speed ejections of material many floors below the point of collapse. These are easily explained as explosive ejections. They are not convincingly explained as escaping jets of compressed air....
>
> There are photographs and video footage of a woman leaning on a girder and waving in the hole where one of the airplanes crashed waiting to be rescued. This would seem to be direct testimony that the fires on the floors where the impact and the jet fuel had their greatest effect, had subsided, and the air and steel temperatures were moderate enough for people to walk around and touch the steel: nowhere near hot enough to cause failure of the structural steel columns. The fact that the fires were emitting black smoke is a sign that they were not burning at high efficiency, so high estimates for fire temperatures are unwarranted. [74]

So: First we have a stunning attack that caught the attention of all the world. We have a following US attack on the nation of Iraq, supposedly due to suspicion that it possessed "weapons of mass destruction," a very broad term that still has yet to be defined. But Iraq had nothing to do with the terrorists.

What Iraq does have to do with, is crude oil, and we know that Standard Oil/Exxon Mobil-Chevron and it's oil conglomerate subordinates deeply desired that oil. Standard Oil/EMC was financed/virtually owned by the Bank of Morgan.

The first suspicion is that a desire to take possession of that the oil lay behind all these murderous events.

Further, some experts have revealed the strong suggestion that the attacks on September 11, 2001, were staged events, designed to terrorize the American people and make everyone "feel attacked" and amenable to any countermeasure the government suggested was appropriate.

A wide range of oppressive measures ensued, and nobody complained. Several hundred people (maybe more) were rounded up and detained — some for months, without any evidence against them; there were roadblocks, the Hudson River was closed to local boaters for a long period, on and on.[1] That, of course, is in addition to launching the War on Terror, a worldwide slaughter.

The message was clear, just as it was for Governor Pickens of South Carolina, the Lindbergh family, the Kennedy family, and all of the others... *If you refuse to do our bidding, no person anywhere is safe, not even the ones in the White House or inside the highest seats of the US military. We will do whatever it takes to see that you go down, so says the banking cartel. What we really want is the nation of America, that is the sweat, flesh, blood, gold and youth of America's free born citizens for our own benefit, and no person or entity is going to stop us from getting it, no matter what it is that we may be forced to do in the name of exemplifying our point!*

Bankers and corporations gained vast wealth from the military invasions that followed. But there was another major development that this event facilitated at the expense of the American citizen base. This most sinister, cynical terror attack on US soil, indeed the most direct since the War of 1812, was a great distraction to the people. This distraction took everyone' mind off the importance of safeguarding Constitutional rights.

The Civil Rights Era, the Cold War and the Vietnam conflict (Congress never did declare war) served to distract the American masses, while the US government in secret embraced aspects of both Communist and fascist ideologies, incorporating them into the functions of government.

While their backs were turned, *what specific event occurred that would further trap the American masses under a corporate-supported tyrant?*

The US Patriot Act

While everyone in the Western world was reeling from the horror of 9/11, in just three weeks' time the US Congress pulled out a voluminous piece of legislation, some two thousand pages, that was, oddly enough, already fully articulated. What struck this author hardest was the observation that

---

[1] "Living in a virtual internment camp," Sound Vision, at https://www.soundvision.com/article/in-a-virtual-internment-camp-muslim-americans-since-911.

those who wanted to shove the massive document through were in heated contest on the congressional floor, with those making the public call for prudence and inquiring hesitation, asking aloud "what specifically is inside this document" never once received any reply.

While the US Patriot Act appeared underneath the guise of preventing terrorism, what it really did was to dismantle all the barriers of privacy that separate the most intimate life specifics of Americans from the ever prying eyes of the US government. Most startling of all, *it allowed the US President to declare the national situations an "emergency," without having to go through Congress for approval.*

Is there any question that, in a real emergency (some massive act of terrorism, such as a suitcase nuclear detonation or a nationwide biological attack), Congress would *not* approve the declaration of a national emergency? Maybe they would refuse to make the call, if a majority in Congress suspected that hands in US government or those closest to it were personally involved!

This new Act gave the President powers he was not meant to have. While recently there has been an effort to quell those voices who equate this to a declaration of martial law, this Act was followed by the National Defense Authorization Act (NDAA) and the National Defense Resources Preparedness Executive Order of 2012. There is no avoiding the fact that the citizen base can be forcibly relocated into "containment facilities," and compelled to provide labor. All rights of trial-by-court-of-law are suspended indefinitely. The Government will directly control, that is, own and use as it sees fit, all food, water, and medical supplies, including any that prudent individuals have set aside for their own families. Gun owners would have to turn in their weapons. And good luck protecting yourself from an abuse of authority by troops and Federal officials at large.[1] The US is not alone in this dismal slide into a police state.[75]

Such realities are why at least one state, *Tennessee*, has disregarded any call for martial law and outlawed their state officials from being able to ever make the declaration. [76] The state's memories of Martial Law are way too clear for its citizens to tolerate a repeat. We might expect to see a bit of inflow of people choosing to relocate to Tennessee.

In the end, the document was simply escorted through, with the true details not known until a number of months later. Once those specifics were known, then we of the future may be readily aware of the truth in exactly what it was that really occurred at the time.

---

[1] "Martial Law by Executive Order," *Huffington Post*, at http://www.huffingtonpost.com/jim-garrison/martial-law-under-another_b_1370819.html. Accessed Jan. 2, 2017.

The title U.S.A. P.A.T.R.I.O.T. stands for "Uniting and Strengthening America by Providing Appropriate Tools Required to Intercept and Obstruct Terrorism Act of 2001."

Following a lack of Congressional approval, parts of the Patriot Act expired on June 1, 2015. But with the passage of the USA Freedom Act on June 2, 2015, the expired parts were restored and renewed through 2019, with minor modifications. Section 215 of the law was amended to stop the National Security Agency from continuing its mass phone data collection program, sort of. Instead, phone companies will retain the data and the NSA can obtain information about targeted individuals with permission from a federal court.

According to Alex Jones in the Infowars Report, "Here are just a couple of ways the FREEDOM Act is worse than the PATRIOT Act:[77]

1) The recent decision of the 2nd U.S. Circuit Court of Appeals that the bulk collection of American citizens' telecommunications information was not authorized by the USA PATRIOT Act means that ... the government was breaking the law each time it grabbed our metadata. The moment the FREEDOM is signed by President Obama that same activity will become legal. How is making an unconstitutional and illegal act into a legal one a benefit to civil liberties?

2) The FREEDOM Act turns private telecommunications companies into agents of state security... and ...

[3] into depositories of "pre-crime" data for future use of state security agencies.

4) The FREEDOM Act provides liability protection for the telecommunications firms who steal and store our private telecommunications information. In other words, there is not a thing you can do about the theft as long as the thief is a "private" agent of the state.

It is very telling that the same Congressional leaders who have supported the PATRIOT Act for all these years are now propagandizing Americans in favor of the FREEDOM Act. FREEDOM Act becomes law; freedom, RIP.

In another interesting report, a former CIA officer, Philip Giraldi, said in an interview with Press TV:

"The Patriot Act was similar to legislation carried out by the Nazis because essentially it was using terrorism in both cases as an excuse to strip civil liberties that were enjoyed in both countries; in the United States and Germany.

"Governments have been willing to use fear, such as fear of terrorism, and fear of the enemy, as a way to get the people lined up in support of government policies. Very often these policies are essentially bad for the people because they take away many of their rights."

He went on to say that the relationship between the American citizens and the US government has changed for the worse since the introduction of the Patriot Act, adding that Americans had not become any safer by their rights being stripped away. The US Patriot Act and desecration of the Constitution has brought a dictatorship surveillance society of phone tapping, hidden cameras and police brutality in the United States, Giraldi said.[78]

In the end, what it is that we are dealing with is a government order that has paved the way for the implementation of Martial Law. The way has now been cleared of all obstructions, such as the need to appeal through the halls of Congress or to sign a Congressional endorsed order. All that must be accomplished is for the masses to become divided, motivated to clash, then the call for a declaration of national emergency; and on the same stroke of the pen, martial law is imposed..

In the same instant America's resource base is given over into the hands of government. America's citizen base then will be rendered chattel. As the great intellectual Jefferson has forewarned us, such shall be the fate of US citizens, *only if they allow it to be so*. In the end, individual freedom, economic and otherwise, *is a choice* that still holds great validity and promise for a most glorious future.

THE FIFTH STEP DOWNWARD: WHEN WE ALL SHALL STAND AT THE GATES OF PURGATORY

The eminent day of atonement for America's sin of complacency [79] shall be ushered in by a number of events. Always as time moves forward, we must remain acutely aware of intentional deception.

Behold the First Herald

The US public school system labors to indoctrinate our youth in order to conceal the true intent of the central bank and its collusive corporations. The real sin against the people is evidenced by the fact that it is all financed with a yearly tax on residential real-estate in flagrant disregard for the Constitutional right of citizens to own property; this annual tax makes a mockery of that right.

This real estate tax goes hand in hand with the right of citizens to choose where their children shall attend school, and among whom their offspring may associate.[80] The authoritarian justification for disregarding this basic Constitutional right to choose where their children may attend school is part of the all-inclusive socialized political objective. The crime of the American public is to quietly accept it, bowing to the appeal to emotion and sympathy.

The sad truth is that the majority of students found throughout America's public schools do not even know how to conduct themselves in a basic professional manner. Professional habits are best taught at home, and the negative habits among one's fellow classmates can only serve to taint those who are well educated in the home, and this eventually serves to corrupt the population at large.

Why it is that the end result is a manufactured uncivilized sub-human, lacking positive interactive manners or the decency to offer any measure of respect toward others? How, at the same time, can our education system fail to provide young people with the most basic skills of reading, writing, arithmetic, and in our day and age, computer acclimation skills? [81]

When is a solid penalty going to fall upon students for failure to perform academically? If we are dealing with fully developed intellectual capacity inside the masses at large, then there should be no problem accepting the hard fact that only one solution works to motivate success in students. When attempts are made to address the situation along these lines, then what specifically is the citizen response to it? If we observe that the response is only negative, yet as we observe that any justification for this response is non-existent, then why do the authorities only continue to placate those who reject the solution by continuing down the same dead end, virtually guaranteed-to-fail road? There most certainly exists a reason for doing so.

We may observe at least two vastly different cultures with entirely different value systems being literally forced into interaction and cohabitation. This mandated mixing was forced in complete disregard for any measure of skill level,[82] developmental levels, professional habits, value systems in general, and so on. Rather than inspiring one group to improve their standing, the less rigorous individuals have had a negative effect on those who could have done better.

According to international studies, today's US level of scholastic achievement ranks last among the developed nations of the earth. [83] Why, when a practical solution is so painfully obvious?

The intent of the central bank, and the corporations that grew up around it, was to totally dominate the resource base and the very lives of the people. By forcing people of divergent economic perception, with alien cultures, social and political views to interact, the tension that resulted served as a huge public distraction, another way to keep people's minds off the bigger questions. We are forced to conclude as a consequence that the authoritarian design from the very beginning was to intentionally cause a dramatic drop in both the quality and level of public education in the United States.

Basic studies such as math, history, writing, especially handwriting, [84] English, grammar and pronunciation, are barely even taught at all. [85] These skills have not been seriously taught for more than a decade, and have been in a state of gradual decline for more than forty years into the past.

Individuals who are well educated in subjects such as mathematics, history, reading and writing, may observe facts developing on the ground, correlate those developments with the facts of history, and anticipate the moves of government, centralized bank and corporations against the people. With both a solid knowledge of historical fact and mathematics, one would possess the ability to devise a plan of resistance, knowing well how to calculate manpower and supply correlations with terrain and distance covered, in unison with others of a like mind.[86]

Behold the Second Herald

According to the presumed endowment of our cherished Constitution, we are innocent until proven guilty in a court of law, as judged by peers of equal standing. To decipher this statement, all claims are to be substantiated by a valid premise, including a set of verifiable facts that support the conclusion that the accused is guilty — otherwise, the accused is deemed innocent. But when the requirement of the premise and the factual verification are held in disregard, and the accused is condemned solely on the basis of an impassioned claim against him, what we are witnessing is the reality of an emerging inquisition.

Inquisitions may assume two forms, political or religious. In present day America the most likely scenario would be for the presence of an extortionist political inquisition (although situations inside America and the West at large [87] is also becoming increasingly conducive to religious inquisition).

In American history, one of the very best examples of religious inquisition may be found in the example of the Salem Witch Trials. What is evident in the historical record is that something else was at stake other than the situation of witchcraft and people casting spells.

From our best indications, it appears that certain impoverished individuals who lacked solid support or influence in the community, yet who were in possession of potentially valuable, coveted land, could be handily expropriated by accusing them of witchcraft. Since the law allowed for accused witches to suffer property confiscation, the judges and the officials could take possession of the property.

As we may recall from the historical record, the first accusation incited fear and quite possibly a retaliatory response from the masses, many of whom were penniless landowners in the identical situation of possessing coveted lands and/or personal enemies of original claimants.

Others among the accused were simply drifting penniless elements who were only impediments to the self-serving goals of the elites, either by speaking out against them and their perceived goals of self-gratification, or possibly by some sort of clandestine intimate relationship, [88] where a cloud of blackmail designing to manipulate was held overhead.

Out of the fear from one angle or another came a host of accusation, with each attempting to lay blame upon the other for his or her accused actions, leading to a blanketed condemning charge of witchcraft from the elitist powers above, who possessed the unchecked ability to levy such immediately damning accusations, and manifest these broad petty accusations into deadly conviction.

In the end, public officials were at liberty to manipulate the tangled web of witchcraft charges, condemn those who it was advantageous to condemn, and purge the community of its non-productive elements at the same time.

On the graves of the dead their last notated claim to innocence may still bring forth tears of sympathy from those who comprehend the reality of what was going on at that time and the way they stoically faced death with the rising of the peach sun.

In the situation of tyranny, the first element to go is legitimate rule of law. The rule of law is replaced by inquisition. Through use of inquisition, any who oppose the extortionist order may be prosecuted and condemned.

Any observation of inquisition being erected must be met with the inclusion of broad, open-ended claims being allowed, [89] where the court condemns based on raw assumption of guilt alone. The only hope of salvation is to hire a very high priced lawyer who knows the system and may be able to negotiate an arrangement whereby the accused may redeem both his reputation and his positive legal standing. Critics may view this situation and declare that the system was designed by lawyers searching to create their own opportunity at the expense of the broad population.

Open ended claims stand as any claim of guilt that cannot be proven or disproven. Thus, the claim either sits in limbo, is held in disregard with the accused then set free, or acted on directly in an effort to condemn the accused. When a political agenda is forwarded to allow a specific claim in an appeal to loyalty from some sort of demographic/political constituency, consequently removing the check against the court accepting it in absence of supporting evidence and in political favoritism, then the court feels at liberty to impute guilt — based on the assumption that the accusation would have never been made unless some level of guilt was present.

But condemnation in the absence of evidence runs counter to the US Constitution, no matter what.

In the beginning, such assertions in the absence of evidence of guilt might be few, but over time they would be more. People might claim that it was just a racket for the benefit of lawyers, the legal system, the privatized prisons that make a bigger profit when they are full; but history has shown that once a nation heads down this path, it picks up speed. Much more is at stake here.

As the foundations of a political inquisition are laid, in the build-up to the Fascist state, one primary realm for such open-ended claims may be in the area of tax evasion. Tax rates in this country have gone up, from a minimal amount 100 years ago to a third to a half of a family's income. And while corporations have whole departments of lawyers helping them find ways to reduce their tax liability, families are less likely to have creative ways to approach the problem.

In addition, the cost of buying a home with a mortgage has risen dramatically. In the 1950s, the typical house cost about two years' salary. Since 1975 it's been over three years' salary for the average family. And in some periods, housing has cost even more. This means that people end up shelling out more for interest payments alone than the price of the house itself: they pay for it twice over. The elevated price of the house also means they pay higher taxes. Thus they are sending more to the IRS than ever, and also raising the bank's profit margin. [90]

This has enslaved citizens to a lifetime of bondage — first to the bank, and later on to the insurance corporations, in cahoots with government interests. On top of that, the owner's Constitutional right to actually possess the property in hand has been stolen out from underneath him, since that interest, tax and insurance must be paid at regular intervals, regardless of the ups and downs of life; rather than on a single occasion upon purchase, for example.

Other problems have come along with the increasing income tax. As the demand increased, so did the need for more regulations to guarantee this extortion from individual funds. The natural response of an individual who is laboring for his own economic progress is to strive to pay no more than necessary, to seek legal loopholes and advantageous ways to plan his finances.

If there was a barrier between the clandestine central banking system and US government officials, who would safeguard the people's concerns, then citizens would have little right, legally or morally, to question the tax system. The sad truth, however is that no such barrier stands and no one is protecting the citizenry; in fact, it is the corporation whose interests have been secured. According to PolitiFact,

> "In 1952, the corporate income tax accounted for 33 percent of all federal tax revenue. Today, despite record-breaking profits, corporate taxes bring in less than 9 percent."[91]

Then, there is the increasing suspicion of anyone who actually comes up with some money. Cash, that is.. People who scrimp and save, and put money in the bank, are now liable to have their savings confiscated, that is, stolen, if a government agent imagines there was an "intent" to break the law. How can any government agent have the right to *guess* what you had in mind? Business owners, and families, are losing their earnings despite having no record of breaking the law. [92]

A second large category of open-ended claims include those made of a sexual nature. Of course, society needs to offer protection primarily to women, children and the severely handicapped. As the situation applies to women and children, there tends to be a bias toward accepting at face value any claim that a predatory male, who lurks somewhere inside the misty shadows of the moon, has committed egregious harm. The problems is that there is also an assumption that the perceived victims never offer a false accusation. It turns out that there are plenty of people convicted for "fabricated crimes," especially when it comes to child sex abuse. [93]

Lawyers, on the other hand, profit handsomely when accused victims make a determined stand to fight the accusation with every element of strength in their being. Police pay their keep when they make arrests. Investigators profit in search for an admission of guilt. Court systems profit when judges try the cases, and correctional officers have secure jobs when inmates are placed behind bars; then parole officers profit when the accused finally exits the system, if he ever does. The biggest loser here is the individual whose life has been ruined by being falsely accused.

The vague claim of sexual harassment is even more liable to be misused. One person's attempt at a friendly comment may be taken as offensive; even more, it can be construed as *potentially* offensive, even if that was not the intent. Again, we have third parties who were not witnesses to the actions simply *imputing* motives.

We all agree that abuse and harassment are bad. We often do *not* agree on what constitutes real abuse or harassment. Even inside the workplace, beyond base actions that would obviously fall into the category of harassment, virtually any gesture or act within the general interactive socialized atmosphere bears the potential for being interpreted as sexual harassment. It is hard to prove a negative, that is, hard to prove no ill intent was present; and it is easiest for the employer to fall back on a raw assumption of guilt. Thus, "some businesses have chosen a 'knee jerk' sexual harassment policy that treats the accused as guilty until proven innocent." [94]

A relatively new category of open-ended claims is that of terrorism — another very broad label. [95] The categories that may be labeled as terrorist are vast and virtually endless; to this very day no legal check exists to give the label of terrorist clear definition. Thus we may perceive that future government action may fit any individual it likes underneath the label of terrorist [96] and give a twisted form of justification to the label, without ever being required to offer solid legal grounds.

All of these categories can be turned into tools for imminent persecution by the police and government agencies. Any citizens who dare to resist increasing government intrusions and demands may well find themselves targeted. Individuals who even dare to speak out in opposition may be intimidated and shut up very effectively.

For quite some time now we have lived with the issue of circumstantial evidence prevailing the situation of courtroom condemnation. Circumstantial evidence involves the issue of events lining up to suggest possibility of guilt, but in absence of hard facts necessary to make a conclusive condemnation.

The acceptance of circumstantial evidence, a bias toward presumption of guilt, and vague definitions of categories of "offense" all make it possible to misinterpret or even to create scenarios that lead to wrongful arrest. Smart phones, smart cars and all the "social media" apps are designed to listen in on private conversations and monitor all your activities. [97] When the time of persecution arrives, one's doors may be suddenly kicked in in the middle of the night. Whoever doesn't end up shot can end up arrested under a presumption of possible "terrorist" activity or "association," or under other broad, ill-defined labels. [98]

Huge groups and even entire communities could potentially be rounded up on a future day in view of a mass protest against an extortionist government mandate. No wonder arrest and condemnation on mere assumption of guilt runs counter to US Constitutional law.

Behold the Third Herald

All through the ages, history shows that when tyranny designs to reign, often its first step is to disarm the people. This is sometimes covered with the excuse of an exaggerated external or internal threat.

The signers of the US Constitution were keenly aware of tyranny's potential to dominate, and they built into the system a system of checks and balances. The final check, as we may clearly recall, lies in the Second Amendment, with the individual citizen's right to keep and bear arms. During Hurricane Katrina, the government confiscated all weapons from New Orleans residents in the interests of maintaining "law and order." Many people saw this as trial run, together with all the FEMA activity that was more geared to putting down an imaginary insurrection than to providing a disaster-struck city with essential aid.

Any terrorist act, now, or any event that can be labelled as terrorism, could be used to justify the confiscation of guns. The US President can call any event a "national emergency." An intentional crash of the US currency by the clandestine central bank, followed by a terror attack, would fit the bill.

Many pension funds are currently being cut drastically; in essence, people are not going to be paid what they were told they would. The terms of their employment have been unilaterally changed, after the fact, and they will be left empty handed. [99] Will Social Security also be cut back? Many people predict that it will.

When the protests begin, it could prompt the President into making the call for "national emergency." In the same instant, martial law is initiated, and the troops then move against the citizens in a feigned effort to restore order.

According to information given to the author by military personnel, exercises are being conducted inside national borders for just such a scenario. We read about the Jade Helm exercises, [100] and we may assume that other exercises (never to be known by the American public) are being conducted as well. [101] A certain tension feels to be charged in the air, as if something huge is about to move upon us, but the date and time cannot be determined.

The charters for both the First and Second Bank of the US were for twenty years each. And it was about twenty years from the time World War Two began (a bank-induced war) [102] [103] until the time Kennedy assumed the US presidency. From Kennedy's inauguration until that of Reagan's was also twenty years. From then to 9/11 was approximately twenty years. And that was almost twenty years ago, now...

Then there is the irony of changing the image on our $20 bill. In 2016, then Secretary of Treasury Jack Lew announced that President Jackson's picture is to be replaced with that of Harriet Tubman. [104] It was Jackson who launched and won a war against the centralized bank of the day. And it was Harriet Tubman who represented the appeal to emotion that fueled the *de facto* centralized bank's attack on the states whose congressional representatives were standing between the bankers and their self-serving interests on one side, and those of the US citizen base and the US Constitution on the other.

Is it an insolent hint from the banks indicating that something ominous lies just ahead? They would obviously assume, in their own amusement, that the masses lack the ability to make the connection.

It is this author's contention that something huge and spectacular is going to occur within the next five to ten years. The attacks that have hampered President Trump in taking up the office he won by election suggest that: a) either he will have to exert something like martial law, if his administration is to get anything done, or, b) those who are opposing him are subverting the democratic order themselves, and are imposing their own totalitarian ways in place of the elected administration, for better or worse.

We are forced by history and necessity to presume that the approach will be indirect, not to set off alarms until it's too late. Increasing gun control is almost a given. But stock market crashes (engineered or otherwise), pension cuts and other maneuvers could effectively confiscate as much as half of US retirement and private investment accounts. With the Federal debt topping $3 trillion, the economy is not stable. Some 20% of people in their prime working years are not in the workforce. Both massive inflation and massive deflation can impoverish the population. If prices go up faster than incomes, the problem is obvious. Conversely, if values drop, then homes and other "assets" purchased on credit (including mortgages and car loans), lose value and are no longer worth the amount that is still due to be paid.

When a population loses all its wealth, all its savings — just like in the olden days, when the villagers might lose all their food supply — typically, people get pretty upset. The resulting unrest is another possible "national emergency." Again, we are back to a ban on all weapon purchases and martial law.

Americans have been increasingly programmed to accept giving up their Constitutional right to bear arms. For a number of years there have been increasing occurrences of mass murders involving the use of firearms. In virtually every instance, the murderers have been on legally prescribed, mind altering drugs, with a long history of mental health issues. [105]

What few Americans realize is that the CIA began a program [106] intending to transform the human body into a weapon in the 1920s. Back in those earliest days the techniques utilized were those of the classic hypnotist. [107] the problem is that the person under hypnosis will not commit every suggested act, and not every person can be hypnotized.

By the 1950s, the process of hypnosis had been improved;[108] thus improving the chances of manipulating a target. Pills, electronic stimuli and other methods were created in attempts to cause the identical effect, and they would work on a much broader range of targets who could be prompted into committing far more serious acts, even if the request violated the target's preconceived notion of morality, and he would never recall doing it upon command. The description reminds one of Edgar Allan Poe's gripping story of Gothic horror, "Berenice."

Crime records from the 1800s on down into the mid-1960s show primarily standard-type crimes, with few incidents that include any "demented," "cult-like," near satanic element. By the late 1960s, however, these statistics appear to have taken an abrupt turn. [109]

With the onset of the 1980s, crimes of mass murder appear to take a more political turn, with mass shootings not only on the streets and in the malls, but also in schools, where they raise the level of horror even higher. Obviously, the appeal to emotion is at its strongest then, and the blatant call for drastically curtailing citizen access to arms (which always accompanies such an event) is hard to argue against.

Martial Law

Martial law is a bizarre concept to most present day Americans. In essence what it means is an outright suspension of the US Constitution and all the rights it provides, including the right to trial by law, and even the most basic right of life or death, since orders for martial law include liberal allowances for summary executions at the discretion of military leadership as situations on the ground dictate, according to their own determination in the matters at hand.

All property, privately held and otherwise, is then under direct ownership of the US Government in the same instant. That includes all financial accounts, all land, food, production tools and materials for cultivating food and/or processing it, and basic utilities in general. In short, every product and structure on the land, as well as the land itself, since the people no longer enjoy the Constitutional right to own any possessions, accumulative or otherwise.

The American people themselves will consequently be rendered chattel to be disposed of as the government sees fit. The population may be rounded up and forcibly relocated,[110] compelled into virtual indefinite labor bondage, in complete service to the corporate dominated nation via its marriage with government, and the new age totalitarian state. The mass containment facilities have already been constructed.[111] The signs are that a forced roundup is being prepared.

Here is how Wikipedia describes martial law:

> Martial law is the imposition of the highest-ranking military officer as the military governor or as the head of the government, thus removing all power from the previous executive, legislative, and judicial branches of government. It is usually imposed temporarily when the government or civilian authorities fail to function effectively (e.g., maintain order and security, or provide essential services).

> Martial law can be used by governments to enforce their rule over the public. Such incidents may occur after a coup d'état (such as Thailand in 2006 and 2014); when threatened by popular protest (China, Tiananmen Square protests of 1989); to suppress political opposition (Poland in 1981); or to stabilize insurrections or perceived insurrections (Canada, the October Crisis of 1970). Martial law may be declared in cases of major natural disasters; however, most countries use a different legal construct, such as a state of emergency.

> ...

Typically, the imposition of martial law accompanies curfews, the suspension of civil law, civil rights, habeas corpus, and the application or extension of military law or military justice to civilians. Civilians defying martial law may be subjected to military tribunal (court-martial).

In US history, quite a few events ended up with a call for martial law. Readers interested in knowing more might look into these events, most of which never represented a threat to national stability.

New Orleans, Louisiana, in the War of 1812
Ex parte Milligan
The Great Chicago Fire, 1871
Coeur d'Alene, Idaho, 1892
San Francisco earthquake of 1906
Colorado Coalfield War
West Virginia Coal Wars
Tulsa Race Riot, 1921
San Francisco, 1934
The Territory of Hawaii
Freedom Riders, 1961

The Resulting Situation

Hurricane Katrina was devastating: first to the people of New Orleans[112] and the Gulf Coast, and second to Americans' sense of civilian rights and the proper role of the military.

The situation on the ground among civilians was complete chaos. Harrowing instances of mass looting, random murders, robbery, and general pillaging went on by what amounted to criminal gangs.[113] In more than a few instances, snipers even fired on fellow citizens from distant roof tops. These snipers, we may presume, were regular rank and file citizen store owners and residential property owners firing on the encroaching gangs, but could also have been return fire by the gangsters themselves or even from private security personnel. [114] And that was *on top* of the destruction from the forces of the storm itself.

Death appeared to be everywhere, [115] although tactfully concealed from view of the public outside of the immediate area by the news media. Some accounts at the time claimed death figures as high as ten thousand, [116] from both the storm and the violence that followed. Prior to the storm, New Orleans was surrounded by a 200-year-old system of dykes with few repairs made over the course of years; and the entire metropolis sat approximately twenty feet below sea level.

The storm that crashed into the city was between category 5 and 6ix, with 200-mile-an-hour winds. New Orleans became a virtual death trap for those who failed to escape during the five-day period while the storm was going around Puerto Rico.

As if this were a rehearsal for something bigger, with a devastating tragedy (one affecting almost exclusively the poor and most vulnerable) as the excuse, the Presidential call for *national emergency and martial law*. To "restore order," the US Military was called in, but so were a number of notorious private security companies such as Blackwater [117] and Triple Canopy. Before any real help was provided, residents witnessed a mass military roundup of all privately-owned weapons. [118] The doors of innocent private citizens were kicked in, [119] even though a situation of threatening violence prevailed all around.

There was also a case of some individuals, [120] who may have chosen to do otherwise for a variety of personal reasons, who were forced to assist in filling sandbags to shore up the dykes. That may have been appropriate, more or less; but it also sets a precedent for compulsion to labor. How far can that be taken, in some future event? Free labor equals huge Corporate profits. We may perceive growing possibility of an eminent nationwide compulsion to labor being justified by a manufactured notion of civic duty, at the expense of liberty in personal choice. This possibility would immediately follow some sort of manufactured *astonishing event* that would both *terrify US citizens* into submission *and distract* the masses from the real truth of what was occurring on the ground.

In our lifetimes, most of us have naturally grown up with a reasonably comfortable sense of security. Most Americans can hardly believe that the military or a militarized police could ever turn its guns on the population here. We are not used to seeing war up close. However, as we may recall, less than 100 years ago such events were not unheard of, and they could happen again. Even the crackdown on Occupy Wall Street, a peaceful protest, was a wake-up call.[1] the US government owned the land, selling it to the large corporations at vastly discounted rates in bulk and with easy-to-access loans, hoping that corporate success would re-attach value to the huge issuance of non-specie backed banknotes of the day. When these corporations expanded, initially the railroads, then later on the mining companies, they did so at the expense of everyone who was already in possession of that land, primarily native nations and their collective communities. Force of government arms

---

[1]   http://www.alternet.org/story/152812/why_are_police_attacking_peaceful_protesters_how_ows_has_exposed_the_militarization_of_us_law_enforcement; see also http://newyork.cbslocal.com/2011/10/14/violence-breaks-out-during-occupy-wall-street-march-on-wall-street/

supported these corporations in their move westward, at times violently against the natives of the land, with the entire might of the US military to back them up.

Not only were practically whole tribes slaughtered, by gunfire, disease, and abuses, but those who survived have suffered ever after. An alien culture was imposed upon the natives by raw might of force. Literally, the youth of these resisting native nations were abducted, delivered into reeducation centers, [121] with the end result of these individuals exchanging their own culture of the most lucid liberty for a culture that held no relevance inside their own ancestral realm.

When we speak of an alien culture, we may also include that to mean an alien religion, complete with a God of whom none were familiar. These people *had no choice but to submit*. In the end, *official authoritarian promises meant nothing*. The might of the Federal Government's military arms crushed the people's resistance — a model we should remember.

In clear notations of the past, we may observe revelations of an unsettling future. All that is needed is a preeminent astonishing event to manifest on the ground [122] that will serve as a justification, provide the motivating fear factor, and trigger the emotions that block rational judgement.

Behold the Great Treasonous Sell Out

Another powerful suggestion of the future can be read in what is known as the financial crisis of 2007 and 2008. The banks and financial corporations were acting like gamblers who know someone else is going to save their hide at the end of the day. Some of the largest financial institutions crashed — or came close. That's how capitalism works. But this time, the national governments bailed out many of them, so that taxpayers got stuck with the bill, paying for the errors that the financiers themselves had made.

Before we draw our conclusions, in our smoldering desire to seek damnation for the guilty, let us examine in a bit more detail how this played out. Even though the banks and financial institutions were bailed out, stock markets dipped drastically, worldwide. The US housing market was nearly shuttered, with mass evictions, foreclosures and rampant unemployment. Key businesses were closed and consumer wealth bled out in amounts that were estimated at trillions of dollars. Many retirees and those nearing retirement lost everything that they held in various banking and investment funds. It was an international tragedy.

This evolved further into the European sovereign debt crisis. An early victim, or rather perpetrator, was *BNP Paribas*, a French multinational bank and financial services firm, one of the largest banks on earth, terminated all withdrawals from three major hedge-funds, for an extreme lack of liquidity. In other words, they were out of money.

Considering how closely the banking world works together, planning and meeting and structuring future events, one suspects this did not come as a complete surprise to others in the industry. This bank was founded by *Louis-Raphael Bischoffsheim*, whose father was considered the founder of what amounted to a family banking dynasty. Louis became close friends with the *Goldschmidt* family, and began working for *Hayum Salomon Goldschmidt*. Louis Bischoffsheim moved to Amsterdam in 1820 to create a bank in his own name. He married Goldschmidt's daughter, and they had two sons. One of them, Maximilian (1843–1940), married *Minna Karoline Freiin Von Rothschild*, daughter of *William Carl Von Rothschild*. Thus, the usual growth of the family tree: the family of *Bischoffshiem* became intermarried with both the *Goldschmidt* family and the family of *Rothschild*.

We must always hold in mind that these banking dynastic families are all closely linked and well connected, regardless of distance or nationality. As we may recall, America is financed and thus, indirectly owned, by the families of Morgan and Rockefeller, who are the American proxy to the family of Rothschild.

Since the name of Rothschild suggests a European heritage that could stir ill ease in the American public, proxies were chosen who would be more comfortable. Morgan had a Welsh heritage, while the Rockefellers were of English, German, and Scots-Irish descent — making them "all-American" by the standards of the day.

When *BNP Paribas* halted withdrawals, securities tied to the US real-estate market via multinational banking investments crashed, damaging the investments of financial institutions worldwide. Additional contributing factors include the following:

Before the crash in securities, banking policies had been changed to allow loans to borrowers who could scarcely afford to pay them back (sub-prime borrowers). It was claimed that housing values would continue to go up, but shaky mortgages were bundled and sold to other investors as if they were quite secure. Investment professionals were paid for prioritizing short-term deals rather than what made good business sense, and banks and insurance companies stretched themselves to the maximum, holding almost nothing in reserve. They had nothing to fall back on when the inevitable losses started to come in.

The moment withdrawals were terminated, no alternative system for retrieving funds was offered. Since the weakness in the US banking system was long known, and no corrections made by the Federal Reserve in anticipation of future troubles, then we must ask how much of this was *calculated*.

Did the banking elites and their collaborating minions have anything to gain from all this, while the populace lost? The situation nearly spiraled completely out of hand, even to the point that national leaders were in a state of absolute bewilderment as to how they could halt this devastating downward spiral. Worldwide, national leaders appealed to the centralized banks within their borders, including US leadership to the Federal Reserve. Next, we see that the CBCC received billions in "stimulus" funds.

The Bush administration and then the Obama administration gained $1 billion in borrowed funds from the Chinese government, since to all appearances the national credit card (from the Federal Reserve) had been maxed out.

Immediately following, with the Obama administration in full control, an additional trillion dollars in "stimulus" debt was assumed from the Chinese government again, via the FR. When the Federal Reserve distributed this huge windfall of borrowed capital, who received the funding?

We are all very aware of the fact that the people on the ground received virtually nothing. They lost the very roof over their heads; [123] and more people filled the food stamp lines than ever before, [124] as unemployment reached levels not witnessed since the Great Depression (another banking-induced phenomenon approximately seventy years earlier). [125]

In response to the situation at hand, President Obama signed the American Recovery And Reinvestment Act of 2009. On the surface, the Act appeared to bear all positive intentions. The act included direct allocations of funds into infrastructure, education, health and energy, with Federal tax incentives, in combination with an expansion of unemployment benefits. The problem is that the bill did not cover even one third of the amounts needed to address these issues alone, according to Paul Krugman, a highly celebrated financial expert.

Therefore, we are forced to conclude that the bill was merely a Band Aid to patch over the bloody wound to body public, while other concerned parties received the lion's share of the borrowed amount. What a surprise. Recall that any debts assumed by the government (with its liberty to borrow from the FR with no checks and safeguards to limit their bottomless thirst) will have to be paid by the tax payer.

This ability to foist debt onto the people, however frugal and responsible they personally may have been and with no regard for the general employment status of economic distress already in place, in the Sixteenth Amendment.

From a casual glance, it seems that most of those who needed the funds *least* received the largest share. These included states and companies that were among the largest supporters of the Obama administration/ Democratic Party. These interests include, but are not limited to, the highly unionized state of Wisconsin, and Washington D.C.; high-end donors who received payback such as Solendra, the "energy green"/solar company, Tesla Motors, NRG solar owners such as Warren Buffett and Steve Cohan. Al Gore managed to get funding to insure a return on his investment into Fisker Automotive, which received $528 million. As for those who suffered when the housing bubble burst, well, let them eat cake.

Still, where did the lion's share of the stimulus funding go? ProPublica provides a chart,[126] demonstrating that most of it went to the large corporations and the banks. Those shaded in red still owe money with no promise to repay, while the others have paid at least part of the funds back or are *promising* to do so.

While we may comprehend the appearance of necessity in lending to these specific institutions, what remains astounding is the fact that huge percentages of the bailout money still lies unaccounted for! The banks and the corporations that grew up around the clandestine central bank received a whopping share of the funds borrowed from the Chinese government and no doubt, other places, with the bill for this massive loan being charged back to the helpless citizens. How in heaven's name can they ever repay such a loan, when the interest alone equals one half of the gross national product or more?

Is it conceivable that private savings and retirement accounts will be confiscated in one way or another? Is it possible that this is one reason behind the drive to go "cashless," so that all our savings must be held in investments and bank accounts that are outside of our control, while every transaction we make is dutifully recorded and reported?

We are dealing with an intentionally motivated crash, followed by a borrowed sum handed over to the CBCC. When the US government decides to move on the private bank holdings of US citizens, and from all appearances it is doing so, the bills for these loans will be paid for by US citizens, with similar scenarios played out worldwide.

Executive Order 12803

EO 12803 was enacted by President George Bush on April 30, 1992, just nine years prior to 9/11. What this bill allowed was a future privatization of America's infrastructure. The term "infrastructure" includes:[127]

Section 1: Definitions; Privatization means disposal or transfer of an infrastructure asset, such as by sale or long term lease, from a state or local government to a private party.

"Infrastructure asset" means asset financed in whole or part by the Federal government and needed for the function of the economy. Examples include, but are not limited to; roads, tunnels, bridges, electricity, supply facilities, mass transit, rail transportation, airports, ports, waterways, water supply facilities, recycling and wastewater treatment facilities, solid waste disposal facilities, housing, schools, prisons and hospitals.

There is no specification that only US corporations could purchase these infrastructure assets which are currently public property — that is, are held for the public good, the taxpayers' good — because they are "needed for the function of the economy." Can a Chinese corporation buy the George Washington Bridge?

In addition to the above facts, consider that during the financial crisis of 2007–2008, Fanny Mae and Freddie Mac, the money lenders behind 85% of America's home mortgage system, were purchased out-right by the US Federal government. With a mortgage, the individual only truly owns the premises when the mortgage has been paid in full. Since tax is imposed every term, it can be debated whether the individual ever truly owns it. What is stopping the US government from simply selling this income-producing asset to either an American firm such as Standard Oil/ExxonMobil, General Electric, Ford Motor Company, or a foreign corporation?

The EU may also be interested in purchasing US housing and real-estate, as well as industrialized prison complexes. No form of check is in place to prevent such a thing.

Barack Obama: The Great Phenomenon (namely, what?)

The Presidency of Obama distinguished itself from all others in a number of significant aspects. One of the most obvious was the superficial appearance of racial combinations.

We may never know if, in fact, he was foreign born.[128] What is certain is that both his parents were loyal to the CIA, regardless of citizenship ad race.

After the trying times of the Bush administrations, which served the needs of the CBCC, facilitating the overwrought corruption inside US government, America's citizens were indeed open to the possibility of positive change and many leapt at the chance Obama seemed to offer. It was on this sole consideration alone that the figure of Barack Obama managed to stride across the threshold of the White House, and into the seat of US Presidency, while riding on what was destined to become a false promise of financial redemption and positive change in US government. But he came from the same CIA as George H. W. Bush.

Furthermore, Obama may well have intended to fulfill his promise to the masses; but the might of the banking cartel was used to dealing with his type. In the end, he had no other choice but to bow before the same master as those before him — to protect his family, and to protect any possibly embarrassing secrets. Right after Trump's inauguration, after all, the Obamas went to vacation with a gay couple in California, then went to visit with Richard Branson, on his island in the Caribbean, where Obama was photographed looking very cozy with Mr. Branson. What else don't we know?

Since the days of the American Civil Rights Movement, the image of the Democratic Party became linked with support for blacks, while the Republican Party was identified more and more as the white party. [129] Today's Democratic Party is the unspoken party of American Socialism, seeking ever greater government "protection," and government control, for the populace. The Republican Party is a party of the CBCC. The RP has never veered from its directional line and is a direct descendant of the old Federalist Party, which was the one that started a war on US soil against the old Democratic Party for demanding checks and balances in government and on currency. The only unrepresented group of citizens is the middle range affectionately known as the "middle class"; whom we may deduce is now the indentured class.

Obama, the person, combined not only black and white, but the party of Socialism and that of the unchecked corporation and clandestine central bank. He strengthened the foundation upon which a future totalitarian regime may take shape, and we should be alert to signs of America heading in the direction of Fascist control.

We have observed that the government is testing levels of reaction, where this reaction originates, and from whom. One example is the powerful appeal to emotion attached to the Confederate flag issue, [130] which reached fevered pitch when the flag was removed from the South Carolina capitol building, as well as the general call for another round in the cultural genocide being imposed on descendants of the Confederate South, strikingly similar to what Chairman Mao did in China during the Cultural Revolution and the Nazi book burning. The message from officials inside US government are understood to mean, "We can dismantle every element that your culture holds dear, even your heritage and identity."

With the homosexual marriage mandate being virtually imposed on all US states, we witnessed an insult to the very fabric of America that transcended all races, economic levels, nationalities of origin and the like. Only a small minority of citizens were in favor. This is shown in the voting statistics alone.

What should disturb all US citizens is not the fact of homosexual marriage achieving Constitutional recognition, but the fact that it was *forced* upon the citizenry by the US *Federal Government/Supreme Court*. This element should even disturb members of the homosexual community, who, generally speaking, tend to be better versed on the issue of Constitutional rights than the average voter. A "good" forced decision today may very well herald a "bad" forced decision tomorrow, one that deeply offends, if not terrifies, the masses.

Another test using the American masses as the mice, with authorities carefully measuring mass reaction, *where*, and from *whom*, can be seen in the authoritarian demand that all Christian churches perform the "marriage" rite [131] even when doing so strictly violates Christian doctrine and beliefs. What happened to freedom of choice in religion? Those who refused [132] have suffered drastic punitive measures. This is a blatant move to say, "We can transform your very ideal of morality, your ways, and the times in which you live."

The collective face of America is being rubbed into the dung heap of the earth by the same central bank and their corporate alliances who have always designed against them from the very beginning. Even more disturbing, the population is *allowing* it to happen, with ne'er a word of protest!

Consider the filthy insults already shoved into the face of America's citizens: First the freedom to work his way up has been wrested from his grasp.

Next, the same CBCC forces are allowed to assume a massive debt for any reason, then force the people to pay for it; all done against the Constitution, since there was no form of check to argue on behalf of America's citizen base.

Third, the government has implemented a socialist in the land founded on ideals of "liberty" and "responsibility," purloining a majority of citizen earnings through a host of regulations and general discouragement of engaging in any form of individual enterprise.

Fourth, even such checks and limitations as had been placed upon corporations have been removed, so that they can fleece the citizen of his earnings and his savings, while they relocate offshore to exploit virtual slave labor.

Now, the supreme insult to the Constitution occurred, when these identical forces of corporation, government, and the clandestine central bank removed the checks and balances through violence and murder, allowing some future Presidential leader whom they support to assume the position of absolute authority over the American people at large.

No wonder bullying in school has become a big issue. It's our national model. We are at the mercy of the schoolyard bully. First there are verbal insults, then threats, then a physical attack that could well be devastating, should we ever allow it to catch us off guard.

Now, if we are near to the point of this unthinkable, vile emanation, what is the most recent event that would precede it, in combination with all that has been discussed as going down before? The response that emerges is one that both astounds and chills the reader into a cold clammy sweat. In the gloomy moonlit distance, if we may dare to listen intensely enough, the spirits of the near future may allow us to perceive the sound of jackboots marching by the collective thousand-horde in perfect rhythm, as they seek us out amid screams of terror.

The Trans Pacific Partnership Agreement — Aborted For Now

The TPP has been defeated for now, but it is a striking model for what could be resurrected any time.

It meant to consolidate corporate power above that of the nation state, and it covered the United States, Brunei, Chili, New Zealand, Singapore, Australia, Canada, Japan, Malaysia, Mexico, Peru and Vietnam. Tariffs were to be dramatically lowered or reduced all together, and internal barriers to corporate progress were calculatingly dismantled.

A propaganda campaign was utilized to court acceptance from those who would have to live under Corporate Boards in lieu of courts of law, under Corporate lawyers and executives in lieu of elected government, those who would have to beg for work in competition with people from the largely "pre-cash" societies of the Third World.

They claimed that TPP would promote economic growth by supporting the creation of jobs, enhance innovation, creativity, productivity and competitiveness, raise living standards, and reduce poverty. In the Third World partners, those results might have been possible. No doubt about it — by outsourcing factories to Mexico, Vietnam and China, for instance, we did improve the economy in those countries, at least for a while. But not in our own.

TPP is a model for the rising possibility of international fascism, since no checks were established to prevent the guaranteed corruption that would accompany it. This is the marriage of corporation and government, the very embodiment of fascism, and without a system of hard checks and balances to protect the people and the management.

TPP also destroys national sovereignty. The terms of the agreement said that corporations could sue any nation whose laws were in their way: environmental laws, sanitary standards for food, anything. The corporation would tell the voters that what was good for corporate profits was good enough for the human cog in the wheel.

No wonder most of Congress was kept in the dark as to the substance of the TPP negotiations, while representatives of U.S. corporations like Halliburton, Chevron, PHRMA, Comcast, and the Motion Picture Association of America were consulted and made privy to details of the agreement.

Here, looming one day into the not-so-distant future, we may see the unemployment rate as high as seventy to ninety percent. Outsourcing, automation and other trends are removing whole categories of jobs. Meanwhile, regulations and other barriers make it increasingly difficult to start, much less maintain, a viable small business.

In the very near future we well may observe that the average American has little to no access to health care. The cams are literally breaking. The streets are rife with crime, and the average US citizens access to weapons of any sort have been seriously curtailed due to vastly taxed price amounts, some insidious unconstitutional future insurance requirement, or the fact that weapons have been made illegal own outright.

In short, over the course of a relatively short time, in this dismal vision revealed here inside our crystal modem, the United States of America is being transformed into a violent, Third-World ghetto-like near apocalyptic environment.

What on earth is the average citizen going to do? What does he have to look forward to as far as any type of reform is concerned? What exactly is going on with leadership in the United States? Why are national leaders allowing this deterioration to occur?

The Terrible Sixth Step: Possible Future Manifestations

With the heavy drone of a midnight cathedral bell and a shocking flash of lightning, the lonesome death knell of liberty rolls out across the American landscape. This astonishing loss was preceded by three primary heralds or signs. The first sign was the fact that America's children were not receiving a true education, although we were inundated with boastful messages claiming our system was the best. If they were not learning facts or history, at least, we were told, they were learning to "think." Yet we see that on average, Americans are not willing to consider any unconventional idea, and they are not the innovative problem solvers and pioneers of yesteryear, but inert receivers of whatever comes to them. Uneducated people tend to be unobservant, complacent and docile, and relatively easy to manipulate with lies, since they are not aware of the complexity of the facts.

The second sign is the call to identity politics, hyped by politicians and the media, and fed and sponsored by NGOs and foundations, that put busloads of protesters on the streets rather than reminding everyone of our common interests, what makes us one nation, the things we can work on together for everyone's good.

There are times when we seem to be goaded to take to the streets, ignoring the fact that provisions for martial law are in place, and it would not take much to see civilians being mass transported by bus, train, transfer truck or van to containment facilities already scattered all across the landscape. Mandated computer chip implants[1] may already have begun, making the program of computer identification far less cumbersome.

Attempts to require people to carry a national ID have been rebuffed for years, but they are closing in now. This is unthinkable, in the land of freeborn America.

The third alarm is heard in the latest buzz about cash-free societies.[133] "Free"? Is that another subliminal trick to make it sound appealing? What's wrong with being able to pay for things, here and there, in cash? What's wrong with being able to hold a bit of our assets at home, instead of in a bank where the ATMs can suddenly be "out of order" or the doors be closed for a "bank holiday" whenever the CBCC decides? Many countries in Europe are already far down that path, and it is being pushed here, too.[134] Why should all our transactions have to go through banks and government institutions? We hear repeated calls to eliminate cash transactions, as if that were the best way to curb corruption.[135] The biggest crooks always have a way around such provisions; this is just to control the "little" people.

All our phone and electronic communications are already monitored. How soon until we are not allowed to meet on the street?

Their Ultimate Goal In Gaining Absolute Authority

And the Destiny of the People Therein

The prevailing purpose of relocating the population into containment facilities would not only accommodate the intention of providing "security" and supplying the minimal needs of citizens in a very cost-effective (cheap) way; the true purpose would be to contain everyone until the corporations, both foreign and stateside, could purchase the residential and commercial real-estate infrastructure from primary mortgage lenders and a system could be put into place that would accommodate the civilians again to the greater benefit of the CBCC, and to more fully enslave the population to those entities.

The new imposter US Constitution would force the population into legalized submission to the new corporate state, when the State was supposed to be serving the people. The rights of the individual would depend on the whim of the CBCC, who would exploit the people in every conceivable manner.

For efficiency's sake, all homes would eventually be basically alike, according to what category the individual was assigned to. That's just like

---

[1] http://beforeitsnews.com/politics/2016/12/congress-passes-bill-to-start-putting-rfid-chips-in-disabled-people-video-2868257.html

the mill houses and the mining towns.[136] The company owned the jobs, the homes, and everything the workers had to buy. We must presume that the same would be true in the new dawning era of Americana. The corporations and the government; state, national, and quite possibly even on a local level, would virtually own everything, including all citizen savings and retirement accounts.

The citizens would have to work wherever, and as much, as they were told. They would eat what they were offered, at whatever price was set. All of the citizen's basic needs would be supplied. No more stress over house or rent payments, taxes, health care, basic utilities, food or transportation. Low level crime would be reduced, due to the omnipresent cameras and personal chips; high level corruption would continue, as services provided to the workforce (never mind those out of the workforce) would gradually be reduced.

Our Present Position In This Coming Saga

Upon release back into the corporate owned towns and cities, those who will remain in the forced labor facility will be those who are deepest in debt, with no chance of a pay-off. Right now we read that personal debt is the highest that it has ever been in history [137], even though the first large burp on this economic health indicator has already occurred, that in itself nearly crashing the entire economy back in 2008. The US is still dealing with shock-waves from the foreclosure situation of 2007-2008, to this very day. [138]

The loans and the revenue lost to investors still have yet to be repaid, both internally on a national scale and externally on an international level. The United States has the highest margin of college debt [139] ever forced onto the backs of the nation's young, through their lack of alternative options for employment by intentional magisterial design, to create wealth for the nation's banks and the corrupt proxies known as tech schools and universities [140] [141], among many others way too numerous to make mention of here , and do so at the expense of its citizen base.

Although this author has deduced that a parent opening up some sort of business franchise with the same money spent on college would be a far better option in eighty percent of college considerations, except when a child performs at the top of his class in one of the very few high-need employment areas, such as chemistry and medicine, for instance.

The truth here is obvious, being that the system is literally pushing individuals to go into such huge volumes of debt, and that the circumstance is intentional by design. First the production base was shipped off shore, and citizens inside national borders had more regulations to deal with that virtually denies them the right to engage in business enterprise on their own. Then the opportunity base contracts to the point that one is forced to attend college, with virtually nothing remaining as a viable employment option. Attending college demands that one go deeply in debt [142] to the banks.

The market caused housing prices to dramatically inflate over the years, [143] with ne'er an authoritarian attempt in neutralizing the negative situation. Thus, we may view clearly that the effort of forcing individual plebeian citizens into massive debt was intentional. [144]

We must give pause and consider that the coming system of forced labor demands the slave camps to be filled into maximum capacity. All debts once taken out shall be paid in full, one way or the other, especially when the corporations, who may well be of international origin, [145] purchase the entire current system of real-estate financed from the Federal Government. We must always recall that the TPP agreement was all but a done deal, allowing foreign corporations as well as US multinationals to function essentially worldwide in complete disregard for national laws, constitutions or otherwise.

Other persons who shall accompany the debtors are those who fall underneath the broad label of terrorist, or any one of the other open ended accusations. Christians will certainly follow very quickly behind, if they are not among the very first group to be persecuted. People who criticize any aspect of the system, Constitutionalists, people who attempt to flee the persecution, engage in any sort of partisan resistance, etc., will fall among ranks of the condemned in this visualization of looming secular American purgatory.

What Can We Do About It?

In our final analysis, we are left with the exasperating question that always accompanies discussions of political, legal or economic problems. What is the best stance to take, and how can we prepare? The sad truth is that there simply are not many options for individuals.

Many groups have sought to change the way decisions are being made, up on the great white throne where these decision-makers perch. Does the vote count? Whether we agree with his priorities or not — assuming we know what those are — a very different sort of president was elected in 2016, only to have the "establishment" brazenly mount protest after protest, and set up an office with the express purpose of getting him overthrown. That's what American democracy has come down to: rule by the mob, with the mob organized by well-funded interest groups, with George Soros and the bankers in the lead.

If things get worse, the first instinct is to go away, somehow. Most people will simply keep a low profile and try to "go along to get along." Some will call that cowardice, an abdication of our responsibilities. Some will simply not find it suits their character to humiliate themselves and cooperate with evil.

For those who choose to do otherwise, the first consideration will be to drop out of sight. There are websites galore that conjecture how this could be accomplished, and others that point out the weaknesses in such schemes. We'll leave it to the reader to ponder that situation. Others will leave the United States. It isn't easy, but if you are independently wealthy or uncommonly resourceful, it should be easier than hiding in the woods for the rest of your life. In any of the three cases, the one thing we will all need most is a handful of trustworthy partners or friends.

Behold the Supreme Vision

When analyzing such major developments, the utmost clarity of mind is required. A complete liberation of both the conscious and subconscious mind, each being independent of the other, helps generate a well-rounded view of the situation. We may accomplish this by a variety of natural means. Getting a good sleep is a start.

This author has discovered that the very best method is to get outdoors and take long walks down winding park roads or woodland paths, or even country roads. The company of large, well-aged trees and scatterings of time-honored architecture, whether ruins or well preserved, seems to buoy the heart. Areas where classical-styled church buildings and timeless graveyards are sheltered by the drooping arms of huge live oaks elegantly draped in quaint vestiges of Spanish moss stand among the very best locales for this purpose; small towns and the forests of the North also have their charms. Where nature and history combine, a sense of spiritual comfort may be palpable.

As the author walks at a comfortable speed, the tranquil scenery gradually passes him by in a virtual blur and his conscious mind begins to disconnect, in graduated phases, allowing the petty concerns of basic daily existence to suspend themselves, to be replaced by translucent reasoning. On some occasions, he finds that his intellect is dominated by intricate visions, allowing him to view splendid details of what might otherwise remain unseen, and fathom that which might otherwise remain incomprehensible.

Indeed, starting with a handful of trustworthy partners or friends, concerned Americans can approach the current and future challenges by keeping a clear vision of what is right and what has to be rolled back. By working small, and working together, we have the best chance of making a difference wherever we are. It requires courage to speak out against every petty abuse of authority, when the neighbors all go along. If we see people making that effort, we should let them know we appreciate them. If we see people exercising the entrepreneurial ambition that made this country great, we should encourage them.[146] We should work together, rather than focusing on our differences. And if we ever see a political representative who is actually promoting the interests of the people, do everything possible to help.

While corruption and greed are endemic, it remains true that most people have a natural inclination to be helpful and do something constructive, if only they could know what that would be. Negativity runs entirely counter to our own motivations for the very best that fellow humanity and the earth at large have to offer. The eventual success of America's people is virtually guaranteed, if individuals can recall their own heritage of determination and continue to persist relentlessly in pursuit of perfect individual liberty, no matter what obstacles fate or the opposition throws them up against.

Notes

1. Nevins, Ordeal of the Union (Vol. IV), pp. 6–17
2. http://www.counterpunch.org/2014/10/07/the-civil-war-and-150-years-of-forgotten-us-military-atrocities/
3. Such as forty acres and a mule; and being instructed to attack Southern neighbors, even while on furlough, with Federal agents informing ex-slaves that they could keep whatever valuables they could seize; and that Federal forces would ride to save them, if prosecution was ever their fate. Never mind incidents such as the one at Natchez, Mississippi, called the Devil's Punch Bowl, where the mass murders were all part of Union Authority in charge there. This all shoes that the war to end slavery was not waged for moralistic reasons. Obviously, something else was going on here.
4. A timeless tactic of survival during times of systemic collapse.
5. From 1865 to 1916 only two Democratic Presidents served in office, Grover Cleveland and Woodrow Wilson, and even these did the CBCC big favors. Cleveland backed the corporation during the Pullman strike, and Wilson approved the new Federal Reserve.
6. Jekyll Island, Secrets of the Federal Reserve, Chapter One, by Eustice Mullins
7. Vanderlip issued war bonds first to the public, then to large corporations.
8. In other words, the strength in resistance held by Southern forces allowed US citizens to live in relative liberty for the next ninety years following the Civil War.
9. "The Return of the Debtors' Prison." The Huffington Post, Sept. 30, 2015,

at   http://www.huffingtonpost.com/entry/the-return-of-the-debtors_1_b_8220964

10. http://www.theroot.com/blogs/journalisms/2014/09/how_media_have_shaped_our_perception_of_race_and_crime.html

11. Jason Sardell, *Economic Origins of the Mafia and Patronage System in Sicily*, 2009.

12. Oriana Bandiera, Private States and the Enforcement of Property Rights: Theory and Evidence on the Origins of the Sicilian Mafia, 2001, pp. 8-10

13. http://www.reformation.org/rockefeller-pentagon-mafia.html

14. The American Monetary Institute acknowledges there is a theory that the "real" reason for the war against Iraq was Saddam Hussein's decision to price Iraqi oil in the new EURO currency. The argument goes that if the price of oil is not denominated exclusively in Dollars, the U.S. would not be able to continue to run up huge deficits. The motivation for other nations to hold accounts and reserves in Dollars is so that they can use them to pay for oil. American Monetary Institute, http://www.monetary.org/was-the-iraqi-shift-to-euro-currency-to-real-reason-for-war/2010/12, accessed Dec. 12, 2016.

15. "On Reclaiming Our Central Bank And Monetary Policy". PublicCentralBank.com. Retrieved 2007-01-31.

16. http://scholarworks.umt.edu/cgi/viewcontent.cgi?article=1587&context=etd, pg 172-174

17. http://humansarefree.com/2015/06/the-federal-reserve-cartel-rothschild.html

18. The following observations come from *Trading With the Enemy*, Charles Higham (1984).

19. Wallace, pp. 360-1

20. https://en.wikipedia.org/wiki/The_Holocaust#Non-Jewish, eleven million victims in total, six million Jews.

21. Information regarding IBM and the Nazi connections is drawn from Edwin Black, *IBM and the Holocaust: the Strategic Alliance Between Nazi Germany and America's Most Powerful Corporation.*

22. http://documents.nytimes.com/confidential-report-provides-new-evidence-of-notorious-nazi-cases?ref=us#p=1

23. http://makeagentorangehistory.org/agent-orange-resources/background/health-effects-of-agent-orange-dioxin/

24. http://www.wnd.com/2015/08/obama-gives-illegals-massive-

health-care-plan/

25. "Bernanke: Federal Reserve caused the Great Depression." Worldnetdaily.com. Read more at http://www.wnd.com/2008/0 3/59405/#fIlSA8mpHfLPOCxP.99

26. https://en.wikipedia.org/wiki/Harlan_County_War

27. https://en.wikipedia.org/wiki/Coal_Creek_War

28. http://kingencyclopedia.stanford.edu/encyclopedia/ encyclopedia/enc_rockefeller_nelson_aldrich_1908_1979/

29. Hermann, Kenneth J. "Killing Me Softly: How Agent Orange Murders Vietnam's Children", *Political Affairs*, April 25, 2006

30. Fleischer, Doris Zames; Zames, Freida (2001). The disability rights movement: from charity to confrontation. Temple University Press. p. 178.

31. http://www.alternet.org/drugs/meet-cias-10-favorite-drug-traffickers

32. The 40th Anniversary of the Illustrated Presidential Report of the Commission on Obscenity and Pornography. http://www. huffingtonpost.com/robert-brenner/sins-of-commission-the-fo_b_779849.html

33. http://www.foxnews.com/opinion/2016/04/14/high-school-wants-to-shut-down-off-campus-jesus-lunch.html

34. http://www.nytimes.com/2013/07/13/us/a-religion-that-embraces-all-religions.html

35. http://www.rense.com/general76/jfkvs.htm

36. http://www.theatlantic.com/business/archive/2014/12/how-common-is-child-labor-in-the-us/383687/

37. http://www.american-historama.org/1866-1881-reconstruction-era/child-labor-america.htm

38. https://www.csun.edu/~ghy7463/mw2.html

39. http://articles.latimes.com/1991-09-04/news/mn-1427_1_north-carolina

40. http://dealbook.nytimes.com/2013/06/24/recent-ex-senators-find-soft-landings-on-corporate-boards/?_r=0

41. http://www.infowars.com/bbc-now-admits-armed-nazis-led-revolution-in-kiev-ukraine/

42. Characteristics of Fascism. http://www.rense.com/general37/char.htm

43. http://www.npr.org/2011/09/28/140869378/americas-love-affair-with-nationalism

44. http://inthesetimes.com/article/16801/UN_US_human_rights_record_report

45. http://www.huffingtonpost.com/keith-gaddie/the-american-nation-probl_b_8733102.html

46. Including free education and first choice of employment, so that they do not have to compete with civilians in a collapsing economy that government and corporate policy intentionally created.

47. http://www.blacklistednews.com/media_now_openly_admitting_the_government_controls_the_news/26077/0/38/38/y/m.html

48. http://www.washingtontimes.com/news/2015/dec/15/charlie-brown-christmas-censored-kentucky-school-d/

49. https://marktwainahf.wikispaces.com/Censorship+History+of+Huck+Finn

50. http://www.southernstudies.org/2016/01/nikki-haleys-troubled-economic-record-in-south-car.html

51. http://www.usatoday.com/story/money/cars/2014/02/20/no-south-carolina-union-jobs/5642031/

52. http://www.nydailynews.com/news/politics/wis-gov-scott-walker-proposes-vast-union-restriction-article-1.2359478

53. http://www.allgov.com/news/controversies/civil-liberty-violations-seen-in-police-interrogations-of-demonstrators-150430?news=856363

54. http://www.wnd.com/2015/05/obamas-national-civilian-security-force-endorsed/

55. http://money.cnn.com/2010/09/08/news/economy/reagan_years_taxes/index.htm

56. https://mises.org/library/sad-legacy-ronald-reagan-0

57. http://www.baltimoresun.com/bal-bz.unions08jun08-story.html

58. http://www.fedsmith.com/2013/10/11/ronald-reagan-and-the-great-social-security-heist/

59. http://www.nytimes.com/2006/10/24/business/retirement/24pension.html?_r-0

60. http://money.usnews.com/money/blogs/planning-to-retire/2010/11/22/7-signs-your-employer-is-looting-your-401k

61. http://www.alternet.org/node/934912

62. http://www.criminaljusticedegreesguide.com/features/10-huge-

u-s-brands-who-profit-from-what-americans-would-call-slave-labor.html

63. http://www.newsmax.com/Finance/StreetTalk/krugman-reagan-crisis-caused/2009/12/17/id/343594/

64. http://fortune.com/2011/05/05/the-rise-of-the-permanently-temporary-worker/

65. http://www.washington.edu/news/2014/11/24/study-us-attracting-fewer-educated-highly-skilled-migrants/

66. http://www.baltimoresun.com/news/opinion/oped/bs-ed-second-amendment-20151003-story.html

67. http://www.theamericanconservative.com/articles/the-critic-as-radical/

68. http://thehill.com/blogs/floor-action/senate/200874-republicans-want-to-allow-states-to-reject-federal-laws

69. Jade Helm. http://www.truthandaction.org/operation-jade-helm-massive-military-drill-across-7-states-unconventional-warfare/; and http://www.truthandaction.org/operation-jade-helm-massive-military-drill-across-7-states-unconventional-warfare/

70. http://www.foxnews.com/story/2008/03/26/spy-in-sky-drone-may-soon-keep-watchful-eye-over-south-florida.html

71. http://www.morningliberty.com/2010/07/28/martial-law-10-regions-for-u-s-are-ready/

72. http://www.pionline.com/article/20130626/ONLINE/130629908/ici-us-retirement-assets-hit-record-208-trillion

73. http://www.investopedia.com/articles/investing/080615/china-owns-us-debt-how-much.asp

74. http://journalof911studies.com/volume/2010/ChandlerDownwardAccelerationOfWTC1.pdf

75. http://www.infowars.com/france-declares-permanent-police-state/

76. https://en.wikipedia.org/wiki/Constitution_of_Tennessee

77. https://www.infowars.com/the-freedom-act-is-worse-than-the-patriot-act/

78. http://www.activistpost.com/2011/01/patriot-act-nazi-law-ex-cia-official.html

79. "This is how consumers turn into debt slaves," Wolf Street, at http://wolfstreet.com/2016/11/08/portrait-of-the-american-debt-slave-as-of-q3/

80. http://www.wsj.com/articles/children-dont-have-constitutional-right-to-switch-schools-appeals-court-rules-1441060163

81. http://psychcentral.com/lib/schools-fail-to-educate-at-least-30-percent-of-our-students/

82. http://www.theatlantic.com/national/archive/2013/03/lets-go-back-to-grouping-students-by-ability/274362/

83. http://www.huffingtonpost.com/2012/07/23/us-students-still-lag-beh_n_1695516.html

84. https://www.washingtonpost.com/local/education/cursive-handwriting-disappearing-from-public-schools/2013/04/04/215862e0-7d23-11e2-a044-676856536b40_story.html

85. http://www.todaysparent.com/blogs/tracys-mama-memoirs/what-kids-arent-learning-at-school/

86. http://www.zerohedge.com/contributed/hidden-dark-agenda-public-education

87. http://digitalcommons.law.lsu.edu/cgi/viewcontent.cgi?article=6405&context=lalrev

88. http://historyofmassachusetts.org/john-proctor-first-male-accused-witch/

89. http://arstechnica.com/tech-policy/2015/12/pre-crime-arrives-in-the-uk-better-make-sure-your-face-stays-off-the-crowdsourced-watch-list/

90. http://www.mybudget360.com/buying-a-home-in-america-today-is-expensive-thanks-to-the-banking-sector-examining-income-and-home-prices-from-1950-to-the-present-can-home-prices-fall-another-38-percent/

91. "Bernie Sanders says tax share paid by corporations has fallen from 33% to 9% since 1952," confirmed by Politfact. http://www.politifact.com/truth-o-meter/statements/2014/aug/28/bernie-s/bernie-sanders-says-tax-share-paid-corporations-ha/

92. "Law Lets I.R.S. Seize Accounts on Suspicion, No Crime Required," The New York Times. Oct. 25, 2014. http://www.nytimes.com/2014/10/26/us/law-lets-irs-seize-accounts-on-suspicion-no-crime-required.html?_r=0

93. Researchers: More than 2,000 false convictions in past 23 years. http://usnews.nbcnews.com/_news/2012/05/21/11756575-researchers-more-than-2000-false-convictions-in-past-23-years?lite

94. http://www.you-can-learn-basic-employee-rights.com/false-sexual-harassment.html

95. http://www.govtslaves.info/mother-charged-with-terrorism-ordered-to-turn-over-guns-after-reading-the-constitution-protesting-property-tax-increase/

96. http://www.washingtonsblog.com/2013/08/u-s-government-may-on-a-whim-label-any-american-a-terrorist.html

97. http://www.dailymail.co.uk/sciencetech/article-2950081/It-s-not-just-smart-TVs-home-gadgets-spy-internet-giants-collecting-personal-data-high-tech-devices.html; and http://www.infowars.com/spy-satellites-used-to-control-american-citizens/

98. http://www.motherjones.com/environment/2009/08/secret-history-hurricane-katrin

99. http://money.cnn.com/2015/10/15/retirement/central-states-pension-fund-cuts/; see also, http://www.teacherpensions.org/blog/teachers-these-4-states-lose-out-double-retirement. See also, https://www.illinoispolicy.org/federal-judge-approves-detroit-pension-cuts/. See also, http://www.kansascity.com/news/business/article60760061.html

100. http://www.latimes.com/nation/la-ff-na-jade-helm-20150508-story.html

101. http://allnewspipeline.com/Military_Drills_All_Across_America_In_December.php

102. http://whatreallyhappened.com/WRHARTICLES/allwarsarebankerwars.php

103. http://www.globalresearch.ca/bankers-are-behind-the-wars/5378240

104. http://nypost.com/2016/04/20/harriet-tubman-will-replace-andrew-jackson-on-the-20-bill/

105. http://www.westernjournalism.com/mass-murders-psychiatric-drugs-and-gun-control/

106. https://en.wikipedia.org/wiki/Project_MKUltra

107. http://www.wanttoknow.info/mind_control/cia_mind_control_experiments_sex_abuse

108. https://en.wikipedia.org/wiki/Project_MKUltra

109. http://quod.lib.umich.edu/h/humfig/11217607.0002.206/—decivilization-in-the-1960s?rgn=main;view=fulltext

110. US Army: Internment And Resettlement Operations, https://info.

publicintelligence.net/USArmy-InternmentResettlement.pdf

111. Internment Camps in "free" America? http://www.crossroad.to/News/internment-camps.htm

112. https://en.wikipedia.org/wiki/Effects_of_Hurricane_Katrina_in_New_Orleans

113. http://www.nytimes.com/2010/08/27/us/27racial.html

114. "There was nothing natural about the disaster that befell New Orleans in Katrina's aftermath." http://www.motherjones.com/environment/2009/08/secret-history-hurricane-katrina

115. http://www.chron.com/news/nation-world/article/5-years-after-Katrina-storm-s-death-toll-remains-1589464.php

116. http://www.usnews.com/news/blogs/data-mine/2015/08/28/no-one-knows-how-many-people-died-in-katrina

117. http://www.washingtonpost.com/wp-dyn/content/article/2005/09/07/AR2005090702214.html

118. http://www.policestateusa.com/2014/large-scale-gun-confiscation/

119. http://www.infowars.com/nra-the-untold-story-of-gun-confiscation-after-katrina/

120. http://www.datacenterresearch.org/reports_analysis/low-wages/

121. https://en.wikipedia.org/wiki/American_Indian_boarding_schools

122. https://www.washingtonpost.com/world/asia_pacific/north-korea-claims-it-could-wipe-out-manhattan-with-a-hydrogen-bomb/2016/03/13/3834cd54-e919-11e5-b0fd-073d5930a7b7_story.html

123. http://money.cnn.com/2009/01/15/real_estate/millions_in_foreclosure/

124. http://www.washingtontimes.com/news/2012/oct/18/welfare-spending-jumps-32-percent-four-years/?page=all

125. For information on the unemployment situation, see: http://www.epi.org/publication/webfeatures_econindicators_jobspict_20081107/, and http://www.cnbc.com/2015/02/06/chart-whats-the-real-unemployment-rate.html; and also: http://www.dollarsandsense.org/archives/2009/0709miller.htm

126. "Bailout Recipients," a chart showing which corporations/banks got what, and who failed to pay it back. At ProPublica, updated Jan. 20., 2017. https://projects.propublica.org/bailout/list

127. https://docs.google.com/file/d/0B-AvzllBOOx7M0VNRnhXMWlCLUE/edit?pref=2&pli=1

128. http://www.rightsidenews.com/editorial/rsn-pick-of-the-day/my-mothers-birth-certificate-and-obamas/

129. http://www.newsweek.com/are-republicans-becoming-party-white-identity-politics-367403

130. http://www.cnn.com/2015/07/10/us/south-carolina-confederate-battle-flag/

131. http://www.snopes.com/politics/religion/hitchingpost.asp

132. On the controversies of same-sex marriage, see:http://www.newsweek.com/can-public-employees-decline-perform-gay-marriages-353741;and also:http://www.nytimes.com/2015/09/04/us/kim-davis-same-sex-marriage.html

133. http://www.cnbc.com/2014/04/23/the-growing-perils-of-the-cashless-future.html

134. https://www.corbettreport.com/the-war-on-cash-a-country-by-country-guide/

135. http://www.washingtonsblog.com/2016/01/cashless-society-war-intensifies-global-epocalypse.html

136. http://ncpedia.org/textiles/mill-villages

137. http://www.prophecynewswatch.com/article.cfm?recent_news_id=200

138. https://www.washingtonpost.com/investigations/lenders-seek-court-actions-against-homeowners-years-after-foreclosure/2013/06/15/3c6a04ce-96fc-11e2-b68f-dc5c4b47e519_story.html

139. http://www.cnbc.com/2015/06/15/the-high-economic-and-social-costs-of-student-loan-debt.html

140. https://www.washingtonpost.com/news/grade-point/wp/2015/01/30/more-than-4-out-of-5-students-graduate-without-a-job-how-could-colleges-change-that/

141. http://www.alternet.org/education/how-parasitic-universities-drain-towns-all-across-america

142. http://www.savingforcollege.com/tutorial101/the_real_cost_of_higher_education.php

143. http://www.curbed.com/2016/1/27/10843266/buying-homes-major-cities-unaffordable-new-york-san-francisco-la

144. http://billmoyers.com/2015/02/14/needless-default/

145. http://www.cnbc.com/2016/01/08/china-stock-swoon-could-

boost-us-real-estate.html

146. http://atlassociety.org/commentary/commentary-blog/4379-america-s-pioneer-spirit-government-vs-new-frontiers

BIBLIOGRAPHY

These are some of the most important sources used in preparing this work.

Books

The Swiss, The Gold And The Dead: How Swiss Bankers Helped Finance the Nazi War Machine. Jean Ziegler (1998).

Behold The Pale Rider, William Cooper (1991). See, especially, page 225:

> "The government encouraged the manufacture and importation of firearms for the criminals to use. This is intended to foster a feeling of insecurity, which would lead the American people to voluntarily disarm themselves by passing laws against firearms. Using drugs and hypnosis on mental patients in a process called Orion, the CIA inculcated the desire in these people to open fire on schoolyards and thus inflame the anti-gun lobby. This plan is well under way, and so far is working perfectly. The middle class is begging the government to do away with the 2nd Amendment."

Websites

https://criminalbankingmonopoly.wordpress.com/

http://www.infowars.com/charleston-shooter-was-on-drug-linked-to-violent-outbursts/

http://www.wnd.com/2015/06/big-list-of-drug-induced-killers/#71dLgiTmuSUZfls6.99

http://reality-bytes.hubpages.com/hub/Americans-Who-Supported-European-Fascism

http://www.truth-out.org/news/item/31168-global-capitalist-crisis-and-the-north-american-free-trade-agreement-reflections-twenty-one-years-on

http://dissidentvoice.org/2014/09/why-the-deep-state-always-wins/

http://www.rt.com/usa/usa-cia-drugs-poor-americas/

http://dissidentvoice.org/2014/09/why-the-deep-state-always-wins/

http://www.nytimes.com/2014/10/27/us/in-cold-war-us-spy-agencies-used-1000-nazis.html?_r=0

http://www.theguardian.com/commentisfree/2014/jul/11/the-ultimate-goal-of-the-nsa-is-total-population-control

http://www.engadget.com/2013/11/21/lg-admits-smart-tv-data-collection/

http://www.thenewamerican.com/usnews/constitution/item/7674-nsa-supercenters-to-store-americans-private-data-permanently

http://www.secretsofthefed.com/china-poised-demand-u-s-land-payment-u-s-debt/

http://ellabakercenter.org/blog/2013/06/prison-labor-is-the-new-slave-labor

https://en.wikipedia.org/wiki/Extermination_through_labor

https://en.wikipedia.org/wiki/Operation_Paperclip

http://www.thetruthseeker.co.uk/?p=108615

http://abcnews.go.com/US/jade-helm-15-facts-training-exercise-causing-jitters/story?id=30915367

https://www.nraila.org/articles/20150911/virginia-senator-kaine-introduces-bill-to-turn-innocent-mistakes-into-felonies

http://personalliberty.com/study-illegal-legal-immigrants-use-social-welfare-more-than-native-citizens/

http://www.zerohedge.com/news/2015-09-16/record-467-million-americans-live-poverty-median-houshold-income-back-1989-levels

http://theantimedia.org/if-you-live-in-one-of-these-states-youll-soon-need-a-passport-for-domestic-flights/

http://www.amazon.com/The-End-America-Warning-Patriot/dp/1933392797

http://www.newyorker.com/news/john-cassidy/is-america-an-oligarchy

http://www.safehaven.com/article/4617/transnational-corporations-the-new-world-order

http://www.washingtontimes.com/news/2015/apr/9/obama-bloomberg-gun-control-agenda-worries-democra/

http://www.wanttoknow.info/mind_control/cia_mind_control_experiments_sex_abuse

http://www.amazon.com/Black-Southerners-Confederate-Armies-

http://www.cnbc.com/2015/10/06/chinese-money-flows-into-us-housing.html

https://en.wikipedia.org/wiki/Elijah_Parish

http://www.americasfreedomfighters.com/2014/04/04/nbc-predicts-all-americans-will-receive-a-microchip-implant-in-2017-per-obamacare/

http://fortune.com/2012/06/20/why-are-the-chinese-investing-in-toledo/

http://www.foxnews.com/politics/2012/03/19/obama-signs-executive-order-revising-authority-to-nationalize-resources-for/

http://www.hangthebankers.com/list-of-school-shootings-on-antidepressants/

https://www.voltairenet.org/IMG/pdf/Sutton_Wall_Street_and_Hitler.pdf

http://humansarefree.com/2015/06/the-federal-reserve-cartel-rothschild.html

http://cnsnews.com/news/article/irs-cheapest-obamacare-plan-will-be-20000-family

http://www.thecommonsenseshow.com/2015/06/26/the-eight-steps-leading-to-the-coming-american-holocaust/

http://www.infowars.com/obama-to-unveil-multiple-gun-control-executive-actions-next-week/

http://www.naturalnews.com/035301_Obama_executive_orders_food_supply.html

http://duncantrussell.com/forum/discussion/7298/the-federal-reserve-killed-jfk-for-printing-dollars-backed-by-silver-what-say-you-yeah-or-nay/p1

http://www.forbes.com/sites/realspin/2015/08/03/final-waters-of-the-u-s-rule-is-more-overreach-by-the-epa/

http://americanholocaustcoming.blogspot.com/2009/05/exposing-coming-terror-state-and-prison.html

http://www.thedailybeast.com/articles/2015/08/04/hillary-clinton-s-mega-donors-are-also-funding-jeb-bush.html

http://theantimedia.org/tpp-trade-deal-will-cost-us-4480000-jobs-say-researchers/

https://shadowproof.com/2016/01/26/congress-quietly-kills-ban-on-funding-neo-nazis-in-ukraine/

http://godfatherpolitics.com/how-black-leaders-exploit-their-people-for-political-and-financial-gain/

http://www.teaparty.org/government-lays-groundwork-confiscate-401k-ira-34778/

https://en.wikipedia.org/wiki/Americans_in_Brazil

http://www.zerohedge.com/news/2016-02-16/larry-summers-launches-war-us-paper-money-its-time-kill-100-bill

http://www.theguardian.com/commentisfree/2016/feb/09/internet-of-things-smart-devices-spying-surveillance-us-government

http://www.marketwatch.com/story/most-americans-have-less-than-1000-in-savings-2015-10-06

http://planetsave.com/2009/03/10/bills-could-reorganizing-farming-and-criminalize-gardening-organic-farming/

http://www.tldm.org/News17/AlienInvasionU.S.MilitaryHasPlans.htm

http://www.amazon.com/Live-Off-Land-City-Country/dp/0873642007

http://www.prophecynewswatch.com/article.cfm?recent_news_id=324

http://www.postandcourier.com/article/20160401/PC1603/160409894

http://www.thepoliticalinsider.com/a-florida-county-just-made-a-bold-announcement-about-the-confederate-flag/

http://endingthefed.com/texas-gov-calls-for-convention-of-the-states-to-stop-obama-this-is-huge.html

http://www.zerohedge.com/print/527927

http://nsarchive.gwu.edu/NSAEBB/NSAEBB146/

http://gizmodo.com/the-government-is-testing-myriad-invasive-biometric-sur-1692480582

http://www.amazon.com/Illuminati-Cult-that-Hijacked-World/dp/1439211485

http://www.thedailybell.com/news-analysis/leaked-tisa-docs-part-of-secret-global-constitution/

http://townhall.com/tipsheet/mattvespa/2016/05/28/wapo-editorial-board-averse-to-blaming-socialism-for-venezuelas-stunning-collapse-n2170028

http://www.theverge.com/2016/6/1/11824118/google-android-location-data-police-warrants

https://www.washingtonpost.com/politics/foreign-governments-gave-millions-to-foundation-while-clinton-was-at-state-dept/2015/02/25/31937c1e-bc3f-11e4-8668-4e7ba8439ca6_story.html

http://www.ibtimes.com/clinton-foundation-donors-got-weapons-deals-hillary-clintons-state-department-1934187

http://www.bloomberg.com/news/articles/2014-10-19/ibm-agrees-to-pay-globalfoundries-1-5-billion-to-take-chip-unit

http://ticdata.treasury.gov/Publish/shlhistdat.html

http://www.bloomberg.com/news/features/2016-05-30/the-untold-story-behind-saudi-arabia-s-41-year-u-s-debt-secret

http://qz.com/690881/the-number-of-new-businesses-in-the-us-is-falling-off-a-cliff/

http://www.dw.com/en/foreign-connected-pacs-spent-10-million-on-the-us-election-so-far/a-19297597

https://www.dollarvigilante.com/blog/2016/05/30/alan-greenspan-warns-venezuelan-style-martial-law-will-soon-come-us.html

http://www.amazon.com/Understanding-Surviving-Martial-Survive-Prosper/dp/B003Q8SNCU

http://www.prophecynewswatch.com/article.cfm?recent_news_id=397

http://www.prophecynewswatch.com/article.cfm?recent_news_id=396

http://www.amazon.com/gp/product/158980466X

http://www.amazon.com/Real-Lincoln-Abraham-Agenda-Unnecessary/dp/0761526463

http://www.amazon.com/Slavery-Was-Cause-Between-States/dp/0985363274

http://www.amazon.com/gp/product/B000M4ZUZO

http://www.amazon.com/gp/product/086597201X

https://theintercept.com/2016/06/07/new-intelligence-bill-gives-fbi-more-secret-surveillance-power/

http://theantimedia.org/bill-congress-ministry-of-truth/

http://www.breitbart.com/texas/2016/06/11/obama-administration-surge-agenda-threatening-u-s-100-syrian-refugees-per-day/

https://www.amazon.com/Wheres-Birth-Certificate-Eligible-President/dp/1936488299

http://www.westernjournalism.com/obama-not-a-citizen-thanks-to-his-own-mother/

http://www.dcclothesline.com/2015/03/29/obama-was-hand-picked-was-not-a-natural-born-citizen-congress-knew-it-and-tried-to-protect-him/

http://worldnewsdailyreport.com/kenya-authorities-release-barack-obamas-real-birth-certificate/

http://www.usnews.com/opinion/articles/2009/11/10/us-taxpayers-should-not-have-to-pay-for-illegal-immigrants-healthcare

http://www.wsj.com/articles/illegal-immigrants-get-public-health-care-despite-federal-policy-1458850082

https://theintercept.com/2016/06/20/fbi-releases-partial-redacted-transcript-orlando-gunmans-911-calls-attack/

http://www.longwarjournal.org/archives/2016/06/orlando-terrorist-swore-allegiance-to-islamic-states-abu-bakr-al-baghdadi.php

http://www.businessinsider.de/cia-director-theres-no-need-to-release-the-28-classified-pages-of-the-911-report-2016-5?r=US&IR=T

http://www.nationalreview.com/article/426419/christian-refugees-syria-religious-minorities-united-states-resettlement-policy

http://www.zerohedge.com/news/2016-06-21/trump-campaign-starts-june-only-13-million-bank-after-making-another-22-million-loan (Author's note: This illustrates how much financing it takes to run state and national candidates. Recall the rising fear in 1913 of the international bankers in regard to estates that generate raw product and/or processed product; now, as a result of new technology, being able to ascend that ladder of prosperity into a level of wealth on par with aristocracy, without needing slave labor to do so. This also suggests that their true purpose in imposing the income tax was to permanently block the US citizen from being able to fund the election of Congressional Representatives that would stand for citizen interests, a representative body that was exterminated by the US Civil War. The bankers and corporations would stop at nothing to prevent the rise of another Congress that would obstruct their ambitions.

http://www.mintpressnews.com/cia-made-google/201521/

http://www.zerohedge.com/news/2016-06-14/contract-orlando-killers-employer-signed-dhs-transport-illegal-immigrants

http://www.middleeasteye.net/news/deleted-official-report-says-saudi-key-funder-hillary-clinton-presidential-campaign-223282807

http://www.activistpost.com/2015/11/hillary-clinton-and-the-funding-of-al-qaeda-terrorists-in-libya-and-syria.html

http://www.inquisitr.com/3054039/john-brennan-fights-release-of-911-reports-secret-chapter/

http://www.nytimes.com/2014/09/07/us/politics/foreign-powers-buy-influence-at-think-tanks.html?_r=1

http://www.pulitzer.org/files/2015/investigative-reporting/lipton/05lipton2015.pdf

http://www.ibtimes.com/texas-secession-brexit-inspires-nationalists-leave-us-texit-vote-2386446

https://en.wikipedia.org/wiki/Texas_secession_movements

http://journal-neo.org/2016/06/28/obama-is-sticking-a-fork-in-america-we-really-could-be-done/

http://christianexaminer.com/article/author-insidious-intolerance-for-christianity-embedding-itself-in-american-culture/50851.htm

https://www.eff.org/deeplinks/2016/06/making-sense-troubling-decision-new-court-ruling-underscores-need-stop-changes

https://www.eff.org/press/releases/fbi-must-not-sidestep-privacy-protections-massive-collection-americans-biometric-data

https://www.yahoo.com/news/dallas-police-chief-negotiations-underway-parking-garage-055053219.html?ref=gs

http://tenthamendmentcenter.com/2009/05/04/lincolns-war/

http://reclaimdemocracy.org/corporate-accountability-history-corporations-us/

https://www.amazon.com/Unequal-Protection-Corporate-Dominance-Rights/dp/1579549551

https://www.amazon.com/AMERICAS-CONCENTRATION-CAMPS-Indian-Reservations/dp/B000GNZGI2

https://www.amazon.com/Thunder-Mountains-West-Virginia-Mine/dp/0822954265

https://www.amazon.com/Battle-Blair-Mountain-Americas-Uprising/dp/0465077730

Official Records, series 1 Vol. 39, page 494, Sherman's policy of total warfare and the crimes he authorized committed.

http://www.prophecynewswatch.com/article.cfm?recent_news_id=486

http://www.ilo.org/global/docs/WCMS_092176/lang--en/index.htm

http://americanhistory.si.edu/museum/mission-history

http://thefederalist.com/2016/07/28/hillary-clinton-wants-to-crack-down-on-the-sharing-economy-millennials-love/

https://cryptome.org/2016/08/deep-politics-rev4.pdf

These links provide further thought-provoking data for everyone who wishes to size up the state of liberty and democracy in the United States today.

http://www.washingtonsblog.com/2013/10/americans-have-lost-virtually-all-of-our-constitutional-rights.html

http://freedomoutpost.com/government-keeps-personal-information-forever/

http://www.theguardian.com/technology/2014/may/04/facial-recognition-technology-identity-tesco-ethical-issues

Foreclosures go up... http://www.cutimes.com/2015/08/21/foreclosures-rise-by-14-realtytrac

Taxes go up... http://www.rense.com/general31/prop.htm

http://www.policestateusa.com/2014/large-scale-gun-confiscation/

https://www.washingtonpost.com/opinions/is-the-united-states-still-the-land-of-the-free/2012/01/04/gIQAvcDlwP_story.html

http://www.heritage.org/research/reports/1993/02/bg926nbsp-how-regulation-is-destroying

https://www.ahip.org/Issues/Rising-Health-Care-Costs.aspx

http://www.naturalnews.com/040429_bank_accounts_confiscation_Ron_Paul.html

https://drstevebest.wordpress.com/2011/11/30/halliburton-confirms-us-concentration-camps-ready-to-detain-up-to-2-million-terrorists/

http://www.thecommonsenseshow.com/2013/06/19/the-forced-depopulation-of-americas-rural-areas/

http://www.sott.net/article/294572-Judge-rules-SWAT-Teams-can-enter-homes-without-a-warrant-and-temporarily-seize-your-property

https://www.lewrockwell.com/2013/03/kelleigh-nelson/killing-the-sick-and-the-elderly/

http://www.shtfplan.com/headline-news/american-concentration-camps-will-be-used-to-enforce-medical-martial-law-for-the-sick-and-to-house-political-dissidents_10302014

Printed in the United States
By Bookmasters